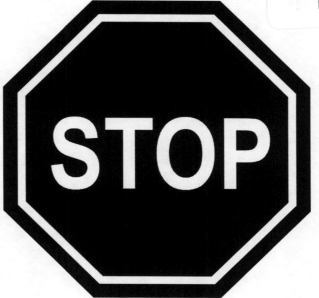

FREE Test Taking Tips Video/DVD Offer

To better serve you, we created videos covering test taking tips that we want to give you for FREE. **These videos cover world-class tips that will help you succeed on your test.**

We just ask that you send us feedback about this product. Please let us know what you thought about it—whether good, bad, or indifferent.

To get your **FREE videos**, you can use the QR code below or email freevideos@studyguideteam.com with "Free Videos" in the subject line and the following information in the body of the email:

  a. The title of your product

  b. Your product rating on a scale of 1-5, with 5 being the highest

  c. Your feedback about the product

If you have any questions or concerns, please don't hesitate to contact us at info@studyguideteam.com.

Thank you!

TOEFL Preparation Book 2023-2024

3 TOEFL iBT Practice Tests and Study Guide
[Includes Audio Links]

Joshua Rueda

Interested in buying more than 10 copies of our product? Contact us about bulk discounts: bulkorders@studyguideteam.com

ISBN 13: 9781637750155
ISBN 10: 1637750153

Table of Contents

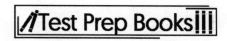

Welcome

Dear Reader,

Welcome to your new Test Prep Books study guide! We are pleased that you chose us to help you prepare for your exam. There are many study options to choose from, and we appreciate you choosing us. Studying can be a daunting task, but we have designed a smart, effective study guide to help prepare you for what lies ahead.

Whether you're a parent helping your child learn and grow, a high school student working hard to get into your dream college, or a nursing student studying for a complex exam, we want to help give you the tools you need to succeed. We hope this study guide gives you the skills and the confidence to thrive, and we can't thank you enough for allowing us to be part of your journey.

In an effort to continue to improve our products, we welcome feedback from our customers. We look forward to hearing from you. Suggestions, success stories, and criticisms can all be communicated by emailing us at info@studyguideteam.com.

Sincerely,
Test Prep Books Team

FREE Videos/DVD OFFER

Doing well on your exam requires both knowing the test content and understanding how to use that knowledge to do well on the test. We offer completely FREE test taking tip videos. **These videos cover world-class tips that you can use to succeed on your test.**

To get your **FREE videos**, you can use the QR code below or email freevideos@studyguideteam.com with "Free Videos" in the subject line and the following information in the body of the email:

 a. The title of your product
 b. Your product rating on a scale of 1-5, with 5 being the highest
 c. Your feedback about the product

If you have any questions or concerns, please don't hesitate to contact us at info@studyguideteam.com.

SCAN HERE

1

Quick Overview

As you draw closer to taking your exam, effective preparation becomes more and more important. Thankfully, you have this study guide to help you get ready. Use this guide to help keep your studying on track and refer to it often.

This study guide contains several key sections that will help you be successful on your exam. The guide contains tips for what you should do the night before and the day of the test. Also included are test-taking tips. Knowing the right information is not always enough. Many well-prepared test takers struggle with exams. These tips will help equip you to accurately read, assess, and answer test questions.

A large part of the guide is devoted to showing you what content to expect on the exam and to helping you better understand that content. In this guide are practice test questions so that you can see how well you have grasped the content. Then, answer explanations are provided so that you can understand why you missed certain questions.

Don't try to cram the night before you take your exam. This is not a wise strategy for a few reasons. First, your retention of the information will be low. Your time would be better used by reviewing information you already know rather than trying to learn a lot of new information. Second, you will likely become stressed as you try to gain a large amount of knowledge in a short amount of time. Third, you will be depriving yourself of sleep. So be sure to go to bed at a reasonable time the night before. Being well-rested helps you focus and remain calm.

Be sure to eat a substantial breakfast the morning of the exam. If you are taking the exam in the afternoon, be sure to have a good lunch as well. Being hungry is distracting and can make it difficult to focus. You have hopefully spent lots of time preparing for the exam. Don't let an empty stomach get in the way of success!

When travelling to the testing center, leave earlier than needed. That way, you have a buffer in case you experience any delays. This will help you remain calm and will keep you from missing your appointment time at the testing center.

Be sure to pace yourself during the exam. Don't try to rush through the exam. There is no need to risk performing poorly on the exam just so you can leave the testing center early. Allow yourself to use all of the allotted time if needed.

Remain positive while taking the exam even if you feel like you are performing poorly. Thinking about the content you should have mastered will not help you perform better on the exam.

Once the exam is complete, take some time to relax. Even if you feel that you need to take the exam again, you will be well served by some down time before you begin studying again. It's often easier to convince yourself to study if you know that it will come with a reward!

Test-Taking Strategies

1. Predicting the Answer

When you feel confident in your preparation for a multiple-choice test, try predicting the answer before reading the answer choices. This is especially useful on questions that test objective factual knowledge. By predicting the answer before reading the available choices, you eliminate the possibility that you will be distracted or led astray by an incorrect answer choice. You will feel more confident in your selection if you read the question, predict the answer, and then find your prediction among the answer choices. After using this strategy, be sure to still read all of the answer choices carefully and completely. If you feel unprepared, you should not attempt to predict the answers. This would be a waste of time and an opportunity for your mind to wander in the wrong direction.

2. Reading the Whole Question

Too often, test takers scan a multiple-choice question, recognize a few familiar words, and immediately jump to the answer choices. Test authors are aware of this common impatience, and they will sometimes prey upon it. For instance, a test author might subtly turn the question into a negative, or he or she might redirect the focus of the question right at the end. The only way to avoid falling into these traps is to read the entirety of the question carefully before reading the answer choices.

3. Looking for Wrong Answers

Long and complicated multiple-choice questions can be intimidating. One way to simplify a difficult multiple-choice question is to eliminate all of the answer choices that are clearly wrong. In most sets of answers, there will be at least one selection that can be dismissed right away. If the test is administered on paper, the test taker could draw a line through it to indicate that it may be ignored; otherwise, the test taker will have to perform this operation mentally or on scratch paper. In either case, once the obviously incorrect answers have been eliminated, the remaining choices may be considered. Sometimes identifying the clearly wrong answers will give the test taker some information about the correct answer. For instance, if one of the remaining answer choices is a direct opposite of one of the eliminated answer choices, it may well be the correct answer. The opposite of obviously wrong is obviously right! Of course, this is not always the case. Some answers are obviously incorrect simply because they are irrelevant to the question being asked. Still, identifying and eliminating some incorrect answer choices is a good way to simplify a multiple-choice question.

4. Don't Overanalyze

Anxious test takers often overanalyze questions. When you are nervous, your brain will often run wild, causing you to make associations and discover clues that don't actually exist. If you feel that this may be a problem for you, do whatever you can to slow down during the test. Try taking a deep breath or counting to ten. As you read and consider the question, restrict yourself to the particular words used by the author. Avoid thought tangents about what the author *really* meant, or what he or she was *trying* to say. The only things that matter on a multiple-choice test are the words that are actually in the question. You must avoid reading too much into a multiple-choice question, or supposing that the writer meant something other than what he or she wrote.

3

5. No Need for Panic

It is wise to learn as many strategies as possible before taking a multiple-choice test, but it is likely that you will come across a few questions for which you simply don't know the answer. In this situation, avoid panicking. Because most multiple-choice tests include dozens of questions, the relative value of a single wrong answer is small. As much as possible, you should compartmentalize each question on a multiple-choice test. In other words, you should not allow your feelings about one question to affect your success on the others. When you find a question that you either don't understand or don't know how to answer, just take a deep breath and do your best. Read the entire question slowly and carefully. Try rephrasing the question a couple of different ways. Then, read all of the answer choices carefully. After eliminating obviously wrong answers, make a selection and move on to the next question.

6. Confusing Answer Choices

When working on a difficult multiple-choice question, there may be a tendency to focus on the answer choices that are the easiest to understand. Many people, whether consciously or not, gravitate to the answer choices that require the least concentration, knowledge, and memory. This is a mistake. When you come across an answer choice that is confusing, you should give it extra attention. A question might be confusing because you do not know the subject matter to which it refers. If this is the case, don't eliminate the answer before you have affirmatively settled on another. When you come across an answer choice of this type, set it aside as you look at the remaining choices. If you can confidently assert that one of the other choices is correct, you can leave the confusing answer aside. Otherwise, you will need to take a moment to try to better understand the confusing answer choice. Rephrasing is one way to tease out the sense of a confusing answer choice.

7. Your First Instinct

Many people struggle with multiple-choice tests because they overthink the questions. If you have studied sufficiently for the test, you should be prepared to trust your first instinct once you have carefully and completely read the question and all of the answer choices. There is a great deal of research suggesting that the mind can come to the correct conclusion very quickly once it has obtained all of the relevant information. At times, it may seem to you as if your intuition is working faster even than your reasoning mind. This may in fact be true. The knowledge you obtain while studying may be retrieved from your subconscious before you have a chance to work out the associations that support it. Verify your instinct by working out the reasons that it should be trusted.

8. Key Words

Many test takers struggle with multiple-choice questions because they have poor reading comprehension skills. Quickly reading and understanding a multiple-choice question requires a mixture of skill and experience. To help with this, try jotting down a few key words and phrases on a piece of scrap paper. Doing this concentrates the process of reading and forces the mind to weigh the relative importance of the question's parts. In selecting words and phrases to write down, the test taker thinks about the question more deeply and carefully. This is especially true for multiple-choice questions that are preceded by a long prompt.

9. Subtle Negatives

One of the oldest tricks in the multiple-choice test writer's book is to subtly reverse the meaning of a question with a word like *not* or *except*. If you are not paying attention to each word in the question, you can easily be led astray by this trick. For instance, a common question format is, "Which of the following is...?" Obviously, if the question instead is, "Which of the following is not...?," then the answer will be quite different. Even worse, the test makers are aware of the potential for this mistake and will include one answer choice that would be correct if the question were not negated or reversed. A test taker who misses the reversal will find what he or she believes to be a correct answer and will be so confident that he or she will fail to reread the question and discover the original error. The only way to avoid this is to practice a wide variety of multiple-choice questions and to pay close attention to each and every word.

10. Reading Every Answer Choice

It may seem obvious, but you should always read every one of the answer choices! Too many test takers fall into the habit of scanning the question and assuming that they understand the question because they recognize a few key words. From there, they pick the first answer choice that answers the question they believe they have read. Test takers who read all of the answer choices might discover that one of the latter answer choices is actually *more* correct. Moreover, reading all of the answer choices can remind you of facts related to the question that can help you arrive at the correct answer. Sometimes, a misstatement or incorrect detail in one of the latter answer choices will trigger your memory of the subject and will enable you to find the right answer. Failing to read all of the answer choices is like not reading all of the items on a restaurant menu: you might miss out on the perfect choice.

11. Spot the Hedges

One of the keys to success on multiple-choice tests is paying close attention to every word. This is never truer than with words like almost, most, some, and sometimes. These words are called "hedges" because they indicate that a statement is not totally true or not true in every place and time. An absolute statement will contain no hedges, but in many subjects, the answers are not always straightforward or absolute. There are always exceptions to the rules in these subjects. For this reason, you should favor those multiple-choice questions that contain hedging language. The presence of qualifying words indicates that the author is taking special care with their words, which is certainly important when composing the right answer. After all, there are many ways to be wrong, but there is only one way to be right! For this reason, it is wise to avoid answers that are absolute when taking a multiple-choice test. An absolute answer is one that says things are either all one way or all another. They often include words like *every*, *always*, *best*, and *never*. If you are taking a multiple-choice test in a subject that doesn't lend itself to absolute answers, be on your guard if you see any of these words.

12. Long Answers

In many subject areas, the answers are not simple. As already mentioned, the right answer often requires hedges. Another common feature of the answers to a complex or subjective question are qualifying clauses, which are groups of words that subtly modify the meaning of the sentence. If the question or answer choice describes a rule to which there are exceptions or the subject matter is complicated, ambiguous, or confusing, the correct answer will require many words in order to be expressed clearly and accurately. In essence, you should not be deterred by answer choices that seem

5

excessively long. Oftentimes, the author of the text will not be able to write the correct answer without offering some qualifications and modifications. Your job is to read the answer choices thoroughly and completely and to select the one that most accurately and precisely answers the question.

13. Restating to Understand

Sometimes, a question on a multiple-choice test is difficult not because of what it asks but because of how it is written. If this is the case, restate the question or answer choice in different words. This process serves a couple of important purposes. First, it forces you to concentrate on the core of the question. In order to rephrase the question accurately, you have to understand it well. Rephrasing the question will concentrate your mind on the key words and ideas. Second, it will present the information to your mind in a fresh way. This process may trigger your memory and render some useful scrap of information picked up while studying.

14. True Statements

Sometimes an answer choice will be true in itself, but it does not answer the question. This is one of the main reasons why it is essential to read the question carefully and completely before proceeding to the answer choices. Too often, test takers skip ahead to the answer choices and look for true statements. Having found one of these, they are content to select it without reference to the question above. Obviously, this provides an easy way for test makers to play tricks. The savvy test taker will always read the entire question before turning to the answer choices. Then, having settled on a correct answer choice, he or she will refer to the original question and ensure that the selected answer is relevant. The mistake of choosing a correct-but-irrelevant answer choice is especially common on questions related to specific pieces of objective knowledge. A prepared test taker will have a wealth of factual knowledge at their disposal, and should not be careless in its application.

15. No Patterns

One of the more dangerous ideas that circulates about multiple-choice tests is that the correct answers tend to fall into patterns. These erroneous ideas range from a belief that B and C are the most common right answers, to the idea that an unprepared test-taker should answer "A-B-A-C-A-D-A-B-A." It cannot be emphasized enough that pattern-seeking of this type is exactly the WRONG way to approach a multiple-choice test. To begin with, it is highly unlikely that the test maker will plot the correct answers according to some predetermined pattern. The questions are scrambled and delivered in a random order. Furthermore, even if the test maker was following a pattern in the assignation of correct answers, there is no reason why the test taker would know which pattern he or she was using. Any attempt to discern a pattern in the answer choices is a waste of time and a distraction from the real work of taking the test. A test taker would be much better served by extra preparation before the test than by reliance on a pattern in the answers.

Introduction to the TOEFL iBT

Function of the Test

The Test of English as a Foreign Language (TOEFL) internet Based Test (iBT) is an exam developed and administered by the Educational Testing Service (ETS) to measure test takers' ability to use and comprehend academic English at a university level. As such, the TOEFL iBT is a widely recognized English language credential for students planning to study in American colleges and universities, as well as in English language academic programs and institutions in over 130 countries. TOEFL scores may also be accepted by some immigration authorities for visas that require an English language proficiency component (policies vary by country and visa type).

According to ETS, over 30 million people have taken the TOEFL. Because of the diverse range of uses for a TOEFL iBT score, the exam is appropriate for a diverse range of test takers. In addition to providing credentials for school admissions and visa applications, TOEFL iBT scores may also be used for hiring criteria or simply for personal evaluation of language progress. (https://www.ets.org/toefl/ibt/about/)

Test Administration

The TOEFL iBT can be taken at an authorized ETS test center, or it can be taken at home. Testing centers located around the world offer the TOEFL iBT more than 60 times a year. To take the test at home, test takers have to meet the Environment and Equipment requirements. These must be met before registering for the exam. At-home testing is offered 24 hours a day and on 4 days out of the week. A third option is to take the test on paper. This method of testing is done in two separate sessions. The paper portion for Reading, Listening, and Writing is taken at a testing center, and the Speaking Section is taken by computer at home. The Speaking section must be done within three days of completing the paper portion. This option is only offered in some areas, so check the website for availability. Test takers must preregister one week before the exam; walk-in registration is not permitted. Refer to the ETS TOEFL website for a list of local test centers and exam dates. Test takers are permitted to retake the exam as many times as they choose, but are limited to one test within a 3-day period.

On the day of the exam, test takers must present the required ID. ID requirements vary based on where the testing will take place as well as citizenship, so refer to the ETS website for accurate information. Other personal belongings are not permitted in the testing room. Electronic devices like phones, cameras, and watches are prohibited, even during break time. Check the ETS website for any additional requirements or restrictions that specific testing centers may have. Food and beverages may be accessed during break time, and longer breaks or extended access to snacks and drinks may be available for test takers in need of exam accommodations. The TOEFL iBT offers a variety of other accommodations for students with disabilities, such as screen magnification, sign language interpretation, and Braille or audio versions of the test. (https://www.ets.org/toefl/ibt/register/disabilities/accommodations)

Test Format

The TOEFL iBT consists of four sections: reading, listening, speaking, and writing. It is necessary to take the entire test at once (it is not possible to take specific sections of the test) unless taking the test in paper form in the two-session format. One ten-minute break is given after the listening section.

Starting July 26, 2023, the type of questions, number of questions, and time limit will vary between subjects as follows:

Subject	Number of questions	Time
Reading	2 passages with 10 questions per passage	35 minutes
Listening	Approximately 3 lectures with 6 questions per lecture and 2 conversations with 5 questions per conversation 28 questions	36 minutes
Speaking	4 questions 1 Independent Speaking task 3 Integrated Speaking tasks	16 minutes total Response time: Independent speaking: 45 seconds per question Integrated speaking: 60 seconds per question
Writing	2 questions 1 Integrated Writing task 1 Academic Discussion Writing task	Integrated writing: 20 minutes Academic Discussion writing: 10 minutes

Test content is based on academic English. Reading and listening passages come from college level textbooks or lectures. Conversations will be related to campus topics and school life. The listening, speaking, and writing sections all include listening components (lectures and/or conversations), and speakers may have accented English from North America, the UK, Australia, or New Zealand.

Because TOEFL iBT is internet based, it is administered via computer. Test takers will use a headset with a microphone to listen to test questions and record their responses. Writing responses must be typed.

Scoring

Test takers can check their scores via their TOEFL online account approximately 10 days after completing the exam. Each section of the test is scored between 0-30 points, with a cumulative score of 0–120 points. Scores are valid for two years, and test takers are able to choose which valid scores from the past two years they wish to report to score recipients (although test scores must be used in their entirety; it is not possible to combine section scores from different test dates).

There are no "passing" or "failing" scores; rather, each institution or program determines its own guidelines for evaluating scores. Many institutions look for scores at or above 80-90 points, while competitive programs may require scores of 100 points or higher. Requirements vary greatly; refer to each institution for their evaluation criteria.

Recent/Future Developments

The TOEFL iBT is the newest version of the test. Previously, TOEFL was a paper-based test (PBT).

Listening Section

We have recorded audio to go along with the listening practice questions. All of the recordings can be found at https://testprepbooks.com/bonus/toefl/, or by scanning the QR code below. The audio is only online. There is no CD.

Study Prep Plan for the TOEFL iBT

1 **Schedule -** Use one of our study schedules below or come up with one of your own.

2 **Relax -** Test anxiety can hurt even the best students. There are many ways to reduce stress. Find the one that works best for you.

3 **Execute -** Once you have a good plan in place, be sure to stick to it.

One Week Study Schedule

Day 1	Reading
Day 2	Listening
Day 3	Writing
Day 4	Practice Test #1
Day 5	Practice Test #2
Day 6	Practice Test #3
Day 7	Take Your Exam!

Two Week Study Schedule

Day 1	Reading	Day 8	Sentences
Day 2	Main Idea	Day 9	Punctuation
Day 3	Authors Use of Evidence to Support	Day 10	Writing Practice
Day 4	Characteristics of Literary Genres	Day 11	Practice Test #1
Day 5	Listening	Day 12	Practice Test #2
Day 6	Speaking	Day 13	Practice Test #3
Day 7	Writing	Day 14	Take Your Exam!

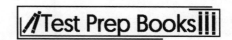

One Month Study Schedule					
Day 1	Reading	Day 11	Practice Quiz	Day 21	Various Homonyms
Day 2	Reading for Tone, Message, and Effect	Day 12	Listening	Day 22	Writing Practice
Day 3	Analysis of Science Excerpts	Day 13	Speaking	Day 23	Academic Discussion
Day 4	Reading Strategies	Day 14	Practice Quiz	Day 24	Practice Test #1
Day 5	Main Idea	Day 15	Writing	Day 25	Answer Explanations #1
Day 6	Meaning of Words in Context	Day 16	Parts of Speech	Day 26	Practice Test #2
Day 7	Authors Use of Evidence to Support.	Day 17	Possessives	Day 27	Answer Explanations #2
Day 8	Literary Elements	Day 18	Sentences	Day 28	Practice Test #3
Day 9	Characteristics of Literary Genres	Day 19	Phrases	Day 29	Answer Explanations #3
Day 10	Literary Nonfiction	Day 20	Punctuation	Day 30	Take Your Exam!

Build your own prep plan by visiting:
testprepbooks.com/prep

11

As you study for your test, we'd like to take the opportunity to remind you that you are capable of great things! With the right tools and dedication, you truly can do anything you set your mind to. The fact that you are holding this book right now shows how committed you are. In case no one has told you lately, you've got this! Our intention behind including this coloring page is to give you the chance to take some time to engage your creative side when you need a little brain-break from studying. As a company, we want to encourage people like you to achieve their dreams by providing good quality study materials for the tests and certifications that improve careers and change lives. As individuals, many of us have taken such tests in our careers, and we know how challenging this process can be. While we can't come alongside you and cheer you on personally, we can offer you the space to recall your purpose, reconnect with your passion, and refresh your brain through an artistic practice. We wish you every success, and happy studying!

Audio Passages

As you are going through this study guide, you will be directed to the online audio recordings for certain passages. All of the recordings can be found at https://testprepbooks.com/bonus/toefl, or by scanning the QR code below:

Reading

The Reading section is the first section on the TOEFL iBT® and is designed to assess the test taker's ability to understand university-level academic texts. The section includes 2 passages, with 10 questions pertaining to each passage, for a total of 20 questions. The total allotted time for the Reading section is 35 minutes.

It should be noted that the questions pertaining to the passage will not appear on the computer screen until the test taker has scrolled all the way to the end of the passage. At that point, the passage text moves to the right side of the screen and the associated questions are listed on left. The passage questions do not need to be answered in order, and test takers can skim them and then refer back to the passage to determine the correct answer.

Each passage is approximately 700 words and comes from an introductory-level university course text from any number of subjects such as biology, sociology, business, and literature. Test takers do not need prior experience or knowledge of the subject to answer the questions successfully; all necessary information is contained within the passages themselves. The test taker only needs to demonstrate their ability to comprehend academic texts, rather than convey an advanced understanding of the specific subject matter.

Test takers should be prepared to critically analyze the point of view and structure of the passage, as there are often multiple perspectives presented, and typically at least one question per passage addresses the organizational structure of the reading exercise.

The questions in the Reading section are of three possible formats, but each passage will have at least one question of each type:

- Multiple-choice questions with four answer options, in which the test taker selects the single best choice.

- Multiple-choice questions that present a sentence in the question and then display four answer options, each which denotes a specific area within the text of the passage. Test takers must select the single best choice that correctly indicates the point in the passage where the new sentence should be inserted.

- "Reading to Learn" questions, which list more than four choices and have more than one correct response and ask test takers to sort the provided answers into gaps in a provided chart or summary statement. Such questions assess the test taker's ability to decode the text's structure or to link ideas from various parts of the passage together.

The first type of multiple-choice questions can address a variety of things. These questions may require that the test taker identify the passage's or main idea or specific factual details that were explicitly stated in the text. Similarly, there are some questions in which the test taker must select the one detail that was *not* in the passage or is incorrectly presented in the answer choice in one way or another. Other questions may ask readers to identify the purpose of the passage in general or of specific statements, such that test takers need to decide *why* the author included a particular point. Some questions pull an entire sentence from the passage and then appear to simplify or paraphrase it in each of the four choices; incorrect choices will either omit important information from the original sentence

14

or contain inaccurate details. Lastly, test takers may need to make logical inferences based on the passage or to determine the meaning of vocabulary words or pronouns referenced in the reading.

Analysis of History/Social Studies Excerpts

The TOEFL iBT® Reading section may include historically-based excerpts. The test may also include one or more passages from social sciences such as economics, psychology, or sociology.

For these types of questions, the test taker will need to utilize all the reading comprehension skills discussed below, but mastery of further skills will help. This section addresses those skills.

Comprehending Test Questions Prior to Reading

While preparing for a historical passage on a standardized test, first read the test questions, and then quickly scan the test answers prior to reading the passage itself. Notice there is a difference between the terms **read** and **scan.** Reading involves full concentration while addressing every word. Scanning involves quickly glancing at text in chunks, noting important dates, words, and ideas along the way. Reading the test questions will help the test taker know what information to focus on in the historical passage. Scanning answers will help the test taker focus on possible answer options while reading the passage.

When reading standardized test questions that address historical passages, be sure to clearly understand what each question is asking. Is a question asking about vocabulary? Is another asking for the test taker to find a specific historical fact? Do any of the questions require the test taker to draw conclusions, identify an author's topic, tone, or position? Knowing what content to address will help the test taker focus on the information they will be asked about later. However, the test taker should approach this reading comprehension technique with some caution. It is tempting to only look for the right answers within any given passage. However, do not put on "reading blinders" and ignore all other information presented in a passage. It is important to fully read every passage and not just scan it. Strictly looking for what may be the right answers to test questions can cause the test taker to ignore important contextual clues that actually require critical thinking in order to identify correct answers. Scanning a passage for what appears to be wrong answers can have a similar result.

When reading the test questions prior to tackling, be sure to understand what skills the test is assessing, and then fully read the related passage with those skills in mind. Focus on every word in both the test questions and the passage itself. Read with a critical eye and a logical mind.

Reading for Factual Information

Standardized test questions that ask for factual information are usually straightforward. These types of questions will either ask the test taker to confirm a fact by choosing a correct answer, or to select a correct answer based on a negative fact question.

For example, the test taker may encounter a passage from Lincoln's Gettysburg Address. A corresponding test question may ask the following:

Which war is Abraham Lincoln referring to in the following passage?: "Now we are engaged in a great civil war, testing whether that nation, or any nation so conceived and so dedicated, can long endure."

This type of question is asking the test taker to confirm a simple fact. Given options such as World War I, the War of Spanish Succession, World War II, and the American Civil War, the test taker should be able to correctly identify the American Civil War based on the words "civil war" within the passage itself, and, hopefully, through general knowledge. In this case, reading the test question and scanning answer options ahead of reading the Gettysburg Address would help quickly identify the correct answer. Similarly, a test taker may be asked to confirm a historical fact based on a negative fact question. For example, a passage's corresponding test question may ask the following:

> Which option is incorrect based on the above passage?

Given a variety of choices speaking about which war Abraham Lincoln was addressing, the test taker would need to eliminate all correct answers pertaining to the American Civil War and choose the answer choice referencing a different war. In other words, the correct answer is the one that contradicts the information in the passage.

It is important to remember that reading for factual information is straightforward. The test taker must distinguish fact from bias. Factual statements can be proven or disproven independent of the author and from a variety of other sources. Remember, successfully answering questions regarding factual information may require the test taker to re-read the passage, as these types of questions test for attention to detail.

Reading for Tone, Message, and Effect

The Reading section does not just address a test taker's ability to find facts within a reading passage; it also determines a reader's ability to determine an author's viewpoint through the use of tone, message, and overall effect. This type of reading comprehension requires inference skills, deductive reasoning skills, the ability to draw logical conclusions, and overall critical thinking skills. Reading for factual information is straightforward. Reading for an author's tone, message, and overall effect is not. It's key to read carefully when asked test questions that address a test taker's ability to identify and analyze these writing devices. These are not questions that can be easily answered by quickly scanning for the right information.

Tone

An author's **tone** is the use of particular words, phrases, and writing style to convey an overall meaning. Tone expresses the author's attitude towards a particular topic. For example, a historical reading passage may begin like the following:

> The presidential election of 1960 ushered in a new era, a new Camelot, a new phase of forward thinking in U.S. politics that embraced brash action and unrest and responded with admirable leadership.

From this opening statement, a reader can draw some conclusions about the author's attitude towards President John F. Kennedy. Furthermore, the reader can make additional, educated guesses about the state of the Union during the 1960 presidential election. By close reading, the test taker can determine that the repeated use of the word *new* and words such as *admirable leadership* indicate the author's tone of admiration regarding President Kennedy's boldness. In addition, the author assesses that the era during President Kennedy's administration was problematic through the use of the words *brash action* and *unrest*. Therefore, if a test taker encountered a test question asking about the author's use of tone and their assessment of the Kennedy administration, the test taker should be able to identify an answer

16

indicating admiration. Similarly, if asked about the state of the Union during the 1960s, a test taker should be able to correctly identify an answer indicating political unrest.

When identifying an author's tone, the following list of words may be helpful. This is not an inclusive list. Generally, parts of speech that indicate attitude will also indicate tone:

- Comical
- Angry
- Ambivalent
- Scary
- Lyrical
- Matter-of-fact
- Judgmental
- Sarcastic
- Malicious
- Objective
- Pessimistic
- Patronizing
- Gloomy
- Instructional
- Satirical
- Formal
- Casual

Message

An author's **message** is the same as the overall meaning of a passage. It is the main idea, or the main concept the author wishes to convey. An author's message may be stated outright, or it may be implied. Regardless, the test taker will need to use careful reading skills to identify an author's message or purpose.

Often, the message of a particular passage can be determined by thinking about why the author wrote the information. Many historical passages are written to inform and to teach readers established, factual information. However, many historical works are also written to convey biased ideas to readers. Gleaning bias from an author's message in a historical passage can be difficult, especially if the reader is presented with a variety of established facts as well. Readers tend to accept historical writing as factual. This is not always the case. Any discerning reader who has tackled historical information on topics such as United States political party agendas can attest that two or more works on the same topic may have completely different messages supporting or refuting the value of the identical policies. Therefore, it is important to critically assess an author's message separate from factual information.

One author, for example, may point to the rise of unorthodox political candidates in an election year based on the failures of the political party in office while another may point to the rise of the same candidates in the same election year based on the current party's successes. The historical facts of what has occurred leading up to an election year are not in refute. Labeling those facts as a failure or a success is a bias within an author's overall message, as is excluding factual information in order to further a particular point. In a standardized testing situation, a reader must be able to critically assess what the author is trying to say separate from the historical facts that surround their message.

17

Using the example of Lincoln's Gettysburg Address, a test question may ask the following:

What message is the author trying to convey through this address?

Then they will ask the test taker to select an answer that best expresses Lincoln's message to his audience. Based on the options given, a test taker should be able to select the answer expressing the idea that Lincoln's audience should recognize the efforts of those who died in the war as a sacrifice to preserving human equality and self-government.

Effect

The **effect** is the particular mood that the author wants the reader to experience while or after reading. An author may want to challenge a reader's intellect, inspire imagination, or spur emotion. An author may present information to appeal to a physical, aesthetic, or transformational sense. Take the following text as an example:

In 1963, Martin Luther King stated "I have a dream." The gathering at the Lincoln Memorial was the beginning of the Civil Rights movement and, with its reference to the Emancipation Proclamation, Dr. King's words electrified those who wanted freedom and equality while rising from hatred and slavery. It was the beginning of radical change.

The test taker may be asked about the effect this statement might have on King's audience. Through careful reading of the passage, the test taker should be able to choose an answer that best identifies an effect of grabbing the audience's attention. The historical facts are in place: King made the speech in 1963 at the Lincoln Memorial, kicked off the civil rights movement, and referenced the Emancipation Proclamation. The words *electrified* and *radical change* indicate the effect the author wants the reader to understand as a result of King's speech. In this historical passage, facts are facts. However, the author's message goes beyond the facts to indicate the effect the message had on the audience and, in addition, the effect the event should have on the reader.

When reading historical passages, the test taker should perform due diligence in their awareness of the test questions and answers up front. From there, the test taker should carefully, and critically, read all historical excerpts with an eye for detail, tone, message (biased or unbiased), and effect. Being able to synthesize these skills will result in success in a standardized testing situation.

Analysis of Science Excerpts

The Reading section may include passages that address the fundamental concepts of Earth science, biology, chemistry, or other sciences. Again, prior knowledge of these subjects is not necessary to determine correct test answers; instead, the test taker's ability to comprehend the passages is key to success. When reading scientific excerpts, the test taker must be able to examine quantitative information, identify hypotheses, interpret data, and consider implications of the material they are presented with. It is helpful, at this point, to reference the above section on comprehending test questions prior to reading. The same rules apply: read questions and scan questions, along with their answers, prior to fully reading a passage. Be informed prior to approaching a scientific text. A test taker should know what they will be asked and how to apply their reading skills. In this section of the test, it is also likely that a test taker will encounter graphs and charts to assess their ability to interpret scientific data with an appropriate conclusion. This section may use the identification of hypotheses, the reading

18

and examination of data, and the interpretation of data representation passages to determine the skill levels of test takers in the comprehension of scientific data.

Examine Hypotheses

When presented with fundamental, scientific concepts, it is important to read for understanding. The most basic skill in achieving this literacy is to understand the concept of hypothesis and, moreover, to be able to identify it in a particular passage. A **hypothesis** is a proposed idea that needs further investigation in order to be proven true or false. While it can be considered an educated guess, a hypothesis goes more in depth in its attempt to explain something that is not currently accepted within scientific theory. It requires further experimentation and data gathering to test its validity and is subject to change, based on scientifically conducted test results. Being able to read a science passage and understand its main purpose, including any hypotheses, helps the test taker understand data-driven evidence. It helps the test taker to be able to correctly answer questions about the science excerpt they are asked to read.

When reading to identify a hypothesis, a test taker should ask, "What is the passage trying to establish? What is the passage's main idea? What evidence does the passage contain that either supports or refutes this idea?" Asking oneself these questions will help identify a hypothesis. Additionally, hypotheses are logical statements that are testable and use very precise language.

Review the following hypothesis example:

> Consuming excess sugar in the form of beverages has a greater impact on childhood obesity and subsequent weight gain than excessive sugar from food.

While this is likely a true statement, it is still only a conceptual idea in a text passage regarding how sugar consumption affects childhood obesity, unless the passage also contains tested data that either proves or disproves the statement. A test taker could expect the rest of the passage to cite data proving that children who drink empty calories gain more weight and are more likely to be obese than children who eat sugary snacks.

A hypothesis goes further in that, given its ability to be proven or disproven, it may result in further hypotheses that require extended research. For example, the hypothesis regarding sugar consumption in drinks, after undergoing rigorous testing, may lead scientists to state another hypothesis such as the following:

> Consuming excess sugar in the form of beverages as opposed to food items is a habit found in mostly sedentary children.

This new, working hypothesis further focuses not just on the source of an excess of calories, but tries an "educated guess" that empty caloric intake has a direct, subsequent impact on physical behavior.

When reading a science passage to determine its hypothesis, a test taker should look for a concept that attempts to explain a phenomenon, is testable, is logical, is precisely worded, and yields data-driven results. The test taker should scan the presented passage for any word or data-driven clues that will help identify the hypothesis, and then be able to correctly answer test questions regarding the hypothesis by using their critical thinking skills.

19

Reading Strategies

A **reading strategy** is a planned method that a reader uses to interact with and think about a text in order to understand its meaning. This is more than just reading a text as it appears. It involves a system that helps the reader categorize and internalize what they are reading.

Pre-Reading Strategies

Pre-reading strategies are important, yet often overlooked. Non-critical readers will often begin reading without taking the time to review factors that will help them understand the text. Skipping pre-reading strategies may result in a reader having to re-address a text passage more times than is necessary. Some pre-reading strategies include the following:

- Previewing the text for clues
- Skimming the text for content
- Scanning for unfamiliar words in context
- Formulating questions on sight
- Recognizing needed prior knowledge

Before reading a text passage, a reader can enhance their ability to comprehend material by **previewing the text for clues**. This may mean making careful note of any titles, headings, graphics, notes, introductions, important summaries, and conclusions. It can involve a reader making physical notes regarding these elements or highlighting anything they think is important before reading. Often, a reader will be able to gain information just from these elements alone. Of course, close reading is required in order to fill in the details. A reader needs to be able to ask what they are reading about and what a passage is trying to say. The answers to these general questions can often be answered in previewing the text itself.

It's helpful to use pre-reading clues to determine the main idea and organization. First, any titles, sub-headings, and chapter headings should be read, and the test taker should make note of the author's credentials if any are listed. It's important to deduce what these clues may indicate as it pertains to the focus of the text and how it's organized.

During pre-reading, readers should also take special note of how text features contribute to the central idea or thesis of the passage. Is there an index? Is there a glossary? What headings, footnotes, or other visuals are included and how do they relate to the details within the passage? Again, this is where any pre-reading notes come in handy, since a test taker should be able to relate supporting details to these textual features.

Next, a reader should **skim** the text for general ideas and content. This technique does not involve close reading; rather, it involves looking for important words within the passage itself. These words may have something to do with the author's theme. They may have to do with structure—for example, words such as *first, next, therefore*, and *last*. Skimming helps a reader understand the overall structure of a passage and, in turn, this helps them understand the author's theme or message.

From there, a reader should quickly **scan** the text for any unfamiliar words. When reading a print text, highlighting these words or making other marginal notation is helpful when going back to read text critically. A reader should look at the words surrounding any unfamiliar ones to see what contextual clues unfamiliar words carry. Being able to define unfamiliar terms through contextual meaning is a critical skill in reading comprehension.

A reader should also **formulate** any questions they might have before conducting close reading. Questions such as "What is the author trying to tell me?" or "Is the author trying to persuade my thinking?" are important to a reader's ability to engage critically with the text. Questions will focus a reader's attention on what is important in terms of ideas and supporting details.

Last, a reader should recognize that authors assume readers bring a prior knowledge set to the reading experience. Not all readers have the same experience, but authors seek to communicate with their readers. In turn, readers should strive to interact with the author of a particular passage by asking themselves what the passage demands they know during reading. If a passage is informational in nature, a reader should ask "What do I know about this topic from other experiences I've had or other works I've read?" If a reader can relate to the content, they will better understand it.

All of the above pre-reading strategies will help the reader prepare for a closer reading experience. They will engage a reader in active interaction with the text by helping to focus the reader's full attention on the details that they will encounter during the next round or two of critical, closer reading.

Strategies During Reading

After pre-reading, a test taker can employ a variety of other reading strategies while conducting one or more closer readings. These strategies include the following:

- Inferring the unspoken/unwritten text
- Clarifying during a close read
- Questioning during a close read
- Organizing the main ideas and supporting details
- Summarizing the text effectively

Inferring the unspoken or unwritten text demands the reader read between the lines in terms of an author's intent or message. The strategy asks that a reader not take everything he or she reads at face value, but instead, he or she will determine what the author is trying to say. A reader's ability to make inference relies on their ability to think clearly and logically about what he or she is reading. It does not ask that the reader make wild speculation or guess about the material but demands he or she be able to come to sound conclusion about the material, given the details provided and those not provided. A reader who can make logical inference from unstated text is achieving successful reading comprehension.

A reader needs to be able to **clarify** what they are reading. This strategy demands a reader think about how and what they are reading. This thinking should occur during and after the act of reading. For example, a reader may encounter one or more unfamiliar ideas during reading, then be asked to apply thoughts about those unfamiliar concepts after reading when answering test questions.

Questioning during a critical read is closely related to clarifying. A reader must be able to ask questions in general about what they are reading and about the author's supporting ideas. Questioning also involves a reader's ability to self-question. When closely reading a passage, it's not enough to simply try to understand the author. A reader must consider critical thinking questions to ensure they are comprehending intent. It's advisable, when conducting a close read, to write out margin notes and questions during the experience. These questions can be addressed later in the thinking process after reading and during the phase where a reader addresses the test questions. A reader who is successful in

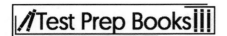
reading comprehension will iteratively question what they read, search text for clarification, then answer any questions that arise.

A reader should **organize** main ideas and supporting details cognitively as they read, as it will help them understand the larger structure at work. The use of quick annotations or marks to indicate what the main idea is and how the details function to support it can be helpful. Understanding the structure of a text passage is sometimes critical to answering questions about an author's approach, theme, messages, and supporting details. This strategy is most effective when reading informational or nonfiction texts. Texts that try to convince readers of a particular idea, that present a theory, or that try to explain difficult concepts are easier to understand when a reader can identify the overarching structure at work.

Post-Reading Strategies

After completing a text, a reader should be able to **summarize** the author's theme and supporting details in order to fully understand the passage. Being able to effectively restate the author's message, sub-themes, and pertinent, supporting ideas will help a reader gain an advantage when addressing standardized test questions. Employing all of these strategies will lead to fuller, more insightful reading comprehension.

Main Idea

It is very important to know the difference between the topic and the main idea of the text. Even though these two are similar because they both present the central point of a text, they have distinctive differences. A **topic** is the subject of the text. This can usually be described in a concise one-to two-word phrase. On the other hand, the **main idea** is more detailed and provides the author's central point of the text. It can be expressed through a complete sentence and can be found in the beginning, middle, or end of a paragraph. In most nonfiction books, the first sentence of the passage usually (but not always) states the main idea. Take a look at the passage below to review the topic versus the main idea:

Cheetahs

Cheetahs are one of the fastest mammals on land, reaching up to 70 miles an hour over short distances. Even though cheetahs can run as fast as 70 miles an hour, they usually only have to run half that speed to catch up with their choice of prey. Cheetahs cannot maintain a fast pace over long periods of time because they will overheat their bodies. After a chase, cheetahs need to rest for approximately 30 minutes prior to eating or returning to any other activity.

In the example above, the topic of the passage is "Cheetahs" simply because that is the subject of the text. The main idea of the text is "Cheetahs are one of the fastest mammals on land but can only maintain this fast pace for short distances." While it covers the topic, it is more detailed and refers to the text in its entirety. The text continues to provide additional details called **supporting details**, which will be discussed in the next section.

Supporting Details

Supporting details help readers better develop and understand the main idea. Supporting details answer questions like *who, what, where, when, why,* and *how*. Different types of supporting details include examples, facts and statistics, anecdotes, and sensory details.

22

Persuasive and informative texts often use supporting details. In persuasive texts, authors attempt to make readers agree with their point of view, and supporting details are often used as "selling points." If authors make a statement, they should support the statement with evidence in order to adequately persuade readers. Informative texts use supporting details such as examples and facts to inform readers. Take another look at the previous "Cheetahs" passage to find examples of supporting details:

Cheetahs

Cheetahs are one of the fastest mammals on land, reaching up to 70 miles an hour over short distances. Even though cheetahs can run as fast as 70 miles an hour, they usually only have to run half that speed to catch up with their choice of prey. Cheetahs cannot maintain a fast pace over long periods of time because they will overheat their bodies. After a chase, cheetahs need to rest for approximately 30 minutes prior to eating or returning to any other activity.

In the example above, supporting details include:

- Cheetahs reach up to 70 miles per hour over short distances.
- They usually only have to run half that speed to catch up with their prey.
- Cheetahs will overheat their bodies if they exert a high speed over longer distances.
- Cheetahs need to rest for 30 minutes after a chase.

Look at the diagram below (applying the cheetah example) to help determine the hierarchy of topic, main idea, and supporting details.

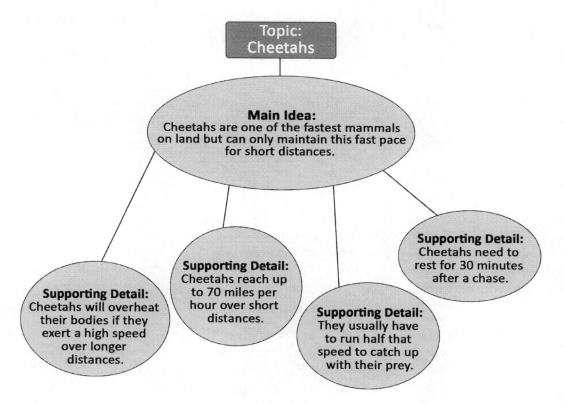

23

Analyzing Nuances of Word Meaning and Figures of Speech

Many words contain two levels of meaning: connotation and denotation. A word's **denotation** is its most literal meaning—the definition that can readily be found in the dictionary. A word's **connotation** includes all of its emotional and cultural associations.

In literary writing, authors rely heavily on connotative meaning to create mood and characterization. The following are two descriptions of a rainstorm:

- The rain slammed against the windowpane, and the wind howled through the fireplace. A pair of hulking oaks next to the house cast eerie shadows as their branches trembled in the wind.

- The rain pattered against the windowpane, and the wind whistled through the fireplace. A pair of stately oaks next to the house cast curious shadows as their branches swayed in the wind.

The first description paints a creepy picture for readers with strongly emotional words like *slammed*, connoting force and violence. *Howled* connotes pain or wildness, and *eerie* and *trembled* connote fear. Overall, the connotative language in this description serves to inspire fear and anxiety.

However, as can be seen in the second description, swapping out a few key words for those with different connotations completely changes the feeling of the passage. *Slammed* is replaced with the more cheerful *pattered*, and *hulking* has been swapped out for *stately*. Both words imply something large, but *hulking* is more intimidating whereas *stately* is more respectable. *Curious* and *swayed* seem more playful than the language used in the earlier description. Although both descriptions represent roughly the same situation, the nuances of the emotional language used throughout the passages create a very different sense for readers.

Selective choice of connotative language can also be extremely impactful in other forms of writing, such as editorials or persuasive texts. Through connotative language, writers reveal their biases and opinions while trying to inspire feelings and actions in readers:

- Parents won't stop complaining about standardized tests.
- Parents continue to raise concerns about standardized tests.

Readers should be able to identify the nuance in meaning between these two sentences. The first one carries a more negative feeling, implying that parents are being bothersome or whiny. Readers of the second sentence, though, might come away with the feeling that parents are concerned and involved in their children's education. Again, the aggregate of even subtle cues can combine to give a specific emotional impression to readers, so from an early age, students should be aware of how language can be used to influence readers' opinions.

Another form of non-literal expression can be found in **figures of speech**. As with connotative language, figures of speech tend to be shared within a cultural group and may be difficult to pick up on for learners outside of that group. In some cases, a figure of speech may be based on the literal denotation of the words it contains, but in other cases, a figure of speech is far removed from its literal meaning. A case in point is **irony**, where what is said is the exact opposite of what is meant:

The new tax plan is poorly planned, based on faulty economic data, and unable to address the financial struggles of middle-class families. Yet legislators remain committed to passing this brilliant proposal.

When the writer refers to the proposal as brilliant, the opposite is implied—the plan is "faulty" and "poorly planned." By using irony, the writer means that the proposal is anything but brilliant by using the word in a non-literal sense.

Another figure of speech is **hyperbole**—extreme exaggeration or overstatement. Statements like "I love you to the moon and back" or "Let's be friends for a million years" utilize hyperbole to convey a greater depth of emotion, without literally committing oneself to space travel or a life of immortality.

Figures of speech may sometimes use one word in place of another. **Synecdoche**, for example, uses a part of something to refer to its whole. The expression "Don't hurt a hair on her head!" implies protecting more than just an individual hair, but rather her entire body. "The art teacher is training a class of Picassos" uses Picasso, one individual notable artist, to stand in for the entire category of talented artists. Another figure of speech using word replacement is **metonymy**, where a word is replaced with something closely associated to it. For example, news reports may use the word *Washington* to refer to the American government or *the crown* to refer to the British monarch.

Meaning of Words in Context

There will be many occasions in one's reading career in which an unknown word or a word with multiple meanings will pop up. There are ways of determining what these words or phrases mean that do not require the use of the dictionary, which is especially helpful during a test where one may not be available. Even outside of the exam, knowing how to derive an understanding of a word via context clues will be a critical skill in the real world. The context is the circumstances in which a story or a passage is happening and can usually be found in the series of words directly before or directly after the word or phrase in question. The clues are the words that hint towards the meaning of the unknown word or phrase.

There may be questions that ask about the meaning of a particular word or phrase within a passage. There are a couple ways to approach these kinds of questions:

- Define the word or phrase in a way that is easy to comprehend (using context clues).
- Try out each answer choice in place of the word.

To demonstrate, here's an example from *Alice in Wonderland*:

Alice was beginning to get very tired of sitting by her sister on the bank, and of having nothing to do: once or twice she <u>peeped</u> into the book her sister was reading, but it had no pictures or conversations in it, "and what is the use of a book," thought Alice, "without pictures or conversations?"

Q: As it is used in the selection, the word <u>peeped</u> means:

Using the first technique, before looking at the answers, define the word *peeped* using context clues and then find the matching answer. Then, analyze the entire passage in order to determine the meaning, not just the surrounding words.

To begin, imagine a blank where the word should be and put a synonym or definition there: "once or twice she _____ into the book her sister was reading." The context clue here is the book. It may be tempting to put *read* where the blank is, but notice the preposition word, *into*. One does not read *into* a book, one simply reads a book, and since reading a book requires that it is seen with a pair of eyes, then *look* would make the most sense to put into the blank: "once or twice she <u>looked</u> into the book her sister was reading."

Once an easy-to-understand word or synonym has been supplanted, readers should check to make sure it makes sense with the rest of the passage. What happened after she looked into the book? She thought to herself how a book without pictures or conversations is useless. This situation in its entirety makes sense.

Now check the answer choices for a match:
a. To make a high-pitched cry
b. To smack
c. To look curiously
d. To pout

Since the word was already defined, Choice *C* is the best option.

Using the second technique, replace the figurative blank with each of the answer choices and determine which one is the most appropriate. Remember to look further into the passage to clarify that they work, because they could still make sense out of context.
a. Once or twice, she <u>made a high pitched cry</u> into the book her sister was reading
b. Once or twice, she <u>smacked</u> into the book her sister was reading
c. Once or twice, she <u>looked curiously</u> into the book her sister was reading
d. Once or twice, she <u>pouted</u> into the book her sister was reading

For Choice *A*, it does not make much sense in any context for a person to cry into a book, unless maybe something terrible has happened in the story. Given that afterward Alice thinks to herself how useless a book without pictures is, this option does not make sense within context.

For Choice *B*, smacking a book someone is reading may make sense if the rest of the passage indicates a reason for doing so. If Alice was angry or her sister had shoved it in her face, then maybe smacking the book would make sense within context. However, since whatever she does with the book causes her to think, "what is the use of a book without pictures or conversations?" then answer Choice *B* is not an appropriate answer. Answer Choice *C* fits well within context, given her subsequent thoughts on the matter. Answer Choice *D* does not make sense in context or grammatically, as people do not *pout into* things.

This is a simple example to illustrate the techniques outlined above. There may, however, be a question in which all of the definitions are correct and also make sense out of context, in which the appropriate context clues will really need to be honed in on in order to determine the correct answer. For example, here is another passage from *Alice in Wonderland*:

> ... but when the Rabbit actually took a watch out of its waistcoat pocket, and looked at it, and then hurried on, Alice <u>started</u> to her feet, for it flashed across her mind that she had never before seen a rabbit with either a waistcoat-pocket or a watch to take out of it, and burning

26

with curiosity, she ran across the field after it, and was just in time to see it pop down a large rabbit-hole under the hedge.

Q: As it is used in the passage, the word <u>started</u> means _____.
    a. to turn on
    b. to begin
    c. to move quickly
    d. to be surprised

All of these words qualify as a definition of *start*, but using context clues, the correct answer can be identified using one of the two techniques above. It's easy to see that one does not turn on, begin, or be surprised to one's feet. The selection also states that she "ran across the field after it," indicating that she was in a hurry. Therefore, to move quickly would make the most sense in this context.

The same strategies can be applied to vocabulary that may be completely unfamiliar. In this case, focus on the words before or after the unknown word in order to determine its definition. Take this sentence, for example:

> Sam was such a <u>miser</u> that he forced Andrew to pay him twelve cents for the candy, even though he had a large inheritance and he knew his friend was poor.

Unlike with assertion questions, for vocabulary questions, it may be necessary to apply some critical thinking skills when something isn't explicitly stated within the passage. Think about the implications of the passage, or what the text is trying to say. With this example, it is important to realize that it is considered unusually stingy for a person to demand so little money from someone instead of just letting their friend have the candy, especially if this person is already wealthy. Hence, a <u>miser</u> is a greedy or stingy individual.

Questions about complex vocabulary may not be explicitly asked, but this is a useful skill to know. If there is an unfamiliar word while reading a passage and its definition goes unknown, it is possible to miss out on a critical message that could inhibit the ability to appropriately answer the questions. Practicing this technique in daily life will sharpen this ability to derive meanings from context clues with ease.

Transitional Words and Phrases

There are approximately 200 transitional words and phrases that are commonly used in the English language. Below are lists of common transition words and phrases used throughout transitions:

Time
    • after
    • before
    • during
    • in the middle

Example about to be Given
    • for example
    • in fact

- for instance

Compare
- likewise
- also

Contrast
- however
- yet
- but

Addition
- and
- also
- furthermore
- moreover

Logical Relationships
- if
- then
- therefore
- as a result
- since

Steps in a Process
- first
- second
- last

Transitional words and phrases are important writing devices because they connect sentences and paragraphs. Transitional words and phrases present logical order to writing and provide more coherent meaning to readers.

Transition words can be categorized based on the relationships they create between ideas:

- General order: signaling elaboration of an idea to emphasize a point—e.g., *for example, for instance, to demonstrate, including, such as, in other words, that is, in fact, also, furthermore, likewise, and, truly, so, surely, certainly, obviously, doubtless*

- Chronological order: referencing the time frame in which the main event or idea occurs—e.g., *before, after, first, while, soon, shortly thereafter, meanwhile*

- Numerical order/order of importance: indicating that related ideas, supporting details, or events will be described in a sequence, possibly in order of importance—e.g., *first, second, also, finally, another, in addition, equally important, less importantly, most significantly, the main reason, last but not least*

28

- Spatial order: referring to the space and location of something or where things are located in relation to each other—e.g., *inside, outside, above, below, within, close, under, over, far, next to, adjacent to*

- Cause and effect order: signaling a causal relationship between events or ideas—e.g., *thus, therefore, since, resulted in, for this reason, as a result, consequently, hence, for, so*

- Compare and contrast order: identifying the similarities and differences between two or more objects, ideas, or lines of thought—e.g., *like, as, similarly, equally, just as, unlike, however, but, although, conversely, on the other hand, on the contrary*

- Summary order: indicating that a particular idea is coming to a close—e.g., *in conclusion, to sum up, in other words, ultimately, above all*

Author's Use of Evidence to Support Claims

Authors utilize a wide range of techniques to tell a story or communicate information. Readers should be familiar with the most common of these techniques. Techniques of writing are also commonly known as rhetorical devices; these are different ways of using evidence to support claims.

In nonfiction writing, authors employ argumentative techniques to present their opinion to readers in the most convincing way. Persuasive writing usually includes at least one type of appeal: an appeal to logic (logos), emotion (pathos), or credibility and trustworthiness (ethos). When a writer appeals to logic, they are asking readers to agree with them based on research, evidence, and an established line of reasoning. An author's argument might also appeal to readers' emotions, perhaps by including personal stories and anecdotes (a short narrative of a specific event). A final type of appeal, appeal to authority, asks the reader to agree with the author's argument on the basis of their expertise or credentials. Consider three different approaches to arguing the same opinion:

Logic (Logos)

Below is an example of an appeal to logic. The author uses evidence to disprove the logic of the school's rule (the rule was supposed to reduce discipline problems, but the number of problems has not been reduced; therefore, the rule is not working) and call for its repeal.

> Our school should abolish its current ban on campus cell phone use. The ban was adopted last year as an attempt to reduce class disruptions and help students focus more on their lessons. However, since the rule was enacted, there has been no change in the number of disciplinary problems in class. Therefore, the rule is ineffective and should be done away with.

Emotion (Pathos)

An author's argument might also appeal to readers' emotions, perhaps by including personal stories and anecdotes.

The next example presents an appeal to emotion. By sharing the personal anecdote of one student and speaking about emotional topics like family relationships, the author invokes the reader's empathy in asking them to reconsider the school rule.

> Our school should abolish its current ban on campus cell phone use. If students aren't able to use their phones during the school day, many of them feel isolated from their loved ones. For

29

example, last semester, one student's grandmother had a heart attack in the morning. However, because he couldn't use his cell phone, the student didn't know about his grandmother's condition until the end of the day—when she had already passed away, and it was too late to say goodbye. By preventing students from contacting their friends and family, our school is placing undue stress and anxiety on students.

Credibility (Ethos)

Finally, an appeal to authority includes a statement from a relevant expert. In this case, the author uses a doctor in the field of education to support the argument. All three examples begin from the same opinion—the school's phone ban needs to change—but rely on different argumentative styles to persuade the reader.

> Our school should abolish its current ban on campus cell phone use. According to Dr. Bartholomew Everett, a leading educational expert, "Research studies show that cell phone usage has no real impact on student attentiveness. Rather, phones provide a valuable technological resource for learning. Schools need to learn how to integrate this new technology into their curriculum." Rather than banning phones altogether, our school should follow the advice of experts and allow students to use phones as part of their learning.

Making Logical Inferences

Critical readers should be able to make inferences. Making an **inference** requires the reader to read between the lines and look for what is implied rather than what is explicitly stated. That is, using information that *is* known from the text, the reader is able to make a logical assumption about information that is not explicitly stated but is probably true. Read the following passage:

> "Hey, do you wanna meet my new puppy?" Jonathan asked.

> "Oh, I'm sorry but please don't—" Jacinta began to protest, but before she could finish Jonathan had already opened the passenger side door of his car and a perfect white ball of fur came bouncing towards Jacinta.

> "Isn't he the cutest?" beamed Jonathan.

> "Yes—achoo!—he's pretty—aaaachooo!!—adora—aaa—aaaachoo!" Jacinta managed to say in between sneezes. "But if you don't mind, I—I—achoo!—need to go inside."

Which of the following can be inferred from Jacinta's reaction to the puppy?
   a.   She hates animals.
   b.   She is allergic to dogs.
   c.   She prefers cats to dogs.
   d.   She is angry at Jonathan.

An inference requires the reader to consider the information presented and then form their own idea about what is probably true. Based on the details in the passage, what is the best answer to the question? Important details to pay attention to include the tone of Jacinta's dialogue, which is overall polite and apologetic, as well as her reaction itself, which is a long string of sneezes. Choices *A* and *D* both express strong emotions ("hates" and "angry") that are not evident in Jacinta's speech or actions. Choice *C* mentions cats, but there is nothing in the passage to indicate Jacinta's feelings about cats.

30

Choice *B*, "she is allergic to dogs," is the most logical choice. Based on the fact she began sneezing as soon as a fluffy dog approached her, it makes sense to guess that Jacinta might be allergic to dogs. Using the clues in the passage, it is reasonable to guess that this is true even though Jacinta never directly states, "Sorry, I'm allergic to dogs!"

Making inferences is crucial for readers of literature because literary texts often avoid presenting complete and direct information to readers about characters' thoughts or feelings, or they present this information in an unclear way, leaving it up to the reader to interpret clues given in the text. In order to make inferences while reading, readers should ask themselves:

- What details are being presented in the text?
- Is there any important information that seems to be missing?
- Based on the information that the author *does* include, what else is probably true?
- Is this inference reasonable based on what is already known?

Recognizing the Structure of Texts in Various Formats

Writing can be classified under four passage types: narrative, expository, descriptive (sometimes called technical), and persuasive. Though these types are not mutually exclusive, one form tends to dominate the rest. By recognizing the *type* of passage you're reading, you gain insight into *how* you should read. If you're reading a narrative, you can assume the author intends to entertain, which means you may skim the text without losing meaning. A technical document might require a close read because skimming the passage might cause the reader to miss salient details.

1. **Narrative writing**, at its core, is the art of storytelling. For a narrative to exist, certain elements must be present. First, it must have characters. While many characters are human, characters could be defined as anything that thinks, acts, and talks like a human. For example, many recent movies, such as *Lord of the Rings* and *The Chronicles of Narnia*, include animals, fantastical creatures, and even trees that behave like humans. Second, it must have a plot or sequence of events. Typically, those events follow a standard plot diagram, but recent trends start *in medias res* or in the middle (near the climax). In this instance, foreshadowing and flashbacks often fill in plot details. Finally, along with characters and a plot, there must also be conflict. Conflict is usually divided into two types: internal and external. Internal conflict indicates the character is in turmoil and is presented through the character's thoughts. External conflicts are visible. Types of external conflict include a person versus nature, another person, or society.

2. **Expository writing** is detached and to the point. Since expository writing is designed to instruct or inform, it usually involves directions and steps written in second person ("you" voice) and lacks any persuasive or narrative elements. Sequence words such as *first*, *second*, and *third*, or *in the first place*, *secondly*, and *lastly* are often given to add fluency and cohesion. Common examples of expository writing include instructor's lessons, cookbook recipes, and repair manuals.

3. Due to its empirical nature, **technical writing** is filled with steps, charts, graphs, data, and statistics. The goal of technical writing is to advance understanding in a field through the scientific method. Experts such as teachers, doctors, or mechanics use words unique to the profession in which they operate. These words, which often incorporate acronyms, are called **jargon**. Technical writing is a type of expository writing but is not meant to be understood by the general public. Instead, technical writers assume readers have received a formal education in a particular field of study and need no explanation

31

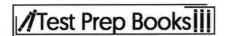

as to what the jargon means. Imagine a doctor trying to understand a diagnostic reading for a car or a mechanic trying to interpret lab results. Only professionals with proper training will fully comprehend the text.

4. **Persuasive writing** is designed to change opinions and attitudes. The topic, stance, and arguments are found in the thesis, positioned near the end of the introduction. Later supporting paragraphs offer relevant quotations, paraphrases, and summaries from primary or secondary sources, which are then interpreted, analyzed, and evaluated. The goal of persuasive writers is not to stack quotes but to develop original ideas by using sources as a starting point. Good persuasive writing makes powerful arguments with valid sources and thoughtful analysis. Poor persuasive writing is riddled with bias and logical fallacies. Sometimes logical and illogical arguments are sandwiched together in the same piece. Therefore, readers should display skepticism when reading persuasive arguments.

Literary Elements

There is no one, final definition of what literary elements are. They can be considered features or characteristics of fiction, but they are really more of a way that readers can examine a text for the purpose of analysis and understanding the meaning. The elements contribute to a reader's literary interpretation of a passage as to how they function to convey the central message of a work. The most common literary elements used for analysis are presented below.

Point of View

The **point of view** is the position the narrator takes when telling the story in prose. If a narrator is incorporated in a drama, the point of view may vary; in poetry, point of view refers to the position the speaker in a poem takes.

First Person
The **first-person point of view** is when the writer uses the word I in the text. Poetry often uses first person, e.g., William Wordsworth's "I Wandered Lonely as a Cloud." Two examples of prose written in first person are Suzanne Collins's *The Hunger Games* and Anthony Burgess's *A Clockwork Orange*.

Second Person
The **second person point of view** is when the writer uses the pronoun *you*. It is not widely used in prose fiction, but as a technique, it has been used by writers such as William Faulkner in *Absalom, Absalom!* and Albert Camus in *The Fall*. It is more common in poetry—e.g., Pablo Neruda's "If You Forget Me."

Third Person
Third person point of view is when the writer utilizes pronouns such as *him, her*, or *them*. It may be the most utilized point of view in prose as it provides flexibility to an author and is the one with which readers are most familiar. There are two main types of third person used in fiction. **Third person omniscient** uses a narrator that is all-knowing, relating the story by conveying and interpreting thoughts/feelings of all characters. In **third person limited**, the narrator relates the story through the perspective of one character's thoughts/feelings, usually the main character.

Plot

The **plot** is what happens in the story. Plots may be singular, containing one problem, or they may be very complex, with many sub-plots. All plots have an exposition, a conflict, a climax, and a resolution.

The **conflict** drives the plot and is something that the reader expects to be resolved. The plot carries those events along until there is a resolution to the conflict.

Tone

The **tone** of a story reflects the author's attitude and opinion about the subject matter of the story or text. Tone can be expressed through word choice, imagery, figurative language, syntax, and other details. The emotion or mood the reader experiences relates back to the tone of the story. Some examples of possible tones are humorous, somber, sentimental, and ironic.

Setting

The **setting** is the time, place, or set of surroundings in which the story occurs. It includes time or time span, place(s), climates, geography—man-made or natural—, or cultural environments Emily Dickinson's poem "Because I could not stop for Death" has a simple setting—the narrator's symbolic ride with Death through town towards the local graveyard. Conversely, Leo Tolstoy's *War and Peace* encompasses numerous settings within settings in the areas affected by the Napoleonic Wars, spanning from 1805 to 1812.

Characters

Characters are the story's figures that assume primary, secondary, or minor roles. Central or major characters are those who are integral to the story—the plot cannot be resolved without them. A central character can be a **protagonist** or hero. There may be more than one protagonist, and they don't always have to possess good characteristics. A character can also be an **antagonist**—the force against a protagonist.

Character development is when the author takes the time to create dynamic characters that add uniqueness and depth to the story. *Dynamic* characters are characters that change over the course of the plot's timeline. **Stock** characters are those that appear across genres and embrace stereotypes—e.g., the cowboy of the Wild West or the blonde bombshell in a detective novel. A **flat** character is one that does not present a lot of complexity or depth, while a **rounded** character does. Sometimes, the **narrator** of a story or the **speaker** in a poem can be a character—e.g., Nick Carraway in F. Scott Fitzgerald's *The Great Gatsby* or the speaker in Robert Browning's "My Last Duchess." The narrator might also function as a character in prose, though not be part of the story—e.g., Charles Dickens's narrator of *A Christmas Carol*.

Development of Themes

Theme or Central Message

The **theme** is the central message of a fictional work, whether that work is structured as prose, drama, or poetry. It is the heart of what an author is trying to say to readers through the writing, and theme is largely conveyed through literary elements and techniques.

In literature, a theme can often be determined by considering the overarching narrative conflict with the work. Though there are several types of conflicts and several potential themes within them, the following are the most common:

- **Individual against the self**—relevant to themes of self-awareness, internal struggles, pride, coming of age, facing reality, fate, free will, vanity, loss of innocence, loneliness, isolation, fulfillment, failure, and disillusionment

33

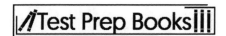

- **Individual against nature**—relevant to themes of knowledge vs. ignorance, nature as beauty, quest for discovery, self-preservation, chaos and order, circle of life, death, and destruction of beauty

- **Individual against society**—relevant to themes of power, beauty, good, evil, war, class struggle, totalitarianism, role of men/women, wealth, corruption, change vs. tradition, capitalism, destruction, heroism, injustice, and racism

- **Individual against another individual**—relevant to themes of hope, loss of love or hope, sacrifice, power, revenge, betrayal, and honor

For example, in Hawthorne's *The Scarlet Letter*, one possible narrative conflict could be the individual against the self, with a relevant theme of internal struggles. This theme is alluded to through characterization—Dimmesdale's moral struggle with his love for Hester and Hester's internal struggles with the truth and her daughter, Pearl. It's also alluded to through plot—Dimmesdale's suicide and Hester helping the very townspeople who initially condemned her.

Sometimes, a text can convey a **message** or **universal lesson**—a truth or insight that the reader infers from the text, based on analysis of the literary and/or poetic elements. This message is often presented as a statement. For example, a potential message in Shakespeare's *Hamlet* could be "Revenge is what ultimately drives the human soul." This message can be immediately determined through plot and characterization in numerous ways, but it can also be determined through the setting of Norway, which is bordering on war.

How Authors Develop Theme

Authors employ a variety of techniques to present a theme. They may compare or contrast characters, events, places, ideas, or historical or invented settings to speak thematically. They may use analogies, metaphors, similes, allusions, or other literary devices to convey the theme. An author's use of diction, syntax, and tone can also help convey the theme. Authors will often develop themes through the development of characters, use of the setting, repetition of ideas, use of symbols, and through contrasting value systems. Authors of both fiction and nonfiction genres will use a variety of these techniques to develop one or more themes.

Regardless of the literary genre, there are commonalities in how authors, playwrights, and poets develop themes or central ideas.

Authors often do research, the results of which contribute to theme. In prose fiction and drama, this research may include real historical information about the setting the author has chosen or include elements that make fictional characters, settings, and plots seem realistic to the reader. In nonfiction, research is critical since information contained within this literature must be accurate.

In fiction, authors present a narrative conflict that will contribute to the overall theme. This conflict may involve the storyline itself and some trouble within characters that needs resolution. In nonfiction, this conflict may be an explanation or commentary on factual people and events.

Authors will sometimes use character motivation to convey theme, such as in the example from *Hamlet* regarding revenge. In fiction, the characters an author creates will think, speak, and act in ways that effectively convey the theme to readers. In nonfiction, the characters are factual, as in a biography, but authors pay particular attention to presenting those motivations to make them clear to readers.

34

Authors also use literary devices as a means of conveying theme. For example, the use of moon symbolism in Mary Shelley's *Frankenstein* is significant as its phases can be compared to the phases that the Creature undergoes as he struggles with his identity.

The selected point of view can also contribute to a work's theme. The use of first-person point of view in a fiction or non-fiction work engages the reader's response differently than third person point of view. The central idea or theme from a first-person narrative may differ from a third-person limited text.

In literary nonfiction, authors usually identify the purpose of their writing, which differs from fiction, where the general purpose is to entertain. The purpose of nonfiction is usually to inform, persuade, or entertain the audience. The stated purpose of a non-fiction text will drive how the central message or theme, if applicable, is presented.

Authors identify an audience for their writing, which is critical in shaping the theme of the work. For example, the audience for J.K. Rowling's *Harry Potter* series would be different than the audience for a biography of George Washington. The audience an author chooses to address is closely tied to the purpose of the work. The choice of an audience also drives the choice of language and level of diction an author uses. Ultimately, the intended audience determines the level to which that subject matter is presented and the complexity of the theme.

Characteristics of Literary Genres

Classifying literature involves an understanding of the concept of genre. A **genre** is a category of literature that possesses similarities in style and in characteristics. Based on form and structure, there are four basic genres.

Fictional Prose
Fictional prose consists of fictional works written in standard form with a natural flow of speech and without poetic structure. Fictional prose primarily utilizes grammatically complete sentences and a paragraph structure to convey its message.

Drama
Drama is fiction that is written to be performed in a variety of media, intended to be performed for an audience, and structured for that purpose. It might be composed using poetry or prose, often straddling the elements of both in what actors are expected to present. Action and dialogue are the tools used in drama to tell the story.

Poetry
Poetry is fiction in verse that has a unique focus on the rhythm of language and focuses on intensity of feeling. It is not an entire story, though it may tell one; it is compact in form and in function. Poetry can be considered as a poet's brief word picture for a reader. Poetic structure is primarily composed of lines and stanzas. Together, poetic structure and devices are the methods that poets use to lead readers to feeling an effect and, ultimately, to the interpretive message.

Literary Nonfiction
Literary nonfiction is prose writing that is based on current or past real events or real people and includes straightforward accounts as well as those that offer opinions on facts or factual events.

Major Forms Within Each Genre

Fictional Prose

Fiction written in prose can be further broken down into **fiction genres**—types of fiction. Some of the more common genres of fiction are as follows:

- **Classical fiction**: a work of fiction considered timeless in its message or theme, remaining noteworthy and meaningful over decades or centuries—e.g., Charlotte Brontë's *Jane Eyre*, Mark Twain's *Adventures of Huckleberry Finn*

- **Fables**: short fiction that generally features animals, fantastic creatures, or other forces within nature that assume human-like characters and has a moral lesson for the reader—e.g., *Aesop's Fables*

- **Fairy tales**: children's stories with magical characters in imaginary, enchanted lands, usually depicting a struggle between good and evil, a sub-genre of folklore—e.g., Hans Christian Anderson's *The Little Mermaid*, *Cinderella* by the Brothers Grimm

- **Fantasy**: fiction with magic or supernatural elements that cannot occur in the real world, sometimes involving medieval elements in language, usually includes some form of sorcery or witchcraft and sometimes set on a different world—e.g., J.R.R. Tolkien's *The Hobbit*, J.K. Rowling's *Harry Potter and the Sorcerer's Stone*, George R.R. Martin's *A Game of Thrones*

- **Folklore**: types of fiction passed down from oral tradition, stories indigenous to a particular region or culture, with a local flavor in tone, designed to help humans cope with their condition in life and validate cultural traditions, beliefs, and customs—e.g., William Laughead's *Paul Bunyan and The Blue Ox*, the Buddhist story of "The Banyan Deer"

- **Mythology**: closely related to folklore but more widespread, features mystical, otherworldly characters and addresses the basic question of why and how humans exist, relies heavily on allegory and features gods or heroes captured in some sort of struggle—e.g., Greek myths, Genesis I and II in the Bible, Arthurian legends

- **Science fiction**: fiction that uses the principle of extrapolation—loosely defined as a form of prediction—to imagine future realities and problems of the human experience—e.g., Robert Heinlein's *Stranger in a Strange Land*, Ayn Rand's *Anthem*, Isaac Asimov's *I, Robot*, Philip K. Dick's *Do Androids Dream of Electric Sheep?*

- **Short stories**: short works of prose fiction with fully-developed themes and characters, focused on mood, generally developed with a single plot, with a short period of time for settings—e.g., Edgar Allan Poe's "Fall of the House of Usher," Shirley Jackson's "The Lottery," Isaac Bashevis Singer's "Gimpel the Fool"

Drama

Drama refers to a form of literature written for the purpose of performance for an audience. Like prose fiction, drama has several genres. The following are the most common ones:

- **Comedy**: a humorous play designed to amuse and entertain, often with an emphasis on the common person's experience, generally resolved in a positive way—e.g., Richard Sheridan's *School for Scandal*, Shakespeare's *Taming of the Shrew*, Neil Simon's *The Odd Couple*

- **History**: a play based on recorded history where the fate of a nation or kingdom is at the core of the conflict—e.g., Christopher Marlowe's *Edward II*, Shakespeare's *King Richard III*, Arthur Miller's *The Crucible*

- **Tragedy**: a serious play that often involves the downfall of the protagonist. In modern tragedies, the protagonist is not necessarily in a position of power or authority—e.g., Jean Racine's *Phèdre*, Arthur Miller's *Death of a Salesman*, John Steinbeck's *Of Mice and Men*

- **Melodrama**: a play that emphasizes heightened emotion and sensationalism, generally with stereotypical characters in exaggerated or realistic situations and with moral polarization—e.g., Jean-Jacques Rousseau's *Pygmalion*

- **Tragi-comedy**: a play that has elements of both tragedy—a character experiencing a tragic loss—and comedy—the resolution is often positive with no clear distinctive mood for either—e.g., Shakespeare's *The Merchant of Venice*, Anton Chekhov's *The Cherry Orchard*

Poetry

The genre of **poetry** refers to literary works that focus on the expression of feelings and ideas through the use of structure and linguistic rhythm to create a desired effect.

Different poetic structures and devices are used to create the various major forms of poetry. Some of the most common forms are discussed in the following chart.

Type	Poetic Structure	Example
Ballad	A poem or song passed down orally which tells a story and in English tradition usually uses an ABAB or ABCB rhyme scheme	William Butler Yeats' "The Ballad of Father O'Hart"
Epic	A long poem from ancient oral tradition which narrates the story of a legendary or heroic protagonist	Homer's *The Odyssey* Virgil's *The Aeneid*
Haiku	A Japanese poem of three unrhymed lines with five, seven, and five syllables (in English) with nature as a common subject matter	Matsuo Bashō "An old silent pond … A frog jumps into the pond, splash! Silence again."

Type	Poetic Structure	Example
Limerick	A five-line poem written in an AABBA rhyme scheme, with a witty focus	From Edward Lear's *Book of Nonsense*: "There was a Young Person of Smyrna Whose grandmother threatened to burn her ..."
Ode	A formal lyric poem that addresses and praises a person, place, thing, or idea	Edna St. Vincent Millay's "Ode to Silence"
Sonnet	A fourteen-line poem written in iambic pentameter	Shakespeare's Sonnets 18 and 130

Literary Nonfiction

Nonfiction works are best characterized by their subject matter, which must be factual and real, describing true life experiences. There are several common types of literary non-fiction.

Biography

A **biography** is a work written about a real person (historical or currently living). It involves factual accounts of the person's life, often in a re-telling of those events based on available, researched factual information. The re-telling and dialogue, especially if related within quotes, must be accurate and reflect reliable sources. A biography reflects the time and place in which the person lived, with the goal of creating an understanding of the person and their human experience. Examples of well-known biographies include *The Life of Samuel Johnson* by James Boswell and *Steve Jobs* by Walter Isaacson.

Autobiography

An **autobiography** is a factual account of a person's life written by that person. It may contain some or all of the same elements as a biography, but the author is the subject matter. An autobiography will be told in first person narrative. Examples of well-known autobiographies in literature include *Night* by Elie Wiesel and *Margaret Thatcher: The Autobiography* by Margaret Thatcher.

Memoir

A **memoir** is a historical account of a person's life and experiences written by one who has personal, intimate knowledge of the information. The line between memoir, autobiography, and biography is often muddled, but generally speaking, a memoir covers a specific timeline of events as opposed to the other forms of nonfiction. A memoir is less all-encompassing. It is also less formal in tone and tends to focus on the emotional aspect of the presented timeline of events. Some examples of memoirs in literature include *Angela's Ashes* by Frank McCourt and *All Creatures Great and Small* by James Herriot.

Journalism

Some forms of **journalism** can fall into the category of literary non-fiction—e.g., travel writing, nature writing, sports writing, the interview, and sometimes, the essay. Some examples include Elizabeth Kolbert's "The Lost World, in the Annals of Extinction series for *The New Yorker* and Gary Smith's "Ali and His Entourage" for *Sports Illustrated*.

Figurative Language

Whereas literal language is the author's use of precise words, proper meanings, definitions, and phrases that mean exactly what they say, **figurative language** deviates from precise meaning and word definition—often in conjunction with other familiar words and phrases—to paint a picture for the reader. Figurative language is less explicit and more open to reader interpretation.

Some examples of figurative language are included in the following graphic.

Term	Definition	Example
Simile	Compares two things using "like" or "as"	Her hair was like gold.
Metaphor	Compares two things as if they are the same	He was a giant teddy bear.
Idiom	Using words with predictable meanings to create a phrase with a different meaning	The world is your oyster.
Alliteration	Repeating the same beginning sound or letter in a phrase for emphasis	The busy baby babbled.
Personification	Attributing human characteristics to an object or an animal	The house glowered menacingly with a dark smile.
Foreshadowing	Giving an indication that something is going to happen later in the story	I wasn't aware at the time, but I would come to regret those words.
Symbolism	Using symbols to represent ideas and provide a different meaning	The ring represented the bond between us.
Onomatopoeia	Using words that imitate sound	The tire went off with a bang and a crunch.
Imagery	Appealing to the senses by using descriptive language	The sky was painted with red and pink and streaked with orange.
Hyperbole	Using exaggeration not meant to be taken literally	The girl weighed less than a feather.

Figurative language can be used to give additional insight into the theme or message of a text by moving beyond the usual and literal meaning of words and phrases. It can also be used to appeal to the senses of readers and create a more in-depth story.

39

Practice Quiz

Questions 1–5 are based upon the following passage:

Walt Whitman (1819–1892) was an American writer who wrote poetry, essays, and more. Whitman was born on Long Island, New York, and grew up in Brooklyn, New York. He received little formal education, as he left school at the age of eleven to work. Whitman worked various jobs, first as a printer at the age of twelve. He read often during this time. His time as a printer ended with a fire that devastated the printing district in which he worked. This led him to pursue teaching at seventeen in 1836. Eventually, he left teaching to become a journalist, founding a newspaper titled *The Long-Islander* and editing for various other papers. Throughout this time, Whitman was writing and eventually published a collection of his own poems titled *Leaves of Grass* (1855) which he released anonymously. **A** Throughout his life, he continued to write various editions of *Leaves of Grass*. The last edition contained over 400 poems, a significant increase from the twelve poems in the original edition. **B**

Whitman played a connective role between the Realist and Transcendentalist literature styles. The Realist style of literature portrayed everyday activities in a truthful way. Realism often focused on the lower and middle classes rather than the wealthy. This was a response to the previous works of Romanticism, which Realists believed had become out of touch with reality. Transcendentalism was both a philosophical and literary movement. In comparison to Realism, it focused more on idealism, nature, and individualism. These themes are common in Whitman's work and can be seen in the titles of some of Whitman's poetry, such as "Song of Myself" and "I Sing the Body Electric." **C** Whitman's work was controversial at the time, in part because of the topics he wrote about and in part because of the free-form style in which he wrote his poetry. **D** Many libraries in the United States banned *Leaves of Grass*, and he was fired from his federal job as a clerk when it was discovered that he was the author. Despite this controversy, Whitman is considered a highly influential writer.

1. The phrase *this was a response* in paragraph 2 refers to:
   a. Transcendentalism
   b. Romanticism
   c. Realism
   d. *Leaves of Grass*

2. According to paragraph 1, all the following are true of *Leaves of Grass* EXCEPT:
   a. There were various editions, which included additional works added throughout Whitman's life.
   b. *Leaves of Grass* was published anonymously.
   c. Whitman first published *Leaves of Grass* after writing as he worked various other jobs.
   d. *Leaves of Grass* is a collection of essays written by Walt Whitman.

40

3. Find the four areas where the letters **A**, **B**, **C**, and **D** are located. These spaces indicate where the following sentence might be added to the passage:

> Other examples of Whitman's work include *Specimen Days & Collect* and *Memoranda During the War.*

In which area does the sentence best fit?
    a. A
    b. B
    c. C
    d. D

4. In paragraph 2, why does the author include explanations of Transcendentalism and Realism?
    a. To explain the way in which Whitman's work was connective between the two
    b. To give a historical background of the time of Whitman
    c. To contrast Whitman's work against other work of the time
    d. To explain the context in which Whitman's work was released

5. An opening sentence is provided to create a summary of the given passage above. Choose THREE answer choices that state the important ideas of the passage.

> Walt Whitman, an American writer, first worked as a printer after leaving school at the age of eleven.

```
1.


2.


3.
```

    a. Whitman worked various jobs as he wrote, leading to him completing the first of many editions of *Leaves of Grass* (1855), a collection of poetry.
    b. Whitman worked as a printer until his time in the printing district ended due to a fire that devastated the area.
    c. Whitman's work connected the Realist movement, which focused on representing everyday life, and the Transcendentalist movement, which focused on idealism and nature.
    d. The Realist movement of literature focused on everyday life, favored the lower and middle classes over the wealthy, and was a response to Romanticism before it.
    e. Whitman's work led to him losing a job upon the discovery that he had authored *Leaves of Grass*.
    f. Whitman, while his work was considered controversial at the time due to content and form, is a highly influential writer.

Answer Explanations

1. C: The phrase *this was a response* in paragraph 2 refers to Realism, as it references that Realism was a response to Romanticism. Transcendentalism, Romanticism, and *Leaves of Grass* are not being referenced at this point, as none of them were mentioned as being in response to something else.

2. D: The correct choice is the one incorrect statement about *Leaves of Grass*, which is that *Leaves of Grass* is a collection of essays written by Walt Whitman. It is not a collection of essays, but a collection of poems. The other choices are all correct: there were various editions released, it was first released anonymously, and Whitman published it after writing while working various other jobs.

3. B: The sentence best fits at Choice *B*, which places it amid an explanation of Whitman's work with *Leaves of Grass*. This allows for more examples of Whitman's work added to the information included in the passage. Choice *A* interrupts the information that is being provided about *Leaves of Grass*. Choice *C* follows an explanation of the themes of Whitman's work and how specific poem titles show these themes. Choice *D* interrupts the explanation of the controversy surrounding his work.

4. A: The author includes explanations of Transcendentalism and Realism to explain how Whitman's work was connective between the two. This feature of Whitman's work is important, so the explanations aid in understanding Whitman's work. Choices *B* and *D* are incorrect because the intention was not to give a historical background or to explain the context of the time in which his work was being released. Choice *C* is incorrect because other work was not specifically mentioned to contrast with these styles.

5. A, C, F: The correct choices are Choice *A,* Choice *C,* and Choice *F:* Whitman worked various jobs as he wrote, leading to him writing the first of many editions of *Leaves of Grass* (1855), a collection of poetry; Whitman's work connected the Realist movement, which focused on representing everyday life, and the Transcendentalist movement, which focused on idealism and nature; Whitman, while his work was considered controversial at the time due to content and form, is a highly influential writer. Including the other choices within the summary would exclude important information from the summary.

42

Listening

The Listening section test of the TOEFL iBT® lasts 36 minutes.

The questions follow each listening clip. There are six questions per lecture or academic discussion and five questions following each conversation. The section will likely contain 3 lectures and academic discussions, each of which is 3–5 minutes in duration, and 2 conversations that each last three minutes.

We have recorded audio to go along with the listening practice questions. You can find all of our audio recordings by going to https://testprepbooks.com/bonus/toefl/ or by scanning the QR code below. The audio is only online. There is no CD.

Most of the questions are multiple choice; the majority offer four answer choices from which test takers must select the single best choice, although some multiple-choice questions may require selecting two or more correct answers. Some questions go beyond regurgitating the information that was presented in the recording and ask test takers to demonstrate deeper listening comprehension by making inferences or describing emotions or other implicit details. Some questions may involve categorizing items using charts or tables or require test takers to order steps or events in a sequence.

It should be noted that not all of the speakers in the audio recordings in the Listening section may speak with native North American English accents. Test takers may encounter English speakers with native accents from the United Kingdom, New Zealand, and Australia.

ETS test administrators model the TOEFL iBT® Listening section exercises after typical classroom lectures, discussions, or common administrative tasks that test takers will encounter in real-world settings long after passing the TOEFL iBT®. Lecture topics pull from a variety of academic disciplines in the arts and sciences, such as history, psychology, earth science, economics, and sociology. Some lecture exercises will be delivered by a single speaker, who is an instructor, or they may feature several speakers in a classroom discussion format, often between the instructor and a handful of students. For example, the instructor may give a short lecture about architecture and then pause to call on a couple of students to answer questions pertaining to the material just presented, or a student may ask the instructor a clarifying question. After the instructor answers the student's question, he or she may continue with the lecture or segue into an organic conversation that deviates from the original lecture topic but more fully answers the student's question.

The conversations are typical of interactions encountered around a university setting between a variety of individuals such as coaches, students, secretaries, administrators, and roommates. Topics may include conversations about registering for classes, purchasing textbooks, asking for directions or locating buildings around campus, meeting a roommate, receiving feedback on an assignment, and asking for academic support, among many others. The speech in the conversations is meant to sound natural and duplicate that which normally occurs between people, including imperfections and pauses. Characters may stumble over their words or even use the wrong word sometimes; in the questions that follow the recording, test takers may be asked to point out these errors.

Test takers are allowed to listen to each exercise only one time, but they are encouraged to take notes while they listen. They can refer to these notes that follow the clip. If headsets are provided, they will have adjustable volume that test takers can experiment with prior to listening to the scored exercises. Each listening exercise begins with a picture of some sort to provide context for the conversation or lecture, and longer recordings will have additional pictures or diagrams scattered throughout the 3–5-minute clip.

ETS presents test takers with three categories of questions on the Listening section and both the lectures and conversations feature questions in each of these categories.

- **Basic Conversation Questions** are one of three types: **Gist-content questions** address the overall general content of the lecture, discussion, or conversation. Instead of addressing the broad content of the lectures or conversations, **gist-purpose questions** require test takers to identify the primary reasons for the given lectures or discussion. Lastly, **detail questions** ask test takers about specific facts provided in the lectures or regarding specific details from the conversations.

- **Pragmatic Understanding Questions** can be one of two types. In the first type, test takers must demonstrate their understanding of the speaker's purpose for delivering certain statements, or the function of what was said. In the second type, test takers must identify the speaker's emotions or preferences, often using nuances in tone of voice, inflection, and intonation to detect attitudes such as sarcasm, frustration, disappointment, or irony.

- **Connecting and Synthesizing Information Questions** can be one of three types. The **understanding organization** questions require test takers to select answer choices that correctly reflect the structure of the listening exercise or the function of specific statements delivered in the lecture or conversation. The **connecting content** questions are the only type of question that is solely found in the lecture-based exercises. It involves demonstrating relationships between explicit and implicit ideas presented in the lecture and often includes charts or tables that test takers must interpret to successfully answer the question. Finally, the **making inferences** questions involve using statements in the conversations or lectures to draw conclusions or surmise information that may not be explicitly discussed in the listening exercise.

Test takers often find the Listening section daunting, particularly because exercises can only be played once. However, the following are a couple of helpful strategies that successful test takers employ to achieve high scores in this section:

- **Use the pictures:** The initial picture helps set the stage and helps provide the context for the conversation or lecture that test takers are about to hear. This picture is crucial in helping the listener imagine what is happening and visualize the speakers before the dialogue even begins. The additional pictures and visual aids that are presented during the course of the audio recordings appear in coordination with the statements or events in the lectures and conversations as they unfurl. Again, these are powerful aids that add context clues about the setting, speakers, and content, which, when taken with the audio information, help provide test takers with a more complete and comprehensive understanding of the exercise.

- **Take notes:** Test takers can, and should, take notes while they listen to the recording to refer to while answering questions. While it is most important to devote attention towards critical listening, jotting down a few key points or details that seem important can help jog one's memory after the recording is over and the questions are presented. Some questions ask very specific information, and this is where careful listening with an ear towards details and a couple of key notes can be quite helpful. For example, from a conversation between two roommates buying course textbooks at the campus store, test takers may be asked to recall the specific subjects for which one speaker was buying books.

- **Practice:** The importance of practice cannot be overstated. Successful test takers listen to spoken English every chance they get and try to understand the main points, supporting details, and the emotions and attitudes of the speakers. There are a variety of media that present listening opportunities from television programs and movies to podcasts and audiobooks. In-person opportunities include class lectures, conversations with peers and friends, and interactions with customer service agents, among others. While formal questions aren't presented after most listening opportunities, candidates can assess their understanding by listening to recordings several times or asking speakers of in-person conversations clarifying questions to verify understanding.

- **Listen for verbal cues:** Listeners can gather clues by appreciating the verbal cues from the recordings. Word emphasis, tone of voice, pauses interjected for effect, and changes in voice inflection can communicate implicit information such as the speaker's emotion (surprise, worry, frustration, etc.) or emphasize that something important is about to happen. Again, understanding these nuances in spoken language will help test takers to more fully grasp the meaning of the conversation or lecture in the recordings.

Practice Quiz

Directions: The Listening section measures your ability to understand conversations and lectures in English. In this test, you will listen to several pieces of content and answer questions after each one. The questions typically ask about the main idea and supporting details. Some questions ask about a speaker's purpose or attitude. Answer the questions based on what is stated or implied by the speakers.

Note that on the actual test, you can take notes while you listen and use your notes to help you answer the questions. Your notes will not be scored.

For your convenience, the transcript is provided after the answer explanations. However, on the actual test, no such transcript will be provided.

Passage: Conversation

Listen to all of these passages by going to https://testprepbooks.com/bonus/toefl/, or by scanning the QR code below:

Recording #1

1. What was Greg looking for help with?
    a. Biology class material
    b. Studying economics
    c. Getting off campus to run errands
    d. Finding the administration building

2. Indicate below whether each task that Greg needs to perform is specifically associated with meeting Deborah to study or with replacing his college ID. Put an "X" in the correct space.

Task	Meeting Deborah to study	Replacing his campus ID
Go to the administration building		
Meet at the front steps		
Have his college ID to get in		
Fill out a form and show a picture ID		
Pay a replacement fee		

3. Where did Greg lose his ID?
   a. At the movies
   b. In biology class
   c. Grocery shopping
   d. At the basketball game

4. Read the following statement from the conversation and then answer the question:

   Greg: I haven't really gotten into a study rhythm yet this semester. That may be part of my problem. I guess I study in my room, when my roommate and I aren't playing video games, that is.

What does Greg mean when he says he has not really gotten into "a study rhythm yet"?
   a. He has not yet studied with music.
   b. He needs to study with video games.
   c. He has not yet established a study routine or habit.
   d. He only studies in the library after class.

5. Why does Deborah say the following: "Well, hey I've got to run to Economics class now."?
   a. She is preparing to end the conversation.
   b. She enjoys running for the school's track team.
   c. She is trying to change the topic of conversation.
   d. She wants a ride to class because she has to get there quickly.

Answer Explanations

1. A: At the beginning of the conversation, listeners should recall that the male student, Greg, was asking the female student, Deborah, how she did on the biology exam. Deborah informs Greg that she did well, earning a 96, while Greg responds that he only got a 69. He says, "This stuff isn't making sense to me." *Stuff,* in this case, refers to the biology class material.

2. Deborah says that a student must go to the administration building with their student ID or another form of picture ID, pay a $15 replacement fee, and fill out a form in order to replace a college ID. Before she finds out that he lost his college ID, Deborah tells Greg that he needs it to get into the library. Toward the end of the conversation Deborah tells Greg to meet him at the front steps of the library.

Task	Meeting Deborah to study	Replacing his campus ID
Go to the administration building		✖
Meet at the front steps	✖	
Have your college ID to get in	✖	
Fill out a form and show a picture ID		✖
Pay a replacement fee		✖

3. D: Choice *D* is the correct answer. Greg says, "I lost my ID at the basketball game last weekend. Do you know where I can get a new one?"

4. C: When Greg says that he has not really gotten into "a study rhythm yet" he means that he has not yet established a study routine or habit. Therefore, Choice *C* is correct.

5. A: Deborah says "Well, hey I've got to run to Economics class now" to signal that she is preparing to end the conversation. This is a common phrase used in casual conversation to convey that one person needs to leave and move on to the next thing and that they want to end the conversation. She may not literally need to "run" to class, but she is wrapping up the conversation.

Listening Practice Quiz Transcript: Conversation

Listen to all of these passages by going to https://testprepbooks.com/bonus/toefl/, or by scanning the QR code below:

Recording #1

(Narrator) Listen to the following conversation between two students and then answer the following questions.

(Greg) Hi Deborah, how did you do on the biology exam?

(Deborah) Pretty well! I got a 96. How about you?

(Greg) Wow. I'm jealous. I got a 69. This stuff isn't making sense to me.

(Deborah) Oh no, I'm sorry to hear that, Greg. I could help you study if you'd like. I usually go to the library after my classes for a couple hours. We could work together on the practice questions and tackle this week's assignment if you want.

(Greg) Actually, that would be great. Are you sure you don't mind?

(Deborah) No, not at all. I have to go to my economics class right now, but I'm usually at the library around 4:00. I sit in the back by the reference section. Do you know where the encyclopedias are?

(Greg) Uh, to be honest, I've never been to the library here. I don't even know where on campus it is. Is it over by the dining hall on the main quad?

(Deborah) Oh wow! You've never been?! Where do you study? And yes, it's over next to the administration building on the main quad. It's directly across from the dining hall. And you need to make sure you have your college ID with you to get in.

(Greg) Yeah, I haven't really gotten into a study rhythm yet this semester. That may be part of my problem. I guess I study in my room, when my roommate and I aren't playing video games, that is. I lost my ID at the basketball game last weekend. Do you know where I can get a new one?

(Deborah) Oh Greg! We need to get you organized. But yes, go to the administration building with another form of picture ID, and you'll need to pay a $15 replacement fee, and fill out a form.

(Greg) Does a driver's license work?

(Deborah) Yes. Do you drive?

(Greg) Yes, I have a Honda Civic parked over by my dorm. I go off campus a lot to buy things at the grocery store or to go to the movies.

(Deborah) That's awesome. I would love to get off campus once in a while and get a breath of "real-world" air, if you know what I mean.

(Greg) Yeah, absolutely. Hey, how about I take you with me when I go shopping tomorrow afternoon in exchange for you tutoring me with the biology stuff?

(Deborah) Sounds perfect! Well, hey I've got to run to Economics class now. I'll see you at the library at 4:00. Let's just meet at the front steps and then we'll go in together and find somewhere to work.

(Greg) Thanks Deborah! I'll work on getting my ID and finding my biology book.

Speaking

The TOEFL Speaking Section assesses the test taker's ability to communicate effectively in English. This section lasts 16 minutes and test takers will encounter four tasks; the first one involves just a prompt. The remaining three ask test takers to listen to a passage and possibly read short passages or conversations. For each task, test takers have about 15–30 seconds to gather their thoughts and prepare, and then they must deliver their verbal response into a microphone. The response is typically expected to last approximately 45-60 seconds, which can be nearly 100 words for a fluent English speaker. Test takers are evaluated on their oral delivery, topic development, content, language use, and grammar of their responses.

While this can sound daunting, the good news is that the Speaking section of the TOEFL is the easiest one to prepare for because the opportunities to practice are endless. Candidates should take advantage of every opportunity to practice their English-speaking skills, not only to optimize their test performance, but also because they will be frequently conversing in English in diverse situations long after passing the exam. Nearly every situation presents a valid opportunity to practice—driving the car, walking the dog, commuting to work, visiting a friend, doing errands, etc.

In addition to capitalizing on every chance to practice speaking, there are some other helpful strategies that successful test takers employ for this section.

Practice, but Don't Memorize

As mentioned, it's impossible to over-practice and the more speaking time a test taker has under their belt, the better. However, memorizing responses, particularly for the first two tasks (which tend to pose only a handful of possible questions), is not recommended. For one thing, scorers are looking for a natural speaking style that feels conversational and relaxed. Rehearsing and memorizing a predetermined response will likely lower one's delivery score even if the content is good. It is better to sound authentic and organic in the delivery of the answer, even if it means slightly less content is delivered in the allotted time.

Listen and Read the Question Carefully

It's easy to jump to an answer when nervous, but successful test takers make sure to pay careful attention to the specific question posed in the task and ensure that their response addresses the exact points desired. For example, the first task usually asks general questions such as what do you enjoy doing in your spare time, what is your family like, or what are your favorite places to visit? Test takers who are overly rehearsed may begin to hear a familiar prompt and then assume they know what the question is asking and prepare to deliver their memorized response. However, this hastiness can lead to mistakes; oftentimes, there are slight changes in the wording of the questions such that the exact question test administrators are looking for is different than that assumed. Instead of what do you enjoy doing on your spare time, the question may be more specific and ask, what do you enjoy doing by yourself in your spare time? If a test taker did not listen carefully or jumped to a prepared answer about enjoying basketball with their team or shopping with friends, points would be deducted for inappropriate content for the intended answer.

Organize

Test takers should take advantage of the 15–30 seconds provided to reflect on the question and organize their thoughts before they have to deliver their response. Many people find it helpful to write down a couple of bullet points that they plan to highlight in their answer. These should be just a word or short phrase, rather than a whole sentence, so as to save time and sound organic and natural in the response. Reading fully composed sentences tends to sound overly rehearsed and may affect one's delivery score.

Speak Clearly and Simply

Many test takers feel anxious or self-conscious about delivering their responses with as little influence of an accent as possible. The good news is that the TOEFL does not expect candidates to speak with any sort of "American" accent and scores are not influenced by the responder's accent one way or another. What is important is that the response is clear, audible, and comprehensible. After all, if scorers cannot hear or understand the recorded answer, they cannot award it with high marks. Test takers should speak as fluidly as possible, without rushing or interjecting long pauses or words of varying volumes. As much as possible, words should be enunciated with all syllables present and emphasizing those necessary for proper pronunciation.

The more even and rhythmic the spoken answer, the better. One more point to note is that many test takers imagine that adding fancy vocabulary words will bolster their score. While demonstrating a rich vocabulary and strong command of English grammar and language skills is important, it is more important to ensure that words are used properly and that sentence structure and intended meaning is on point. If test takers are not confident in the meaning or proper usage of a word, it is better to use a seemingly simpler word whose meaning they are sure of.

Make Speech Flow

As mentioned, answers should flow as naturally and fluidly as possible. With that said, short pauses should be interjected at the end of each sentence or where commas would be used in written text to help listeners understand the thoughts and the organization of the response. Rushing into each subsequent sentence without an adequate pause tends to make answers sound confusing. To connect thoughts together and create a logical flow to the response, test takers should demonstrate command of the use of conjunctions and employ effective connecting words and phrases such as *because, due to, for example, after this, if...then,* and *however.*

Structure the Answer

Although spoken language is often not as formal as written communication, answers should still be organized, with well-developed thoughts presented in a logical order. Successful test takers generate their ideas and plan their delivery during the reflection time prior to recording their responses. It is wise to start the answer by stating the topic thought (like a topic sentence in a written essay) and then expand or describe that thought in the subsequent sentences. Adding a concluding sentence that ties back to the beginning thought gives the listener clarity and pulls all the details together into a comprehensive and intelligent answer.

Tell a Story

The most memorable conversations are those that include a captivating story. Speakers should try to make responses engaging and personal, when appropriate. This may not only make for a more enjoyable listen for scorers, but may also improve one's score by garnering more delivery points.

52

Be Confident

Everyone has important things to say. Test takers should not worry about saying something "stupid" or "boring." They should speak from the heart and be confident in their command of English as well as their comprehension of the posed question. There is no need to rush when delivering the response; there is plenty of time in 45 seconds to get out a complete answer. On that note, if there is extra time at the end of the allotted recording time, it is generally recommended to simply end the response when the question has been fully answered rather than fill every last second with speaking. It is unnecessary to speak aimlessly at the end, as this can reduce one's content score if the answer starts deviating from what was asked. Test takers should just pace themselves, stay relaxed, and speak with authority.

Practice Quiz

Listen to all of these passages by going to https://testprepbooks.com/bonus/toefl or by scanning the QR code below:

Recording #2

1. Listen to the following audio recording and answer the question:

- Preparation Time: 15 seconds
- Response Time: 45 seconds

2. Read the following announcement and then listen to the conversation. Lastly, answer the question that follows.

New Community Garden Opening

Due to public support, we will be opening a community garden on campus. This garden will be available to all students. Students will be able to come to the garden at any time and collect fresh vegetables, fruits, and even flowers for free. Due to the high cost of living, we know that students are dealing with food insecurity. We hope that this free garden will help alleviate that struggle.

Healthy eating is one of our top concerns for students. While there are healthy options on campus, there are far more fast-food establishments available. We hope that by opening the garden, we will help students feel more inclined to make healthy choices by eating fresh fruits and vegetables.

Recording #3

Listen to the following conversation between two students:

Question: What is the female student's opinion regarding the community garden? Be sure to address her comments regarding both of the reasons given for opening a community garden.

- Preparation Time: 20 seconds
- Response Time: 60 seconds

Sample Responses

Listen to all of these passages by going to testprepbooks.com/bonus/toefl or by scanning the QR code below:

Recording #4

Recording #5

Speaking Practice Quiz Transcripts

Recording #2

1. If a recent high school graduate has to make the decision between starting a full-time job with good benefits and a $60,000 per year starting salary or starting college and paying tuition of $50,000 per year plus living expenses and spending four years to get the degree, but with the possibility of earning a starting salary of $75,000 once the degree is obtained, which do you think they should choose? Explain the reasons for your opinion.

Recording #3

2. **(Male Student)** Oh, that's cool. They are opening a community garden.

(Female Student) Really? That's awesome. I struggle to find fresh food on campus. The grocery store is far away, so I usually just stop to get fast food near my dorm. Do students have to pay a fee?

(Male Student) They said everything will be free for students.

(Female Student) That's great. I've noticed that it's way easier to eat unhealthy due to the cost. A salad and smoothie at the food hall is $12, while a burger and milkshake is $7. For a student who doesn't make a ton of money, it's not hard to decide which option to take.

(Male Student) I wonder who is running the garden.

(Female Student) I'm not sure, but it'd be cool to see them incorporate a gardening club so students can volunteer! This garden will provide so many opportunities for the school. This was a great decision.

Sample Response Transcripts

Recording #4

1. The better choice in my opinion is to take the job right after high school. If $60,000 is the starting salary, then they might be making $75,000 by the time they would have earned the degree anyway. Rather than spending money right away on college, a person can save some money for college and also save money for other things that will come up in the future. Maybe they could by a house or a car and get that done and then attend school part time if they still want to earn a degree. Sometimes work experience is as important as an education. I think this would be a smart way to get both. I would tell the person to choose this instead of paying $50,000 a year for four years to earn a degree.

Recording #5

2. The female student said that it was a great decision for the school to start a community garden where students can get free vegetables and fruits. The decision was made because not many options are there for students to find fresh food. It costs a lot and it can be harder to find. This student usually gets fast food because it's closer than the grocery store is to her dorm. The garden will make it easier to get fresh food because it's there on campus. Another reason for the garden is so students can get free food. Food costs a lot of money. The female student agrees that this is a good idea. It costs her more to eat healthy food than unhealthy food. So being able to get free fresh food makes sense to her. Instead of paying $12 for something healthy, she can get fruits and vegetables for free.

Writing

The TOEFL writing section consists of two different writing questions. The first writing section gives you a passage to read about a topic. Then, you will listen to a short lecture around two minutes long over the same topic. Though the two different mediums are over the same topic, they may have differing opinions. You will then have twenty minutes to write an essay synthesizing the two pieces.

The second writing section simulates an online academic discussion where a professor asks a question and students respond online, giving their opinions. Two responses from other students are given. The test taker has ten minutes to type their answer, using one hundred words or more to explain their own opinion and add to the discussion.

Writing the Essay

Brainstorming

One of the most important steps in writing an essay is prewriting. Before drafting an essay, it's helpful to think about the topic for a moment or two, in order to gain a more solid understanding of the task. Then, spending about five minutes jotting down the immediate ideas that could work for the essay is recommended. It is a way to get some words on the page and offer a reference for ideas when drafting. Scratch paper is provided for writers to use any prewriting techniques such as webbing, free writing, or listing. The goal is to get ideas out of the mind and onto the page.

Considering Opposing Viewpoints

In the planning stage, it's important to consider all aspects of the topic, including different viewpoints on the subject. There are more than two ways to look at a topic, and a strong argument considers those opposing viewpoints. Considering opposing viewpoints can help writers present a fair, balanced, and informed essay that shows consideration for all readers. This approach can also strengthen an argument by recognizing and potentially refuting opposing viewpoint(s).

Drawing from personal experience may help to support ideas. For example, if the goal for writing is a personal narrative, then the story should come from the writer's own life. Many writers find it helpful to draw from personal experience, even in an essay that is not strictly narrative. Personal anecdotes or short stories can help to illustrate a point in other types of essays as well.

Moving from Brainstorming to Planning

Once the ideas are on the page, it's time to turn them into a solid plan for the essay. The best ideas from the brainstorming results can then be developed into a more formal outline. An outline typically has one main point (the thesis) and at least three sub-points that support the main point. Here's an example:

Main Idea

- Point #1
- Point #2
- Point #3

Of course, there will be details under each point, but this approach is the best for dealing with timed writing.

Staying on Track

Basing the essay on the outline aids in both organization and coherence. The goal is to ensure that there is enough time to develop each sub-point in the essay, roughly spending an equal amount of time on each idea. Keeping an eye on the time will help. If there are fifteen minutes left to draft the essay, then it makes sense to spend about 5 minutes on each of the ideas. Staying on task is critical to success and timing out the parts of the essay can help writers avoid feeling overwhelmed.

Parts of the Essay

The **introduction** has to do a few important things:

- Establish the **topic** of the essay in original wording (i.e., not just repeating the prompt)
- Clarify the significance/importance of the topic or purpose for writing (not too many details, a brief overview)
- Offer a **thesis statement** that identifies the writer's own viewpoint on the topic (typically one to two brief sentences as a clear, concise explanation of the main point on the topic)

Body paragraphs reflect the ideas developed in the outline. Three to four points is probably sufficient for a short essay, and they should include the following:

- A **topic sentence** that identifies the sub-point (e.g., a reason why, a way how, a cause or effect)
- A detailed **explanation** of the point, explaining why the writer thinks this point is valid
- Illustrative **examples**, such as personal examples or real-world examples, that support and validate the point (i.e., "prove" the point)
- A **concluding sentence** that connects the examples, reasoning, and analysis to the point being made

The **conclusion**, or final paragraph, should be brief and should reiterate the focus, clarifying why the discussion is significant or important. It is important to avoid adding specific details or new ideas to this paragraph. The purpose of the conclusion is to sum up what has been said to bring the discussion to a close.

Don't Panic!

Writing an essay can be overwhelming, and performance panic is a natural response. The outline serves as a basis for the writing and helps writers keep focused. Getting stuck can also happen, and it's helpful to remember that brainstorming can be done at any time during the writing process. Following the steps of the writing process is the best defense against writer's block.

Timed essays can be particularly stressful, but assessors are trained to recognize the necessary planning and thinking for these timed efforts. Using the plan above and sticking to it helps with time management. Timing each part of the process helps writers stay on track. Sometimes writers try to cover too much in their essays. If time seems to be running out, this is an opportunity to determine whether all of the ideas in the outline are necessary. Three body paragraphs are sufficient, and more than that is probably too much to cover in a short essay.

More isn't always *better* in writing. A strong essay will be clear and concise. It will avoid unnecessary or repetitive details. It is better to have a concise, five-paragraph essay that makes a clear point, than a ten-paragraph essay that doesn't. The goal is to write one to two pages of quality writing. Paragraphs

59

should also reflect balance; if the introduction goes to the bottom of the first page, the writing may be going off-track or be repetitive. It's best to fall into the one to two-page range, but a complete, well-developed essay is the ultimate goal.

The Final Steps

Leaving a few minutes at the end to revise and proofread offers an opportunity for writers to polish things up. Putting one's self in the reader's shoes and focusing on what the essay actually says helps writers identify problems—it's a movement from the mindset of writer to the mindset of editor. The goal is to have a clean, clear copy of the essay. The following areas should be considered when proofreading:

- Sentence fragments
- Awkward sentence structure
- Run-on sentences
- Incorrect word choice
- Grammatical agreement errors
- Spelling errors
- Punctuation errors
- Capitalization errors

The Short Overview

The essay may seem challenging, but following these steps can help writers focus:

- Take one to two minutes to think about the topic.
- Generate some ideas through brainstorming (three to four minutes).
- Organize ideas into a brief outline, selecting just three to four main points to cover in the essay (eventually the body paragraphs).
- Develop essay in parts:
- Introduction paragraph, with intro to topic and main points
- Viewpoint on the subject at the end of the introduction
- Body paragraphs, based on outline
- Each paragraph: makes a main point, explains the viewpoint, uses examples to support the point
- Brief conclusion highlighting the main points and closing
- Read over the essay (last five minutes).
- Look for any obvious errors, making sure that the writing makes sense.

Parts of Speech

Nouns

A **common noun** is a word that identifies any of a class of people, places, or things. Examples include numbers, objects, animals, feelings, concepts, qualities, and actions. *A, an,* or *the* usually precedes the

60

common noun. These parts of speech are called *articles*. Here are some examples of sentences using nouns preceded by articles.

A building is under construction.

The girl would like to move to *the* city.

A **proper noun** (also called a **proper name**) is used for the specific name of an individual person, place, or organization. The first letter in a proper noun is capitalized. "My name is *Mary*." "I work for *Walmart*."

Nouns sometimes serve as adjectives (which themselves describe nouns), such as "hockey player" and "state government."

Pronouns

A word used in place of a noun is known as a **pronoun**. Pronouns are words like *I, mine, hers,* and *us.*

Pronouns can be split into different classifications (as shown below) which make them easier to learn; however, it's not important to memorize the classifications.

- **Personal pronouns:** refer to people

- **First person pronouns:** we, I, our, mine

- **Second person pronouns:** you, yours

- **Third person pronouns:** he, she, they, them, it

- **Possessive pronouns:** demonstrate ownership (mine, his, hers, its, ours, theirs, yours)

- **Interrogative pronouns:** ask questions (what, which, who, whom, whose)

- **Relative pronouns:** include the five interrogative pronouns and others that are relative (whoever, whomever, that, when, where)

- **Demonstrative pronouns:** replace something specific (this, that, those, these)

- **Reciprocal pronouns:** indicate something was done or given in return (each other, one another)

- **Indefinite pronouns:** have a nonspecific status (anybody, whoever, someone, everybody, somebody)

Indefinite pronouns such as *anybody, whoever, someone, everybody,* and *somebody* command a singular verb form, but others such as *all, none,* and *some* could require a singular or plural verb form.

Antecedents

An **antecedent** is the noun to which a pronoun refers; it needs to be written or spoken before the pronoun is used. For many pronouns, antecedents are imperative for clarity. In particular, a lot of the

61

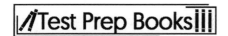

personal, possessive, and demonstrative pronouns need antecedents. Otherwise, it would be unclear who or what someone is referring to when they use a pronoun like *he* or *this*.

Pronoun reference means that the pronoun should refer clearly to one, clear, unmistakable noun (the antecedent).

Pronoun-antecedent agreement refers to the need for the antecedent and the corresponding pronoun to agree in gender, person, and number. Here are some examples:

> The *kidneys* (plural antecedent) are part of the urinary system. *They* (plural pronoun) serve several roles.

> The kidneys are part of the *urinary system* (singular antecedent). *It* (singular pronoun) is also known as the renal system.

Pronoun Cases

The **subjective pronouns** —*I, you, he/she/it, we, they,* and *who*—are the subjects of the sentence.

> Example: *They* have a new house.

The **objective pronouns**—*me, you* (*singular*), *him/her, us, them,* and *whom*—are used when something is being done for or given to someone; they are objects of the action.

> Example: The teacher has an apple for *us*.

The **possessive pronouns**—*mine, my, your, yours, his, hers, its, their, theirs, our,* and *ours*—are used to denote that something (or someone) belongs to someone (or something).

> Example: It's *their* chocolate cake.

> Even Better Example: It's *my* chocolate cake!

One of the greatest challenges and worst abuses of pronouns concerns *who* and *whom*. Just knowing the following rule can eliminate confusion. *Who* is a subjective-case pronoun used only as a subject or subject complement. *Whom* is only objective-case and, therefore, the object of the verb or preposition.

> *Who* is going to the concert?

> You are going to the concert with *whom*?

Hint: When using *who* or *whom*, think of whether someone would say *he* or *him*. If the answer is *he*, use *who*. If the answer is *him*, use *whom*. This trick is easy to remember because *he* and *who* both end in vowels, and *him* and *whom* both end in the letter *M*.

Many possessive pronouns sound like contractions. For example, many people get *it's* and *its* confused. The word *it's* is the contraction for *it is*. The word *its* without an apostrophe is the possessive form of *it*.

> I love that wooden desk. It's beautiful. (contraction)

> I love that wooden desk. Its glossy finish is beautiful. (possessive)

If you are not sure which version to use, replace *it's/its* with *it is* and see if that sounds correct. If so, use the contraction (*it's*). That trick also works for *who's/whose, you're/your*, and *they're/their*.

Adjectives

"The *extraordinary* brain is the *main* organ of the central nervous system." The adjective *extraordinary* describes the brain in a way that causes one to realize it is more exceptional than some of the other organs while the adjective *main* defines the brain's importance in its system.

An **adjective** is a word or phrase that names an attribute that describes or clarifies a noun or pronoun. This helps the reader visualize and understand the characteristics—size, shape, age, color, origin, etc.— of a person, place, or thing that otherwise might not be known. Adjectives breathe life, color, and depth into the subjects they define. Life would be *drab* and *colorless* without adjectives!

Adjectives often precede the nouns they describe.

> She drove her <u>new</u> car.

However, adjectives can also come later in the sentence.

> Her car is <u>new</u>.

Adjectives using the prefix *a*– can only be used after a verb.

> Correct: The dog was alive until the car ran up on the curb and hit him.

> Incorrect: The alive dog was hit by a car that ran up on the curb.

Other examples of this rule include *awake, ablaze, ajar, alike,* and *asleep*.

Other adjectives used after verbs concern states of health.

> The girl was finally *well* after a long bout of pneumonia.

> The boy was *fine* after the accident.

An adjective phrase is not a bunch of adjectives strung together, but a group of words that describes a noun or pronoun and, thus, functions as an adjective. *Very happy* is an adjective phrase; so are *way too hungry* and *passionate about traveling*.

Possessives

In grammar, *possessive nouns* show ownership, which was seen in previous examples like *mine, yours,* and *theirs*.

Singular nouns are generally made possessive with an apostrophe and an *s* ('*s*).

> My *uncle's* new car is silver.

> The *dog's* bowl is empty.

> *James's* ties are becoming outdated.

Plural nouns ending in *s* are generally made possessive by just adding an apostrophe ('):

> The pistachio nuts' saltiness is added during roasting. (The saltiness of pistachio nuts is added during roasting.)

> The students' achievement tests are difficult. (The achievement tests of the students are difficult.)

If the plural noun does not end in an *s* such as *women,* then it is made possessive by adding an *apostrophe s* ('s)—*women's.*

Indefinite possessive pronouns such as *nobody* or *someone* become possessive by adding an *apostrophe s*— *nobody's* or *someone's.*

Verbs
A verb is the part of speech that describes an action, state of being, or occurrence.

A verb forms the main part of a predicate of a sentence. This means that the verb explains what the noun (which will be discussed shortly) is doing. A simple example is *time <u>flies</u>.* The verb *flies* explains what the action of the noun, *time,* is doing. This example is a *main* verb.

Helping (auxiliary) verbs are words like *have, do, be, can, may, should, must,* and *will.* "I *should* go to the store." Helping verbs assist main verbs in expressing tense, ability, possibility, permission, or obligation.

Particles are minor function words like *not, in, out, up,* or *down* that become part of the verb itself. "I might *not.*"

Participles are words formed from verbs that are often used to modify a noun, noun phrase, verb, or verb phrase.

> The *running* teenager collided with the cyclist.

Participles can also create compound verb forms.

> He is *speaking.*

Verbs have five basic forms: the **base** form, the **-s** form, the **-ing** form, the **past** form, and the **past participle** form.

The past forms are either **regular** (*love/loved; hate/hated*) or **irregular** because they don't end by adding the common past tense suffix "-ed" (*go/went; fall/fell; set/set*).

Adverbs
Adverbs have more functions than adjectives because they modify or qualify verbs, adjectives, or other adverbs as well as word groups that express a relation of place, time, circumstance, or cause. Therefore, adverbs answer any of the following questions: *How, when, where, why, in what way, how often, how much, in what condition,* and/or *to what degree. How good looking is he? He is <u>very</u> handsome.*

Here are some examples of adverbs for different situations:

- how: quickly
- when: daily
- where: there
- in what way: easily
- how often: often
- how much: much
- in what condition: badly
- what degree: hardly

As one can see, for some reason, many adverbs end in *-ly*.

Adverbs do things like emphasize (*really, simply,* and *so*), amplify (*heartily, completely,* and *positively*), and tone down (*almost, somewhat,* and *mildly*).

Adverbs also come in phrases.

The dog ran as <u>though his life depended on it.</u>

Prepositions

Prepositions are connecting words and, while there are only about 150 of them, they are used more often than any other individual groups of words. They describe relationships between other words. They are placed before a noun or pronoun, forming a phrase that modifies another word in the sentence. **Prepositional phrases** begin with a preposition and end with a noun or pronoun, the **object of the preposition.** *A pristine lake is <u>near the store</u> and <u>behind the bank</u>.*

Some commonly used prepositions are *about, after, anti, around, as, at, behind, beside, by, for, from, in, into, of, off, on, to,* and *with*.

Complex prepositions, which also come before a noun or pronoun, consist of two or three words such as *according to, in regards to,* and *because of.*

Interjections

Interjections are words used to express emotion. Examples include *wow, ouch,* and *hooray.* Interjections are often separate from sentences; in those cases, the interjection is directly followed by an exclamation point. In other cases, the interjection is included in a sentence and followed by a comma. The punctuation plays a big role in the intensity of the emotion that the interjection is expressing. Using a comma or semicolon indicates less excitement than using an exclamation mark.

Conjunctions

Conjunctions are vital words that connect words, phrases, thoughts, and ideas. Conjunctions show relationships between components. There are two types:

Coordinating conjunctions are the primary class of conjunctions placed between words, phrases, clauses, and sentences that are of equal grammatical rank; the coordinating conjunctions are *for, and,*

nor, *but*, *or*, *yet*, and *so*. A useful memorization trick is to remember that the first letter of these conjunctions collectively spell the word *fanboys*.

I need to go shopping, *but* I must be careful to leave enough money in the bank.

She wore a black, red, *and* white shirt.

Subordinating conjunctions are the secondary class of conjunctions. They connect two unequal parts, one **main** (or **independent**) and the other **subordinate** (or **dependent**). I must go to the store *even though* I do not have enough money in the bank.

Because I read the review, I do not want to go to the movie.

Notice that the presence of subordinating conjunctions makes clauses dependent. *I read the review* is an independent clause, but *because* makes the clause dependent. Thus, it needs an independent clause to complete the sentence.

Sentences

First, let's review the basic elements of sentences.

A **sentence** is a set of words that make up a grammatical unit. The words must have certain elements and be spoken or written in a specific order to constitute a complete sentence that makes sense.

1. A sentence must have a **subject** (a noun or noun phrase). The subject tells whom or what the sentence is addressing (i.e. what it is about).

2. A sentence must have an **action** or **state of being** (*a* verb). To reiterate: A verb forms the main part of the predicate of a sentence. This means that it explains what the noun is doing.

3. A sentence must convey a complete thought.

When examining writing, be mindful of grammar, structure, spelling, and patterns. Sentences can come in varying sizes and shapes; so, the point of grammatical correctness is not to stamp out creativity or diversity in writing. Rather, grammatical correctness ensures that writing will be enjoyable and clear. One of the most common methods for catching errors is to mouth the words as you read them. Many typos are fixed automatically by our brain, but mouthing the words often circumvents this instinct and helps one read what's actually on the page. Often, grammar errors are caught not by memorization of grammar rules but by the training of one's mind to know whether something *sounds* right or not.

Types of Sentences

There isn't an overabundance of absolutes in grammar, but here is one: every sentence in the English language falls into one of four categories.

- Declarative: a simple statement that ends with a period

  The price of milk per gallon is the same as the price of gasoline.

- Imperative: a command, instruction, or request that ends with a period

  Buy milk when you stop to fill up your car with gas.

66

- Interrogative: a question that ends with a question mark

    Will you buy the milk?

- Exclamatory: a statement or command that expresses emotions like anger, urgency, or surprise and ends with an exclamation mark

    Buy the milk now!

Declarative sentences are the most common type, probably because they are comprised of the most general content, without any of the bells and whistles that the other three types contain. They are, simply, declarations or statements of any degree of seriousness, importance, or information.

Imperative sentences often seem to be missing a subject. The subject is there, though; it is just not visible or audible because it is *implied*. Look at the imperative example sentence.

    Buy the milk when you fill up your car with gas.

You is the implied subject, the one to whom the command is issued. This is sometimes called *the understood you* because it is understood that *you* is the subject of the sentence.

Interrogative sentences—those that ask questions—are defined as such from the idea of the word *interrogation*, the action of questions being asked of suspects by investigators. Although that is serious business, interrogative sentences apply to all kinds of questions.

To exclaim is at the root of **exclamatory sentences**. These are made with strong emotions behind them. The only technical difference between a declarative or imperative sentence and an exclamatory one is the exclamation mark at the end. The example declarative and imperative sentences can both become an exclamatory one simply by putting an exclamation mark at the end of the sentences.

    The price of milk per gallon is the same as the price of gasoline!
    Buy milk when you stop to fill up your car with gas!

After all, someone might be really excited by the price of gas or milk, or they could be mad at the person that will be buying the milk! However, as stated before, exclamation marks in abundance defeat their own purpose! After a while, they begin to cause fatigue! When used only for their intended purpose, they can have their expected and desired effect.

Independent and Dependent Clauses

Independent and dependent clauses are strings of words that contain both a subject and a verb. An **independent clause** *can* stand alone as complete thought, but a **dependent clause** *cannot*. A dependent clause relies on other words to be a complete sentence.

    Independent clause: The keys are on the counter.
    Dependent clause: If the keys are on the counter

Notice that both clauses have a subject (*keys*) and a verb (*are*). The independent clause expresses a complete thought, but the word *if* at the beginning of the dependent clause makes it *dependent* on other words to be a complete thought.

67

Independent clause: If the keys are on the counter, please give them to me.

This example constitutes a complete sentence since it includes at least one verb and one subject and is a complete thought. In this case, the independent clause has two subjects (*keys* & an implied *you*) and two verbs (*are* & *give*).

> Independent clause: I went to the store.
> Dependent clause: Because we are out of milk,
>
> Complete Sentence: Because we are out of milk, I went to the store.
> Complete Sentence: I went to the store because we are out of milk.

Sentence Structures

A **simple sentence** has one independent clause.

> I am going to win.

A **compound sentence** has two independent clauses. A conjunction—*for, and, nor, but, or, yet, so*—links them together. Note that each of the independent clauses has a subject and a verb.

> I am going to win, but the odds are against me.

A **complex sentence** has one independent clause and one or more dependent clauses.

> I am going to win, even though I don't deserve it.

Even though I don't deserve it is a dependent clause. It does not stand on its own. Some conjunctions that link an independent and a dependent clause are *although, because, before, after, that, when, which,* and *while*.

A **compound-complex sentence** has at least three clauses, two of which are independent and at least one that is a dependent clause.

> While trying to dance, I tripped over my partner's feet, but I regained my balance quickly.

The dependent clause is *While trying to dance*.

Run-Ons and Fragments

Run-Ons

A common mistake in writing is the run-on sentence. A **run-on** is created when two or more independent clauses are joined without the use of a conjunction, a semicolon, a colon, or a dash. We don't want to use commas where periods belong. Here is an example of a run-on sentence:

> Making wedding cakes can take many hours I am very impatient, I want to see them completed right away.

There are a variety of ways to correct a run-on sentence. The method you choose will depend on the context of the sentence and how it fits with neighboring sentences:

68

Making wedding cakes can take many hours. I am very impatient. I want to see them completed right away. (Use periods to create more than one sentence.)

Making wedding cakes can take many hours; I am very impatient—I want to see them completed right away. (Correct the sentence using a semicolon, colon, or dash.)

Making wedding cakes can take many hours, and I am very impatient and want to see them completed right away. (Correct the sentence using coordinating conjunctions.)

I am very impatient because I would rather see completed wedding cakes right away than wait for it to take many hours. (Correct the sentence by revising.)

Fragments

Remember that a complete sentence must have both a subject and a verb. Complete sentences consist of at least one independent clause. Incomplete sentences are called **sentence fragments**. A sentence fragment is a common error in writing. Sentence fragments can be independent clauses that start with subordinating words, such as *but, as, so that,* or *because,* or they could simply be missing a subject or verb.

A fragment error can be corrected by adding the fragment to a nearby sentence or by adding or removing words to make it an independent clause. For example:

Dogs are my favorite animals. Because cats are too lazy. (Incorrect; the word because creates a sentence fragment)

Dogs are my favorite animals because cats are too lazy. (Correct; this is a dependent clause.)

Dogs are my favorite animals. Cats are too lazy. (Correct; this is a simple sentence.)

Subject and Predicate

Every complete sentence can be divided into two parts: the subject and the predicate.

Subjects: Subjects are needed in sentences to tell the reader who or what the sentence describes. Subjects can be simple or complete, and they can be direct or indirect. There can also be compound subjects.

Simple subjects are the noun or nouns the sentence describes, without modifiers. The simple subject can come before or after the verb in the sentence:

The big brown <u>dog</u> is the calmest one.

Complete subjects are the subject together with all of its describing words or modifiers.

The <u>big brown dog</u> is the calmest one. (The complete subject is big brown dog.)

Direct subjects are subjects that appear in the text of the sentence, as in the example above. **Indirect subjects** are implied. The subject is "you," but the word *you* does not appear.

Indirect subjects are usually in imperative sentences that issue a command or order:

Feed the short skinny dog first. (The understood you is the subject.)

Watch out—he's really hungry! (The sentence warns you to watch out.)

Compound subjects occur when two or more nouns join together to form a plural subject.

<u>Carson</u> and <u>Emily</u> make a great couple.

Predicates: Once we have identified the subject of the sentence, the rest of the sentence becomes the predicate. Predicates are formed by the verb, the direct object, and all words related to it.

We <u>went to see the Cirque du' Soleil performance</u>.

The gigantic green character <u>was funnier than all the rest</u>.

Direct objects are the nouns in the sentence that are receiving the action. Sentences don't necessarily need objects. Sentences only need a subject and a verb.

The clown brought the acrobat the <u>hula-hoop</u>. (What is getting brought? the hula-hoop)

Then he gave the trick pony a <u>soapy bath</u>. (What is being given? (a soapy bath)

Indirect objects are words that tell us to or for whom or what the action is being done. For there to be an indirect object, there first must always be a direct object.

The clown brought <u>the acrobat</u> the hula-hoop. (Who is getting the direct object? the hula-hoop)

Then he gave <u>the trick pony</u> a soapy bath. (What is getting the bath? a trick pony)

Phrases

A **phrase** is a group of words that go together but do not include both a subject and a verb. They are used to add information, explain something, or make the sentence easier for the reader to understand. Unlike clauses, phrases can never stand alone as their own sentence. They do not form complete thoughts. There are noun phrases, prepositional phrases, verbal phrases, appositive phrases, and absolute phrases. Here are some examples of phrases:

I know <u>all the shortest routes</u>.

<u>Before the sequel</u>, we wanted to watch the first movie. (introductory phrase)

The jumpers have hot cocoa <u>to drink right away</u>.

Subject-Verb Agreement

The subject of a sentence and its verb must agree. The cornerstone rule of subject-verb agreement is that subject and verb must agree in number. Whether the subject is singular or plural, the verb must follow suit.

Incorrect: The houses is new.

Correct: The houses are new.

Also Correct: The house is new.

In other words, a singular subject requires a singular verb; a plural subject requires a plural verb.

The words or phrases that come between the subject and verb do not alter this rule.

Incorrect: The houses built of brick is new.

Correct: The houses built of brick are new.

Incorrect: The houses with the sturdy porches is new.

Correct: The houses with the sturdy porches are new.

The subject will always follow the verb when a sentence begins with *here* or *there.* Identify these with care.

Incorrect: Here *is* the *houses* with sturdy porches.

Correct: Here *are* the *houses* with sturdy porches.

The subject in the sentences above is not *here*, it is *houses*. Remember, *here* and *there* are never subjects. Be careful that contractions such as *here's* or *there're* do not cause confusion!

Two subjects joined by *and* require a plural verb form, except when the two combine to make one thing:

Incorrect: Garrett and Jonathan is over there.

Correct: Garrett and Jonathan are over there.

Incorrect: Spaghetti and meatballs are a delicious meal!

Correct: Spaghetti and meatballs is a delicious meal!

In the example above, *spaghetti and meatballs* is a compound noun. However, *Garrett and Jonathan* is not a compound noun.

Two singular subjects joined by *or, either/or,* or *neither/nor* call for a singular verb form.

Incorrect: Butter or syrup are acceptable.

Correct: Butter or syrup is acceptable.

71

Plural subjects joined by *or*, *either/or*, or *neither/nor* are, indeed, plural.

The chairs or the boxes are being moved next.

If one subject is singular and the other is plural, the verb should agree with the closest noun.

Correct: The chair or the boxes are being moved next.

Correct: The chairs or the box is being moved next.

Some plurals of money, distance, and time call for a singular verb.

Incorrect: Three dollars *are* enough to buy that.

Correct: Three dollars *is* enough to buy that.

For words declaring degrees of quantity such as *many of, some of,* or *most of,* let the noun that follows *of* be the guide:

Incorrect: Many of the books is in the shelf.

Correct: Many of the books are in the shelf.

Incorrect: Most of the pie *are* on the table.

Correct: Most of the pie *is* on the table.

For indefinite pronouns like anybody or everybody, use singular verbs.

Everybody *is* going to the store.

However, the pronouns *few, many, several, all, some,* and *both* have their own rules and use plural forms.

Some *are* ready.

Some nouns like *crowd* and *congress* are called *collective nouns* and they require a singular verb form.

Congress *is* in session.

The news *is* over.

Books and movie titles, though, including plural nouns such as *Great Expectations*, also require a singular verb. Remember that only the subject affects the verb. While writing tricky subject-verb arrangements, say them aloud. Listen to them. Once the rules have been learned, one's ear will become sensitive to them, making it easier to pick out what's right and what's wrong.

Dangling and Misplaced Modifiers

A **modifier** is a word or phrase meant to describe or clarify another word in the sentence. When a sentence has a modifier but is missing the word it describes or clarifies, it's an error called a **dangling modifier**. We can fix the sentence by revising to include the word that is being modified. Consider the following examples with the modifier underlined:

72

Incorrect: <u>Having walked five miles</u>, this bench will be the place to rest. (This implies that the bench walked the miles, not the person.)

Correct: <u>Having walked five miles</u>, Matt will rest on this bench. (*Having walked five miles* correctly modifies *Matt*, who did the walking.)

Incorrect: <u>Since midnight</u>, my dreams have been pleasant and comforting. (The adverb clause *since midnight* cannot modify the noun *dreams*.)

Correct: <u>Since midnight</u>, I have had pleasant and comforting dreams. (*Since midnight* modifies the verb have had, telling us when the dreams occurred.)

Sometimes the modifier is not located close enough to the word it modifies for the sentence to be clearly understood. In this case, we call the error a **misplaced modifier**. Here is an example with the modifier underlined.

Incorrect: We gave the hot cocoa to the children <u>that was filled with marshmallows</u>. (This sentence implies that the children are what are filled with marshmallows.)

Correct: We gave the hot cocoa <u>that was filled with marshmallows</u> to the children. (The cocoa is filled with marshmallows. The modifier is near the word it modifies.)

Parallel Structure in a Sentence

Parallel structure, also known as **parallelism**, refers to using the same grammatical form within a sentence. This is important in lists and for other components of sentences.

Incorrect: At the recital, the boys and girls were dancing, singing, and played musical instruments.
Correct: At the recital, the boys and girls were dancing, singing, and playing musical instruments.

Notice that in the second example, *played* is not in the same verb tense as the other verbs, nor is it compatible with the helping verb *were*. To test for parallel structure in lists, try reading each item as if it were the only item in the list.

The boys and girls were dancing.
The boys and girls were singing.
The boys and girls were played musical instruments.

Suddenly, the error in the sentence becomes very clear. Here's another example:

Incorrect: After the accident, I informed the police *that Mrs. Holmes backed* into my car, *that Mrs. Holmes got out* of her car to look at the damage, and *she was driving* off without leaving a note.

Correct: After the accident, I informed the police *that Mrs. Holmes backed* into my car, *that Mrs. Holmes got out* of her car to look at the damage, and *that Mrs. Holmes drove off* without leaving a note.

Correct: After the accident, I informed the police that Mrs. Holmes *backed* into my car, *got out* of her car to look at the damage, and *drove off* without leaving a note.

73

Note that there are two ways to fix the nonparallel structure of the first sentence. The key to parallelism is consistent structure.

Punctuation

Commas

A **comma** (,) is the punctuation mark that signifies a pause—breath—between parts of a sentence. It denotes a break of flow. As with so many aspects of writing structure, authors will benefit by memorizing all of the different ways in which commas can be used so as not to abuse them.

In a complex sentence—one that contains a subordinate (dependent) clause or clauses—the use of a comma is dictated by where the subordinate clause is located. If the subordinate clause is located before the main clause, a comma is needed between the two clauses.

> I will not pay for the steak, *because I don't have that much money*.

Generally, if the subordinate clause is placed after the main clause, no punctuation is needed.

> I did well on my exam because I studied two hours the night before.

Notice how the last clause is dependent because it requires the earlier independent clauses to make sense.

Use a comma on both sides of an interrupting phrase.

> I will pay for the ice cream, *chocolate and vanilla*, and then will eat it all myself.

The words forming the phrase in italics are nonessential (extra) information. To determine if a phrase is nonessential, try reading the sentence without the phrase and see if it's still coherent.

A comma is not necessary in this next sentence because no interruption—nonessential or extra information—has occurred. Read sentences aloud when uncertain.

I will pay for his chocolate and vanilla ice cream and then will eat it all myself.

If the nonessential phrase comes at the beginning of a sentence, a comma should only go at the end of the phrase. If the phrase comes at the end of a sentence, a comma should only go at the beginning of the phrase.

Other types of interruptions include the following:

- interjections: Oh no, I am not going.
- abbreviations: Barry Potter, M.D., specializes in heart disorders.
- direct addresses: Yes, Claudia, I am tired and going to bed.
- parenthetical phrases: His wife, lovely as she was, was not helpful.
- transitional phrases: Also, it is not possible.

The second comma in the following sentence is called an Oxford comma.

> I will pay for ice cream, syrup, and pop.

74

It is a comma used after the second-to-last item in a series of three or more items. It comes before the word *or* or *and*. Not everyone uses the Oxford comma; it is optional, but many believe it is needed. The comma functions as a tool to reduce confusion in writing. So, if omitting the Oxford comma would cause confusion, then it's best to include it.

Commas are used in math to mark the place of thousands in numerals, breaking them up so they are easier to read. Other uses for commas are in dates (*March 19, 2016*), letter greetings (*Dear Sally,*), and in between cities and states (*Louisville, KY*).

Apostrophes
This punctuation mark, the apostrophe ('), is a versatile little mark. It has a few different functions:

- Quotes: Apostrophes are used when a second quote is needed within a quote.

- In my letter to my friend, I wrote, "The girl had to get a new purse, and guess what Mary did? She said, 'I'd like to go with you to the store.' I knew Mary would buy it for her."

- Contractions: Another use for an apostrophe in the quote above is a contraction. *I'd* is used for *I would.*

The basic rule for making *contractions* is one area of spelling that is pretty straightforward: combine the two words by inserting an apostrophe (') in the space where a letter is omitted. For example, to combine *you* and *are*, drop the *a* and put the apostrophe in its place: *you're.*

he + is = he's

you + all = y'all (informal but often misspelled)

- Possession: An apostrophe followed by the letter *s* shows possession (*Mary's* purse). If the possessive word is plural, the apostrophe generally just follows the word.

- The trees' leaves are all over the ground.

Ellipses
An **ellipsis** (...) is used to show that there is more to the quoted text than is necessary for the current discussion. Writers use them in place of words, lines, phrases, list content, or paragraphs that might just as easily have been omitted from a passage of writing. This can be done to save space or to focus only on the specifically relevant material.

Exercise is good for some unexpected reasons. Watkins writes, "Exercise has many benefits such as...reducing cancer risk."

In the example above, the ellipsis takes the place of the other benefits of exercise that are more expected.

The ellipsis may also be used to show a pause in sentence flow.

"I'm wondering...how this could happen," Dylan said in a soft voice.

Semicolons

The **semicolon** (;) might be described as a heavy-handed comma. Take a look at these two examples:

> I will pay for the ice cream, but I will not pay for the steak.
> I will pay for the ice cream; I will not pay for the steak.

What's the difference? The first example has a comma and a conjunction separating the two independent clauses. The second example does not have a conjunction, but there are two independent clauses in the sentence, so something more than a comma is required. In this case, a semicolon is used.

Two independent clauses can only be joined in a sentence by either a comma and conjunction or a semicolon. If one of those tools is not used, the sentence will be a run-on. Remember that while the clauses are independent, they need to be closely related in order to be contained in one sentence.

Another use for the semicolon is to separate items in a list when the items themselves require commas.

> The family lived in Phoenix, Arizona; Oklahoma City, Oklahoma; and Raleigh, North Carolina.

Colons

Colons (:) have many miscellaneous functions. Colons can be used to precede further information or a list. In these cases, a colon should only follow an independent clause.

> Humans take in sensory information through five basic senses: sight, hearing, smell, touch, and taste.

The meal includes the following components:

- Caesar salad
- spaghetti
- garlic bread
- cake

The family got what they needed: a reliable vehicle.

While a comma is more common, a colon can also precede a formal quotation.

> He said to the crowd: "Let's begin!"

The colon is used after the greeting in a formal letter.

> Dear Sir:
> To Whom It May Concern:

In the writing of time, the colon separates the minutes from the hour (*4:45 p.m.*). The colon can also be used to indicate a ratio between two numbers (*50:1*).

Hyphens

The **hyphen** (-) is a little hash mark that can be used to join words to show that they are linked.

76

Hyphens can connect two words that work together as a single adjective (a compound adjective).

> honey-covered biscuits

Some words always require hyphens even if not serving as an adjective.

> merry-go-round

Hyphens always go after certain prefixes like *anti-* & *all-*.

Hyphens should also be used when the absence of the hyphen would cause a strange vowel combination (*semi-engineer*) or confusion. For example, *re-collect* should be used to describe something being gathered twice rather than being written as *recollect*, which means to remember.

Parentheses and Dashes

Parentheses are half-round brackets that look like this: *( )*. They set off a word, phrase, or sentence that is an afterthought, explanation, or side note relevant to the surrounding text but not essential. A pair of commas is often used to set off this sort of information, but parentheses are generally used for information that would not fit well within a sentence or that the writer deems not important enough to be structurally part of the sentence.

> The picture of the heart (see above) shows the major parts you should memorize.
> Mount Everest is one of three mountains in the world that are over 28,000 feet high (K2 and Kanchenjunga are the other two).

See how the sentences above are complete without the parenthetical statements? In the first example, *see above* would not have fit well within the flow of the sentence. The second parenthetical statement could have been a separate sentence, but the writer deemed the information not pertinent to the topic.

The **em-dash** (—) is a mark longer than a hyphen used as a punctuation mark in sentences and to set apart a relevant thought. Even after plucking out the line separated by the dash marks, the sentence will be intact and make sense.

> Looking out the airplane window at the landmarks—Lake Clarke, Thompson Community College, and the bridge—she couldn't help but feel excited to be home.

The dashes use is similar to that of parentheses or a pair of commas. So, what's the difference? Many believe that using dashes makes the clause within them stand out while using parentheses is subtler. It's advised to not use dashes when commas could be used instead.

Quotation Marks

Quotation marks ("") are used in a number of ways. Here are some instances where quotation marks should be used: to indicate a quote that was taken from somewhere else, either from a verbal or written source...

- Dialogue for characters in narratives. When characters speak, the first word should always be capitalized, and the punctuation goes inside the quotes. For example:

> Janie said, "The tree fell on my car during the hurricane."

77

- Around titles of songs, short stories, essays, and chapters in books
- To emphasize a certain word
- To refer to a word as the word itself

Capitalization

Here's a non-exhaustive list of things that should be capitalized:

- The first word of every sentence
- The first word of every line of poetry
- The first letter of proper nouns (World War II)
- Holidays (Valentine's Day)
- The days of the week and months of the year (Tuesday, March)
- The first word, last word, and all major words in the titles of books, movies, songs, and other creative works (In the novel, *To Kill a Mockingbird*, note that *a* is lowercase since it's not a major word, but *to* is capitalized since it's the first word of the title.)
- Titles when preceding a proper noun (President Roberto Gonzales, Aunt Judy)

When simply using a word such as president or secretary, though, the word is not capitalized.

Officers of the new business must include a *president* and *treasurer*.

Seasons—spring, fall, etc.—are not capitalized.

North, *south*, *east*, and *west* are capitalized when referring to regions but are not when being used for directions. In general, if it's preceded by *the* it should be capitalized.

I'm from the South.
I drove south.

Various Homonyms

That/Which

The pronouns *that* and *which* are both used to refer to nouns—but they are not interchangeable. The rule is to use the word that in essential clauses and phrases that help convey the meaning of the sentence. Use the word *which* in nonessential (less important) clauses. Typically, *which* clauses are enclosed in commas.

The morning <u>that I fell asleep in class</u> caused me a lot of trouble.

This morning's coffee, <u>which had too much creamer</u>, woke me up.

Who/Whom

We use the pronouns *who* and *whom* to refer to people. We always use *who* when it is the subject of the sentence or clause. *Whom* is always the object of a verb or preposition.

<u>Who</u> hit the baseball for the home run? (subject)

The baseball fell into the glove of <u>whom</u>? (object of the preposition of)

78

The umpire called <u>whom</u> "out"? (object of the verb called)

To/Too/Two

to: a preposition or infinitive (*to walk, to run, walk to the store, run to the tree*)

too: means also, as well, or very (*She likes cookies, too.; I ate too much.*)

two: a number (*I have two cookies. She walked to the store two times.*)

There/Their/They're

there: an adjective, adverb, or pronoun used to start a sentence or indicate place (*There are four vintage cars over there.*)

their: a possessive pronoun used to indicate belonging (*Their car is the blue and white one.*)

they're: a contraction of the words "they are" (*They're going to enter the vintage car show.*)

Your/You're

your: a possessive pronoun (*Your artwork is terrific.*)

you're: a contraction of the words "you are" (*You're a terrific artist.*)

Its/It's

its: a possessive pronoun (*The elephant had its trunk in the water.*)

it's: a contraction of the words "it is" (*It's an impressive animal.*)

Affect/Effect

affect: as a verb means "to influence" (*How will the earthquake affect your home?*); as a noun means "emotion or mood" (*Her affect was somber.*)

effect: as a verb means "to bring about" (*She will effect a change through philanthropy.*); as a noun means "a result of" (*The effect of the earthquake was devastating.*)

Other mix-ups: Other pairs of words cause mix-ups but are not necessarily homonyms. Here are a few of those:

Bring/Take

bring: when the action is coming toward (*Bring me the money.*)

take: when the action is going away from (*Take her the money.*)

Can/May

can: means "able to" (*The child can ride a bike.*)

may: asks permission (*The child asked if he may ride his bike.*)

Than/Then

than: a conjunction used for comparison (*I like tacos better than pizza.*)

then: an adverb telling when something happened (*I ate and then slept.*)

Disinterested/Uninterested

disinterested: used to mean "neutral" (*The jury remains disinterested during the trial.*)

uninterested: used to mean "bored" (*I was uninterested during the lecture.*)

Percent/Percentage

percent: used when there is a number involved (*Five percent of us like tacos.*)

79

percentage: used when there is no number (*That is a low percentage.*)

Fewer/Less

fewer: used for things you can count (*He has fewer playing cards.*)

less: used for things you cannot count, as well as time (*He has less talent. You have less than a minute.*)

Farther/Further

farther: used when discussing distance (*His paper airplane flew farther than mine.*)

further: used to mean "more" (*He needed further information.*)

Lend/Loan

lend: a verb used for borrowing (*Lend me your lawn mower. He will lend it to me.*)

loan: a noun used for something borrowed (*She applied for a student loan.*)

Note

- Some people have problems with these:
-
  - regardless/irregardless
  - a lot/alot

Irregardless and *alot* are always incorrect. Don't use them

Writing Practice

Integrated Writing

First, read the article below:

Fracking is a controversial subject in the United States. Natural gas is available in the United States, but fracking must be performed to obtain it. Fracking would help the United States in multiple ways due to its abundance, affordability, and low carbon emissions.

Fracking is a current necessity due to how reliant the United States is on natural gas. This country requires a lot of natural gas and oil. By fracking, the U.S. could bolster its reserves of natural gas while also increasing exports. Natural gas is necessary for stoves and heating in homes, schools, and hospitals. It's also used to produce fertilizer and chemicals needed for agriculture. The transportation of buses, trucks, and cars require natural gas. Simply put, the U.S. requires a huge amount of natural gas to operate.

The United States currently relies on other countries to provide natural gas and oil. Around 35 percent of the nation's supply comes from foreign sources. To increase independence, the U.S. should focus on producing it within the country. This would be paramount in in case of a national emergency where the U.S. cannot rely on other countries. Producing within the country would lower prices drastically. Citizens would not face drastic price fluctuations. The economy would overall be bolstered by the lowered prices, increased exports, and new jobs.

Fracking is often accused of being environmentally damaging. However, fracking uses less water than coal and nuclear power. Water usage is important as America faces water shortages. Natural gas is also much cleaner burning than coal and produces far less greenhouse gases. Burning coal creates harmful particles and releases nitrogen oxide and sulfur dioxide into the air. These things can be immediately deadly to those who are living and working in the vicinity of coal. Natural gas is much better for air quality.

Now listen to the following lecture: testprepbooks.com/bonus/toefl

Recording #6

Prompt: Summarize the points presented in the lecture. Explain how they relate to specific points in the reading passage.

You have 20 minutes to write your essay.

The following pages are provided for writing your essay.

83

Academic Discussion

First, read the following online academic discussion between a professor and some students:

Instructor: Religion seeks to answer many of life's questions. Different religions are integral to cultures across the world. However, religion can also be a highly divisive topic and can quickly become political. Should religion be a required course in schools?

Student 1: I do not believe that religion should be taught in schools. It goes against the separation of church and state. It may go against some students' personal beliefs to learn about religions other than their own. If students want to learn about religion, they have plenty of time to do so at home. Otherwise, it opens the door for teachers to impose their beliefs and make students uncomfortable.

Student 2: Religion should be a required topic in schools. Teaching about different cultures, religions, and ideologies opens up a student to a whole world outside of their own. It is key to understanding other people and respecting their beliefs. Part of why religion is so divisive is because nobody is teaching mutual understanding and respect. The only way to ensure that people do not remain close-minded is to teach them about ways of living that differ from their own. There is a way to teach religion without imposing beliefs onto the students, so that concern is unwarranted.

Next, add your opinion to the conversation using 100 words or more.

You have 10 minutes to write your response.

The following pages are provided for writing your essay.

Writing Practice Sample Responses

Integrated Writing Task Sample Response

In the lecture, it was explained that fracking is not something that the United States should consider doing. The consequences outweigh the benefits that were described in the passage.

The first point is that fracking is unnecessary. The United States produces more natural gas than other countries and they already have enough to last for another decade, as long as it's used at the same rate as it is used now. There could be less dangerous ways of obtaining natural gas that could be found. The focus could be on finding those ways rather than fracking while it's not needed. This is the opposite of what the passages states. The passage states that fracking is necessary now, but this is not true.

The second reason that fracking should not be considered is because the damage that will be done to the communities and the wildlife would leave a burden. Fracking would be done in rural areas and poor areas. It will create pollution, and it's linked to health problems. Any health problems caused to people in these communities is not worth the independence or a better economy for the United States. The communities would have to deal with all of the negative issues created by fracking. Creating this burden to their infrastructure would not help their economy, but the passage says that the economy will be bolstered.

Finally, fracking causes pollution by releasing many contaminants into the air. It also releases methane, which traps more heat than carbon dioxide does. To prove that fracking is not environmentally damaging, the passage claims that fracking uses less water and that natural gas is cleaner to burn. While this may be so, fracking still causes damage to the environment. The lecture points out that there is no need for this when there are sources of clean energy.

The lecture explains why the United States should not use fracking for natural gas. It is not needed at this time, it will cause problems to the community and wildlife where it is done, and it will cause air pollution and damage the environment. All of these points contradict what was said in the passage.

Academic Discussion Writing Task Sample Response

Religion should be offered electively in schools. Students should not be forced to learn about religion, as it may go against their personal beliefs or be highly uncomfortable based on their background. However, religion is important to understanding cultures around the world. For example, in many Middle Eastern countries, religion greatly affects their citizens' daily lives. Their clothing, food, and daily activities are based on their religious beliefs. In order to understand their culture, the students must also understand the basics of their religion. History also has many religious components. Wars have been fought over religion. Countries have been divided over religion. To understand why history has played out in the way that it has, students should have the opportunity to learn about religion.

Integrated Writing Practice Lecture Transcript

Listen to all of these passages by going to testprepbooks.com/bonus/toefl or by scanning the QR code below:

Recording #6

(Professor) Fracking is dangerous and should not be allowed in the United States. It creates permanent consequences for the environment and is currently unnecessary. A ban on fracking would help the Earth and all its inhabitants.

Fracking is not necessary for the United States at this time. The United States has large reserves of natural gas and oil. The current reserves could last over a decade at the current levels of consumption. The nation already produces more natural gas than any other country on the planet, so fracking for more is unnecessary. By holding off on fracking, we may discover less invasive and damaging methods of obtaining natural gas. The health risks and environmental damage fracking creates do not outweigh the potential economic benefits. Instead of ignoring environmental and health concerns, the U.S. should focus on alternative energy that does not require dirty fossil fuels.

The mission for energy independence is not worth the consequences it brings for local citizens. Fracking places a burden on local infrastructure because it is generally approved in poor and rural areas. These communities will have to deal with the health problems and environmental destruction that come with fracking. In order to begin fracking, large areas of land must be taken over. Waterways may become polluted and no longer accessible. The chemicals used for fracking are especially harmful to pregnant women. They have also been linked to cancer, heart problems, and asthma. Wildlife and biodiversity will suffer as habitats are destroyed. These issues will become a burden for the communities that are taken over by fracking companies.

Claims that natural gas is cleaner than coal are only true to an extent. Fracking for natural gas releases methane. This greenhouse gas traps over 80 times the amount of heat that carbon dioxide does. This means that it is actually a bigger contributor to pollution. Volatile organic compounds, nitrogen oxides, and other air contaminants are released during the process as well. Fracking is not a better solution to coal and should not be considered a worthwhile method of energy production when clean energy is available.

90

Reading

Questions 1–10 are based on the following passage:

Behaviorism played a large role in the beginnings of the field of psychology. Behavioral psychology deals with a theory of learning. The basis of behaviorism is the idea that conditioning teaches behaviors through the interaction between an individual and their environment or environmental stimuli. Because this understanding of learning is based upon purely external factors, behaviorism relies on observable behaviors rather than inherited or internal factors. **A** Observable behaviors, compared to the internal workings of the mind, are easier to note through experimentation and can be better controlled for. A number of notable scientists, such as Ivan Pavlov, were involved in the early days of behaviorism.

Ivan Pavlov (1849–1936) was a Russian physiologist who studied conditioning. More specifically, Pavlov studied conditioned reflex, in which conditioning causes a human or animal to respond to a stimulus with a reflex that was previously associated with a different original stimulus. Pavlov conducted experiments with dogs regarding their salivatory response to food. **B** He trained them to salivate at the sound of a bell. In his experiment, dogs were presented with food—the original stimulus—shortly after a bell—the new stimulus—was rung. At the end of the conditioning process, the dogs began to salivate at the sound of the bell alone, without being presented food. This process is called classical conditioning. Two stimuli are paired, one of which elicits an initial response. Through this pairing, the other stimulus alone comes to elicit the same response. **C** Another early experiment in behaviorism was performed by Edward Thorndike (1874–1949), an American psychologist. Thorndike created puzzle boxes for animals that could only be exited if a bar was pressed or a lever was pulled. He placed cats in the boxes and measured how long each animal took to execute the task needed to exit the box. Upon learning the response, the cat would receive a reward; often that reward was food. Thorndike ran the experiment with various animals and measured their learning curves. He found that, while different animals learned at different speeds, the learning curve was generally the same. Animals would at first find the box difficult to escape, but with each success, they escaped more quickly until the speed with which they could solve the puzzle leveled off. In addition to his experimentation, Thorndike's Law of Effect is another important part of his work. He theorized that in learning, if a stimulus and its response is followed by satisfaction, this association is strengthened, whereas if the stimulus and response are followed by annoyance, the association is weakened.

A 1913 article by American psychologist John B. Watson (1878–1958) was an important factor in the field of behavioral psychology coming together with more defined goals. In the article, titled "Psychology as the Behaviorist Views It," Watson discussed the underlying beliefs of both behavioral analysis and the methodology its adherents used. **D** One of the beliefs it stated was that the theoretical goal of behaviorism is the

anticipation and control of behavior. Watson preferred to measure behavior because it is more objective than the internal workings of the mind. He found behavior easier to observe and he wanted to learn how to control it. B. F. Skinner (1904–1990), an American psychologist, is another behaviorist whose work was important to the field. Skinner was interested in how consequence affects behavior and called the specific area of his interest radical behaviorism, which deals with the philosophy of behavioral science. Rather than simply predicting behavior, Skinner wanted to comprehend behavior as a part of an environmental history of consequences that have been reinforced. This view of behaviorism is associated with operant conditioning. Operant conditioning is similar to classical conditioning in that both concepts are learning processes. While classical conditioning focuses on producing reflexive behaviors in response to stimuli, operant conditioning modifies behavior by associating stimuli with either punishment or reinforcement. This controls behavior by either encouraging or discouraging certain behaviors based on whether they are associated with a positive or negative response from the environment surrounding someone. This became known as the principles of reinforcement.

1. The use of the word *observable* in this passage is closest in meaning to:
   a. Perceptible
   b. Invisible
   c. Prominent
   d. Superficial

2. Find the four areas where the letters **A**, **B**, **C**, and **D** are located. These spaces indicate where the following sentence might be added to the passage.

   This is an example of one original area of research in behavioral psychology, as there are many different forms of conditioning and other behaviors that were studied, as well as some that are still being studied.

In which area does the sentence best fit?
   a. A
   b. B
   c. C
   d. D

3. The phrase *it stated* in paragraph 3 refers to:
   a. John B. Watson
   b. Ivan Pavlov's experiment
   c. The article written by John B. Watson
   d. B. F. Skinner

4. Which of the following choices best communicates the important information of the sentence that is highlighted? Incorrect answer choices exclude pertinent information or misrepresent information.
   a. When a stimulus and its response become associated with a positive feeling that follows it, their association becomes strengthened.
   b. A stimulus and response are strengthened if followed by gratification and weakened if followed by irritation.
   c. When a stimulus and its response become associated with a negative feeling that follows it, their association is weakened.
   d. When followed by satisfaction, a stimulus and response become weakened in association.

5. Which of the following can be inferred about behaviorism from paragraph 1?
   a. Behaviorism balances the understanding of internal factors with external factors.
   b. Behaviorism seeks to understand how the mind responds to external factors that influence behavior.
   c. Because behaviorism only focuses on the external rather than the internal or an even balance of both, it is not a valid area of psychology.
   d. Behaviorism sought to understand psychology and learning through what was more easily measurable—behavior, rather than internal mental processes.

6. According to paragraph 2, what is an example of classical conditioning?
   a. Cats learning more quickly after solving a puzzle box by being rewarded with food
   b. A bell eliciting salivation alone after being previously presented along with food
   c. Mice receiving a shock after performing a task incorrectly
   d. Thorndike's Law of Effect

7. In paragraph 2, why does the author include examples of experiments completed in the early days of behaviorism?
   a. To illustrate the type of research that was done in the early days of behaviorism
   b. To contrast the field of behaviorism from other areas of psychology
   c. To explain the potential uses of the experiments as it applies to daily life
   d. To illustrate classical conditioning and Thorndike's Law of Effect

8. According to paragraph 3, all of the following statements are true about operant conditioning EXCEPT:
   a. Operant conditioning focuses on how behavior is reinforced or discouraged based on the environment.
   b. B. F. Skinner conducted research in operant conditioning.
   c. Operant conditioning also focuses on reflexive responses, much like classical conditioning.
   d. Operant conditioning is an example of one type of learning process studied by behaviorists.

9. The phrase *He placed cats* in paragraph 2 refers to:
   a. Ivan Pavlov
   b. John B. Watson
   c. B. F. Skinner
   d. Edward Thorndike

93

10. An opening sentence is provided to create a summary of the given passage above. Choose THREE answer choices that state the important ideas of the passage.

Behaviorism is an area of psychology and a theory of learning based on conditioning and observable behaviors.

1.

2.

3.

a. Observable behaviors can be documented in experimentation and are easier to observe than the internal aspects of psychology.
b. Ivan Pavlov studied classical conditioning through an experiment with salivation, food, bells, and dogs.
c. Many important experiments have been done in the field of behaviorism, but behaviorism did not exist until John B. Watson's article.
d. Thorndike also conducted important work in behaviorism, including experiments that demonstrated the learning curve and his Law of Effect.
e. John B. Watson and B. F. Skinner are important figures in behaviorism—Watson by writing an article that laid out the goals of behaviorism and its methodology, and B. F. Skinner by conducting work in operant conditioning and the principles of reinforcement.
f. Operant conditioning is a form of conditioning, different from classical conditioning studied by Pavlov, that deals with learning behaviors as they are reinforced or not reinforced by either positive or negative responses from environmental factors.

Questions 11–20 are based on the following passage:

The Impressionist art movement lasted around twenty years in the mid-to-late nineteenth century (1860–1886). Impressionism consisted of a number of artists living in Paris, France, and followed the art movements such as Neoclassicism and Romanticism. Many of its characteristics were in opposition to these previous movements. The Neoclassical era of art lasted from the late eighteenth century through the early-to-mid nineteenth century. It took inspiration from Greek and Roman art as well as various archaeological discoveries of the time. The artists of this movement favored more particular aspects of art, such as straight lines opposed to curved lines or color. The Romantic movement of art first began in the early nineteenth century and was at its strongest through the mid-nineteenth century in France and Britain. This movement began as a response to the French Revolution's aftermath and featured more violent imagery, unpredictability, and terror. Impressionism was more of a

94

response to classical art than Romantic art, favoring different techniques to represent daily life.

Impressionism rejected the classical in the interest of modernity. Impressionist artists wanted their work to represent their reality. They longed for color as opposed to the classical emphasis on lines and precision. Many Impressionist artists partook in plein air painting, in which they would set up their materials outside and paint the scenery directly. **A** Plein air painting was made easier due to an invention by John Rand—paint contained in a tube—which made paint much more portable. The work of Edouard Manet was highly inspirational to Impressionist painters, though he never considered himself to be a part of Impressionism. One example of his work is *Olympia* (1865), which was accepted into the Académie des Beaux-Arts' Salon de Paris (a.k.a. the Salon). The Salon was an art exhibition that began in 1667. The Salon's juries often rejected the art of Impressionists. When Impressionist art was accepted, it often placed poorly. This was due to the juries' disapproval of the way Impressionists strayed from a more traditional style of painting. Following much rejection, many Impressionist artists joined together to host independent exhibitions of their rejected work. The first of these exhibitions was held in 1874 and included the work of artists such as Monet, Renoir, and Degas. Impressionist work was often critiqued, and the name Impressionism itself came from a critiqued piece by Monet titled Impression, Sunrise, after which the artists began calling themselves Impressionists. There are several notable artists of this movement, two of which were Claude Monet and Pierre-Auguste Renoir.

Claude Monet (1840–1926) is among the most well-known Impressionist artists. In his early days in Paris, Monet began painting plein air after being introduced to it by Eugene Boudin (1824–1898). In 1862, Monet then joined the studio of Charles Gleyre and met artists such as Pierre-Auguste Renoir, Alfred Sisley, and Frédéric Bazille. **B** Monet's early work was first accepted with praise by the Salon and its jury in 1865 with works such as *Mouth of the Seine at Honfleur* and *La Pointe de la Hève at Low Tide*. More of his work was accepted in the years 1866 and 1868; one of these pieces was his famous *The Woman in the Green Dress* (1866). But for many years following these acceptances, Monet's work was rejected. After he received these rejections, Monet chose to join the independent exhibition of 1874. **C** Monet's work often featured his proximate surroundings, both in terms of people and places, though he favored landscapes over portraits.

Pierre-Auguste Renoir (1841–1919) is another of the most well-known Impressionist artists. Prior to Impressionism, Renoir was first a porcelain painter. As he aspired to become a professional artist, Renoir began to study art in the studio of Charles Gleyre in 1862, just as Monet did. Renoir's early work was initially accepted by the Salon starting in 1864. Years later, after receiving many rejections, he also joined the first independent exhibition of Impressionist painters. Impressionism sought to reflect reality, which can be seen in Renoir's work. Renoir's paintings of this time focused on surroundings, streets, and people. He often would paint in plein air. **D** In contrast to Monet, Renoir often favored painting young women along with his landscapes. An example of this preference is Renoir's painting *The Large Bathers* (1887).

95

11. The use of the word *interest* in this passage is closest in meaning to:
    a. Fascination
    b. Boredom
    c. Preference
    d. Concern

12. The phrase *they longed for* in paragraph 2 refers to:
    a. Neoclassical artists
    b. Impressionist artists
    c. Romantic artists
    d. The Salon's juries

13. Which of the following choices best communicates the important information of the sentence that is highlighted? Incorrect answer choices exclude pertinent information or misrepresent information.
    a. The name of the Impressionist art movement came from a critic assigning them that name.
    b. A painting done by Renoir inspired the name of the Impressionist movement following the critique of his work.
    c. Impressionist artists decided on the name *Impressionism* themselves to describe their style of art.
    d. After a critique of Monet's *Impression, Sunrise*, artists of this time and style began calling themselves Impressionists.

14. Find the four areas where the letters **A**, **B**, **C**, and **D** are located. These spaces indicate where the following sentence might be added to the passage.

    Upon meeting each other, the four artists would often paint in plein air together.

In which area does the sentence best fit?
    a. A
    b. B
    c. C
    d. D

15. Which of the following can be inferred about Impressionism from paragraph 1?
    a. Impressionism rejected the art and techniques that came before it in favor of representing everyday life.
    b. Impressionism was more of a response to Romantic art than classical art.
    c. Impressionism favored technicality and linework over color.
    d. Impressionism favored unpredictability and terror, due to the reality of life following the French Revolution.

16. According to paragraph 2, what can be said about the Salon juries' opinion of Impressionism?
    a. The Salon approved of the work of Impressionist artists.
    b. Though the Salon often rejected the work of Impressionists, their art placed well when it was accepted.
    c. The Salon did not approve of the techniques of Impressionism and favored the more technical work that preceded it.
    d. The Salon was supportive of Monet, but not other Impressionist artists of the time.

96

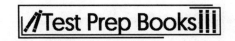

17. In paragraph 1, why does the author include explanations of the art movements that preceded Impressionism?
   a. To illustrate why the shift toward Impressionism was important
   b. To support the superiority of the art movements that came before Impressionism
   c. To note the similarities of Impressionism with the art of the Neoclassical and Romantic movements
   d. To contrast the work of Impressionism against the art that came before it

18. According to paragraph 4, all the following statements are true about Renoir EXCEPT:
   a. Renoir was generally solitary in his work and never really associated with or worked alongside any other Impressionist artists.
   b. Renoir was initially accepted by the Salon, though like many other Impressionist artists, he faced many rejections from its juries.
   c. Renoir enjoyed plein air painting.
   d. Renoir liked painting women along with the landscapes that he would paint.

19. According to paragraph 3, what can be said about the work of Claude Monet?
   a. Monet enjoyed working with things that he was unfamiliar with.
   b. Monet preferred to paint the people and places that surrounded him.
   c. Monet seldom painted in plein air, preferring to paint indoors.
   d. Though he also received many rejections from the Salon, Monet chose to not participate in the independent exhibition of 1874.

20. An opening sentence is provided to create a summary of the given passage above. Choose THREE answer choices that state the important ideas of the passage.

   Impressionist art began as a rejection of the technicality of the classical art that came before it; artists of the movement preferred to represent the livelihood of day-to-day people and their surroundings.

   1.

   2.

   3.

   a. Impressionist artists faced much criticism for the techniques they used and were frequently rejected by the Salon.
   b. The Académie des Beaux-Arts' Salon de Paris was an art exhibition that began in 1667 and rejected many Impressionist pieces.
   c. Edouard Manet, though the inspiration for many Impressionist artists, never considered himself to be an Impressionist painter.

97

d. Monet is one of the most famous Impressionist painters; one of his most well-known pieces was one of the few that the Salon accepted, titled *The Woman in the Green Dress* (1866).

e. After many rejections, Impressionist artists held an independent exhibition in 1874 to display the many pieces that were rejected by the juries of the Salon.

f. Monet and Renoir, two well-known Impressionist artists, met in the studio of Charles Gleyre; they both enjoyed plein air painting, although they had different preferences for the focus of their work, and they faced many rejections by the Salon.

Listening

Directions: The Listening section measures your ability to understand conversations and lectures in English. In this test, you will listen to several pieces of content and answer questions after each one. The questions typically ask about the main idea and supporting details. Some questions ask about a speaker's purpose or attitude. Answer the questions based on what is stated or implied by the speakers.

Listen to all of these passages by going to testprepbooks.com/bonus/toefl, or by scanning the QR code below:

Note that on the actual test, you can take notes while you listen and use your notes to help you answer the questions. Your notes will not be scored.

For your convenience, the transcripts of all of the audio passages are provided after the answer explanations. However, on the actual test, no such transcripts will be provided.

Recording #1: Conversation

1. Which of the following is NOT something the two students discuss in this conversation?
    a. Concerns about the final exam
    b. A surprise party for the professor
    c. How Julia's volleyball team is doing
    d. Plans to study for the final exam together

2. Who is the surprise party being planned for?
    a. Julia
    b. The volleyball coach
    c. Aaron
    d. The economics professor

3. Which of these topics is discussed before the surprise party?
   a. Plans to study for the final exam together
   b. When volleyball practice is taking place
   c. How Aaron is doing in biology class
   d. A mutual friend's new car

4. What is Aaron implying when he says, "Whoa, really? No way, not happening."?
   a. He is also worried about his performance on the upcoming final exam.
   b. He doesn't believe Julia isn't confident about the final exam.
   c. He is expressing confidence that the final exam will be easy.
   d. He is supporting Julia's decision to focus on volleyball practice instead.

5. What can be inferred about what Julia and Aaron think of their economics professor?
   a. They don't have any strong feelings about the professor.
   b. They wish the professor wasn't so strict on them during class.
   c. They respect and appreciate the effort he puts in as their teacher.
   d. They dislike the professor because he assigns so much homework.

Recording #2: Lecture

6. What is the main topic of the lecture?
   a. The range of learning disabilities that future teachers should be aware of
   b. The ways in which Executive Functioning Disorder impacts students
   c. The cures for Executive Functioning Disorder
   d. How to teach students who are interested in psychology

7. What is the role of the executive function of the brain?
   a. To make business decisions for the brain and body
   b. To plan, organize, and manage tasks, processes, and deadlines
   c. To prevent learning disabilities
   d. To help take notes, listen to lectures, and perform well on exams

8. Why does the professor explain in detail how teachers can modify their instruction to help students with Executive Functioning Disorder?
   a. Because many of the students listening to the lecture want to become teachers
   b. Because many of the students listening to the lecture have Executive Functioning Disorder
   c. Because Executive Functioning Disorder only affects students in school
   d. Because the students listening to the lecture are teachers

9. According to the professor, when is having executive functioning issues especially challenging for a person?
   a. Executive function issues are especially challenging when a person has to focus on both writing and listening.
   b. Executive functioning issues are especially challenging when seeking help.
   c. Executive functioning issues are especially challenging for CEOs.
   d. Executive functioning issues are especially challenging when a person also has ADHD or dyslexia.

10. Why does the professor add the clause "Like in our class" to the beginning of the sentence: "Like in our class, teachers should review prior material briefly before building upon it in the new lesson"?
   a. To help students connect the lesson with their own experience
   b. To remind students of their learning disabilities
   c. To show students that he is a good professor
   d. To persuade students to become teachers

11. Based on the information in the lecture, which of the following would someone with Executive Functioning Disorder likely struggle with?
   a. Reading a fantasy novel
   b. Playing sports on a team
   c. Remembering what to buy in the grocery store without a list
   d. Painting or drawing realistic landscapes

Recording #3: Lecture

12. What was the main topic addressed in the lecture?
   a. The contributions of various historical astronomers to our understanding of modern astronomy
   b. The importance of the telescope in our understanding of the Universe
   c. The history of how the Universe and Solar System formed billions of years ago
   d. The geocentric model of the Solar System

13. According to the professor, what was Copernicus' main contribution to our understanding?
   a. He proposed the geocentric model of the Solar System
   b. He invented the telescope, which we have used to make more discoveries
   c. He proposed the three laws of motion
   d. He developed the idea that Earth, and the other planets, rotate around the Sun

14. How was the information in the lecture organized?
   a. In order of importance of each scientist's discoveries
   b. In chronological order of the scientists' work
   c. In the order presented in the course textbook
   d. In the order of how many discoveries each scientist made

15. What does the professor imply about the scientists discussed in the lecture?
   a. That only their accurate discoveries or proposals were important to our understanding
   b. That they made a lot of mistakes in their discoveries
   c. That they did not know very much about the Universe
   d. That their contributions, even when inaccurate, helped shape our current understanding

16. Match the following items in the table with the correct astronomer by placing an "X" in the appropriate box.

	Galileo	Copernicus	Newton
He proposed the three laws of motion.			
He said the Sun was a star.			
He invented the telescope.			
He lay the foundation for scientific thought and experimentation.			

17. What is the professor implying when she makes the following statement?

> "He thought the Earth was not moving and that the Sun and Moon revolved around the stationary planet, so we know now that this part was off-base but he's still a key player in our evolution."

    a. That his ideas were wrong and not important in the discussion of astronomy
    b. That other scientists and other humans continued to evolve from his DNA
    c. That he made a bunch of discoveries we have verified as correct
    d. That he is important in any discussion of the history of astronomy, even if some of his ideas were incorrect

Recording #4: Lecture and Discussion

18. What is the main topic of the lecture?
    a. The scientific method and how to conduct experiments
    b. How gemstones are used for jewelry
    c. Why rubies are rare and how they form
    d. How to read articles in *Discover* magazine

19. Why did Penn State University Geosciences professor Peter Heaney refer to rubies as a "minor geological miracle"?
    a. Because conditions must be perfect for them to form and this is rare
    b. Because they are important gemstones that contribute to our economy
    c. Because they can be discovered through scientific experiments
    d. Because they are red

20. According to the professor, how do gemstones get their colors?
    a. By the different temperature under which they form
    b. By forming in volcanoes or in the Himalayas, areas that have lots of color
    c. By various elemental substitutions to the normal arrangement of aluminum and oxygen atoms.
    d. By jewelers looking to design beautiful, ornate designs that consumers will buy

21. Based on what the professor says about conducting scientific experiments, which of the following experiments would he likely recommend for making the best chocolate chip cookies?
    a. An experiment that manipulates baking conditions by cooking batches at different temperatures and for different lengths of time
    b. An experiment that adds different amounts of sugar and bakes them for different lengths of time
    c. An experiment that adds different proportions of whole wheat and white flower, different amounts of sugar, and bakes them for different lengths of time
    d. An experiment that uses the same exact recipe but bakes them for different lengths of time

22. According to the discussion, which of the following are true about rubies? Select two correct answers.
    a. They are gemstones
    b. They readily form
    c. They are a variety of corundum
    d. We have no idea how old they are

23. Put an "X" in the boxes next to all of the elements that must be present for a ruby to form.

Titanium	
Molten granite	
Salt	
Silica	
Chromium	
Sapphire	

Recording #5: Conversation

24. What is the main problem the student is having?
    a. She does not know which classes to register for
    b. She needs to get a job on campus
    c. Her bill is higher than she predicted
    d. She is looking for financial aid forms

25. Which of the following were components of the student's bill? *Select all that apply.*
    a. Tuition
    b. Technology fee
    c. Meal plan and housing
    d. Activities fee

26. The financial aid officer explains to the student what she needs to do to fill out her FASFA, apply for a work-study, and fix the hold on her account. In the chart provided, put the following steps in the correct order:
   A. Register for classes
   B. Apply for a campus job
   C. Wait for evaluation of financial aid package
   D. Pay balance on the account
   E. Register to fill out the FAFSA
   F. Input prior year's tax information
   G. Ask for tuition reduction

1	
2	
3	
4	
5	
6	

27. What is the most likely reason that the student says, "Back home I worked as a computer programmer at my mom's software company."?
   a. There's a glitch in the system at the financial aid office and she thinks she can fix it.
   b. She's letting the financial aid officer know that she has experience that might be helpful for a work-study job on campus.
   c. She'll telling the financial aid officer that she'll be able to work with her mom if she can't register for classes and has to move back home.
   d. She's implying that she's earned too much money to qualify for financial aid.

28. Based on the conversation, which job is the student most likely to apply for?
   a. A job at the financial aid office
   b. A job at the computer lab
   c. A job at the sports center
   d. A job at the library

Speaking

Listen to all of these passages by going to testprepbooks.com/bonus/toefl, or by scanning the QR code below:

Recording #6

1. Listen to the following recording and then answer the question:
   - Preparation Time: 15 seconds
   - Response Time: 45 seconds

2. Read the following announcement and then listen to the conversation. Lastly, answer the question at the end.

Chess Program Shut Down by University Officials

Today we are disappointed to announce that the intramural chess program has been banned from competing on campus. We have received reports of cheating in the program. One team captain and two members were caught using computer algorithms to cheat during online matches. In addition to cheating, there have been reports of hazing. Our source has shown proof of team captains embarrassing new members before allowing them on the team.

As a university, we do not approve of these actions. Both cheating and hazing are banned on this campus. To mitigate any damage done by the chess program, we are shutting it down for the remainder of the semester. Any members involved in the incidents above will be facing disciplinary action. We apologize to those affected.

Recording #7

Listen to the following conversation:

Question: The male student expresses his opinions about the university's decision to ban chess competitions. What are his opinions? Be sure to compare them with the reasons given for banning chess competitions.

   - Preparation Time: 30 seconds
   - Response Time: 60 seconds

3. Read the following academic passage and then listen to the lecture. Finally, follow the instructions below.

> A supervolcano is a volcanic center that can produce an eruption with the magnitude of a Level 8 on the Volcanic Explosivity Index, the highest on the scale. This can be referred to as a supereruption. They are capable of creating craters in the earth called calderas that can be up to 50 kilometers wide. There are around twenty supervolcanoes on Earth. It is very rare to see a major eruption from a supervolcano. It is much more common to see normal, less disastrous eruptions from these volcanoes. The last supereruption was 26,500 years ago.

Recording #8

Listen to the following lecture:

Instructions: Explain supervolcanoes and discuss the examples provided by the professor.

- Preparation Time: 30 seconds
- Response Time: 60 seconds

Recording #9

4. Listen to the following lecture in an earth science course and then follow the instructions below:
Instructions: Using points and information from the lecture, describe the two different examples of minor members of the Solar System detailed by the professor.

- Preparation Time: 20 seconds
- Response Time: 60 seconds

Writing

Listen to all of these passages by going to testprepbooks.com/bonus/toefl, or by scanning the QR code below:

Integrated Writing

First, read the passage below:

Zoos are institutions that contribute to the conservation of various animals. The goal of most zoos is to help animals through advocacy, breeding programs, and rehabilitation. Overall, zoos aim to improve the well-being and population of various species of animals.

One major way that zoos help animals is through educating the public about protecting animals. They allow visitors to see animals they otherwise would never be able to. This helps foster an appreciation for and connection to animals. Education about habitat conservation and the dangers of poaching keeps people invested in personally supporting the wildlife they have come to appreciate. This support may include making the choice not to hunt animals for sport, as well as financial donations. Donations and fundraising are critical for zoos, allowing them to maintain the costs of caring for animals.

Another way that zoos help animal conservation is through breeding programs for endangered species. When few animals are left in a species, finding potential mates and protecting their offspring against potential predators can be difficult. Zoo employees can help animals avoid illnesses and injuries that may prevent healthy pregnancy and birth. A catered diet and supplementation also foster strong breeding. When zoos take on these endangered animals and help produce healthy offspring, they may be able to maintain or even increase the animal's population. This helps avoid critical endangerment and extinction.

A third way that zoos help animals is through rescue and rehabilitation. Many times, the animals that can be seen in the zoo are no longer in the wild for good reason. In some cases, they have physical ailments that would lead to a death sentence in their natural habitat. Some of these animals will stay in the safe environment of a zoo indefinitely,

but others are put on a path of rehabilitation and re-release. This keeps animals alive when they would otherwise die in the wild, which ultimately contributes to stronger population levels.

Now listen to the following lecture:

Recording #9

Prompt: Summarize the points presented in the lecture. Explain how they contrast with specific points in the reading passage.

You have 20 minutes to write your essay.

The following pages are provided for writing your essay.

107

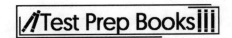

Academic Discussion

First, read the following online academic discussion between a professor and some students:

Instructor: In recent years, the evolution of media has greatly changed the way that we view news journalism. Many fear that the news has become too biased and is no longer a credible source of information. What do you think has contributed to the landscape changes of news journalism? How would you suggest restoring faith in journalism?

Student 1: I think that politics are the main reason that journalism has changed. Every news outlet has a political affiliation now. This means that people are only receiving news from one side or the other. To restore faith in journalism, there needs to be more focus on teaching people how to consume unbiased news and identify misinformation.

Student 2: I disagree with the idea that the media has changed the way we view news. The news has always been full of propaganda and biased information. The people have no direct control over this except to not consume biased media that they do not support. Our best hope is to elect political officials who can pass laws regarding misinformation in the news.

Next, add your opinion to the conversation using 100 words or more.

You have 10 minutes to write your response.

The following pages are provided for writing your essay.

111

Test Prep Books

114

Answer Explanations #1

Reading

1. A: In this passage, *observable* describes behavior that can be watched and noted. It most closely fits perceptible, as this means seeing the behavior as it occurs. Choice *B* is the opposite of observable. Choices *C* and *D* are more similar, but do not have the same intention with how *observable* is used in the passage—*observable* in the passage means to be noticeable, whereas *prominent* implies something that is projecting and *superficial* implies occurring on the surface.

2. C: The given sentence best fits after an example of research that was done in the early days of behaviorism. Choice *C* is the best option, given that it follows an explanation of classical conditioning, which was studied in Ivan Pavlov's work. Choices *A* and *D* follow more general statements about behaviorism and are not specific examples that could be referenced by the sentence given in this question. Choice *B* is incorrect, as it interrupts the idea being explained.

3. C: The phrase *it stated* in paragraph 3 refers to what was stated in John B. Watson's article "Psychology as the Behaviorist Views It." Choices *A* and *C* are both individuals, and *it stated* does not refer to them. Choice *D*, Pavlov's experiments, is referenced in the second paragraph, not in this sentence of paragraph 3.

4. B: A stimulus and response are strengthened if followed by something positive, and the opposite is the case if they are followed by something negative. Choice *B* best states this connection without leaving out or misrepresenting information. Choices *A* and *C* explain half of the information within the highlighted section, and Choice *D* states incorrect information.

5. D: Behaviorism measures behavior because it is observable and not as subjective as mental processes. Choices *A* and *B* include a reference to behaviorism incorporating internal aspects, which is not true. Choice *C* makes a judgment about behaviorism that is an opinion, rather than an assumption that is inherently true or false.

6. B: This choice explains the work of Pavlov, who studied classical conditioning. The other choices are relevant to behaviorism, but none are classical conditioning. Choices *A* and *D* are associated with Thorndike, and Choice *C* is related to operant conditioning experiments that are not mentioned in the passage—though based upon the passage, there is no negative response given in the studies of classical conditioning, which makes Choice *C* incorrect.

7. A: The experiments are included to explain the early days of behaviorism and the kind of work that was conducted during that time, which then influenced future work and research. Choices *B* and *C* are incorrect, as there are no mentions of other areas of psychology and there is no mention of how the work applies to daily life. Choice *D* is incorrect because while classical conditioning and Thorndike's Law of Effect are illustrated in the paragraph, the purpose of illustrating these is best explained by Choice *A* in the context of the passage.

8. C: Classical conditioning works with reflexive responses, while operant conditioning does not. The other choices are all correct statements about operant conditioning: it focuses on the impact of

environmental factors on whether behavior is reinforced or discouraged, B.F. Skinner studied operant conditioning, and it is an example of a learning process that has been studied by behaviorists.

9. D: The phrase *he placed cats* in paragraph 2 refers to Edward Thorndike in a description of an experiment that he completed. Choice *A*, Ivan Pavlov, is not being referenced at this point but is referenced earlier in the paragraph. Choice *B* is incorrect, as John B. Watson is not referenced until paragraph 3. Choice *C* is incorrect because B.F. Skinner is not referenced until paragraph 3.

10. B, C, E: The three correct answers are as follows. Choice *B*: Ivan Pavlov studied classical conditioning through an experiment with salivation, food, bells, and dogs; Choice *C*: Thorndike also conducted important work in behaviorism, including experiments that demonstrated the learning curve and the Law of Effect; and Choice *E*: John B. Watson and B. F. Skinner are important figures in behaviorism, Watson writing an article that laid out the goals of behaviorism and its methodology, and B. F. Skinner conducting work in operant conditioning and the principles of reinforcement. The other options would require the exclusion of one of these notable aspects of behaviorism. While observable behaviors and operant conditioning are important parts of behaviorism, they are included in other sentences that allow for a more thorough summary of key information. Behaviorism was made clear through John B. Watson's article, and it is a key part of the history of behaviorism, but behaviorism began with work such as Pavlov and Thorndike's.

11. C: The use of *interest* in this passage is within the phrase *in the interest of*. Of all choices, this most closely relates to *preference*. Choice *A* implies a curiosity and Choice *D* implies a benefit for the group, neither of which accurately portrays the intention of *interest* in this sentence. Choice *B* is the opposite of the use of *interest*.

12. B: The phrase *they longed for* references the Impressionist artists longing to use color and represent everyday life in comparison to the technicality of classical artists before them. Choices *A* and *C* (classical and Romantic artists) are not being referenced at that point and did not necessarily prefer the use of color. The juries of the Salon (Choice *D*) also are not referenced at this point in the passage; they preferred the techniques of previous artists and did not enjoy the style of the Impressionists' art.

13. D: The name of the Impressionist art movement came from a critique of one of Monet's works titled *Impression, Sunrise*. Choices *A* and *B* misrepresent the information in the sentence. A critic did not assign them the name, and the painting was by Monet, not Renoir. Choice *C* leaves out important information, specifically about the painting done by Monet and the criticism it received.

14. B: The given sentence mentions the four artists and plein air painting. The only space for that sentence that is preceded by the mention of four artists is Choice *B* in reference to Monet joining the studio of Charles Gleyre. The other choices follow references to aspects of the sentence but do not suit the placement of the provided sentence. Choice *A* mentions plein air painting, but there is no context given regarding the four artists. Choice *C* follows a sentence about the independent exhibitions, though there are no artists mentioned. Choice *D* follows a sentence that references Renoir and plein air painting, though it is not the right fit due to no mention of three other artists.

15. A: Impressionism rejected the technique and work of art movements that preceded it. The Impressionists also wanted to represent their reality. Choice *B* is incorrect since Impressionism was more of a response to classical art than Romantic. Choice *C* is incorrect, as Impressionism strayed from

precision in favor of color. Choice *D* is also incorrect, as Impressionism did not favor those things, Romantic art did.

16. C: The Salon rejected most Impressionist art and did not like the techniques used. They preferred the more precise works of art that were more common prior to Impressionism. The other choices state more support from the Salon jury than was true. Choice *A* overstates the jury's support of Impressionist art overall. Choice *B* states more support when the work was accepted. Choice *D* states that Monet received more support than other artists did. Each of these statements is incorrect.

17. D: The explanation of the art of movements that came before Impressionism is used to contrast the techniques and goals of Impressionism against the art that came before it. Choices *A* and *B* include opinions regarding the few art movements mentioned, which is not the intention of the author in explaining the different movements. Choice *C* is also incorrect, as the intention of explaining these movements was not to show similarities (there are no similarities that are mentioned) but to show the ways in which Impressionism differed.

18. A: Renoir was not a solitary member of the Impressionist art movement. Rather, he worked alongside various Impressionist artists such as Monet, Bazille, and Sisley. Each of the other choices is an accurate statement about Renoir: he was initially accepted by the Salon, enjoyed plein air painting, and painted many women along with his landscape work.

19. B: Monet worked most often with his proximate surroundings, both in terms of people and places that he painted. The other choices are incorrect statements about the work of Monet: he did not work more often with unfamiliar things, he frequently painted in plein air, and he did participate in the 1874 independent exhibition held by Impressionist artists.

20. A, E, F: The three correct choices are as follows. Choice *A*: Impressionist artists faced much criticism for the techniques they used and were frequently rejected by the Salon; Choice *E*: after many rejections, Impressionist artists held an independent exhibition in 1874 to display the many pieces that were rejected by the juries of the Salon; and Choice *F*: Monet and Renoir, two well-known Impressionist artists, met in the studio of Charles Gleyre; they both enjoyed plein air painting, although they had different preferences for the focus of their work, and they faced many rejections by the Salon. Though the Salon, Manet, and Monet are all important parts of Impressionism, any of the other options would leave out important information from the passage or would mention some of the same information twice.

Listening

Listen to all of these passages by going to testprepbooks.com/bonus/toefl, or by scanning the QR code below:

Recording #1: Conversation

1. C: How well Julia's volleyball team is doing is not discussed in this conversation. The final exam, study plans, and the surprise party are all discussed, so Choices A, B, and D are all incorrect.

2. D: The surprise party is being planned for the economics professor, Professor Evans. Julia and Aaron are taking part in the planning of the party. They are not the subjects of the party, so Choices A and C are incorrect. The volleyball coach is not mentioned, so Choice B is incorrect.

3. A: Before the topic of the surprise party comes up, Julia and Aaron talk about plans to study for their economics final together. Volleyball practice is mentioned after the party planning, so Choice B is incorrect. Biology class isn't mentioned, so Choice C is incorrect. There's also no mention of a mutual friend's new car, so Choice D is incorrect.

4. B: Aaron is expressing disbelief that Julia isn't confident about the final exam because she is one of the best students in the class. He is not referring to his own confidence in the final exam or that the exam will be easy, making Choices A and C incorrect. It isn't a statement of support for Julia focusing on volleyball practice instead of studying, so Choice D is incorrect.

5. C: Because the students are planning a surprise party and mention how much the professor does to help them, it can be inferred that Julia and Aaron think highly of the professor and respect him, making Choice C correct. If they were indifferent about their professor, they likely wouldn't be planning a surprise party for him, so Choice A is incorrect. They mention how helpful the professor is, so Choice B is incorrect since the behavior of being strict in class doesn't match up. They make no mention of disliking the professor, so Choice D is incorrect.

Recording #2: Lecture

6. B: The main topic of the lecture is the ways in which Executive Functioning Disorder impacts students. Listeners hear about the symptoms of the disorder, how these symptoms play out in the classroom, and various techniques or accommodations that teachers may provide to assist a student with the disorder. Choice A is incorrect because while Executive Functioning Disorder is a learning disability and the professor mentions that the lecture is building upon previously discussed learning disabilities, the focus

118

of the lecture is on the specific issue of Executive Functioning Disorder, not learning disabilities at large. Cures for the disorder are not mentioned, so Choice C is incorrect, and while the students listening to the lecture are in a psychology class, the lecture is not about how to teach them, so Choice D is incorrect.

7. B: The professor equates executive function of the brain to a CEO of a company because it is involved in the planning, organizing, and managing of tasks, processes, and deadlines. While it is helpful for the tasks in Choice D (taking notes, listening to lectures, and performing well on exams), these are examples of instances where it is used but does not refer to its general function overall.

8. A: The professor explains how teachers can modify their instruction to help students with Executive Functioning Disorder because many of the students listening to the lecture want to become teachers. This is evidenced by the fact that he says, "I know many of you have expressed an interest in teaching someday so uh...it's important to think about how this will affect students in your classrooms."

9. D: Choice D is correct. The professor says that executive functioning issues often occur "concurrently with other learning disorders like ADHD or dyslexia." This means that they occur at the same time. Later, the professor says, "This can make it, uh...especially challenging." Therefore, Choice D is correct. Choice A is incorrect because the professor refers to focus on both writing and listening when discussing accommodations for assessments and testing. There is no mention of this being especially challenging. Choice B is incorrect because although the professor does say that people with executive functioning difficulties find it challenging to identify when and how to seek help, the questions asks to identify what the professor said is "especially" challenging. Choice C is incorrect because the professor only use the term CEO when saying that some people "equate executive function with the CEO of the brain."

10. A: The professor says, "Like in our class, teachers should review prior material briefly before building upon it in the new lesson" to help students connect the lesson with their own experience in his classroom. Listeners get a glimpse into the fact that he has done this at the very beginning of the lecture. "Today, we are going to pick up where we left off last class talking about learning disabilities. Now, we will turn our attention to another common learning disability known as Executive Functioning Disorder." Teachers often try to connect concepts in the classroom to students' own experiences so that new material makes more sense and is relatable.

11. C: Listeners learn that Executive Functioning Disorder causes difficulties with planning, organizing, and managing of tasks, processes, and deadlines. We also hear that they struggle to "memorize and especially retrieve things from their memory" which would make remembering what to buy in the grocery store without a list quite difficult.

Recording #3: Lecture

12. A: This lecture is mainly focused on the contributions of various historical astronomers to our understanding of modern astronomy. While the telescope's importance is mentioned, Choice B,, this is not the main topic of the lecture. Choice C is incorrect because the history of how the Universe and Solar System formed billions of years ago is not mentioned at all. The history of advancements in astronomy is, instead. Lastly, while the geocentric model of the Solar System is briefly discussed, it is not the primary topic in the lecture, as a much more significant portion of the talk is about notable advancements and discoveries, making Choice D incorrect.

119

13. D: The professor says, "Copernicus, in many ways, can be thought of as the first in the modern astronomy scientists because he overturned the geocentric model of the solar system that had stood for over two thousand years, and instead, correctly (but shockingly at the time) suggested that the sun was the center of the solar system and the planets revolved around the sun. This was basically the birth of our present understanding of the solar system – the Heliocentric model." This means that Copernicus developed the idea that Earth, and the other planets, rotate around the Sun, which overturned the geocentric model of the Solar System, making Choice A incorrect. Galileo invented the telescope so Choice B is incorrect, and Newton proposed the three laws of motion, so Choice C is incorrect.

14. B: The professor structures the lecture in chronological order of the scientists' work. Although dates are not provided, listeners can answer this correctly based on what the professor says at the beginning of the lecture: "We are *continuing* our discussion today of the history of astronomers *from ancient times working up to the present day*. So, remember, we are talking about the key contributors that have helped build our understanding of astronomy today."

15. D: The professor implies that the contributions of the discussed scientists, even when inaccurate, helped shape our current understanding of astronomy. Perhaps the best evidence for this argument comes from when she is talking about Brahe's importance, even though some of his ideas were incorrect. "He thought the Earth was not moving and that the Sun and Moon revolved around the stationary planet, so we know now that this part was off-base, *but he's still a key player in our evolution.*"

16.

	Galileo	Copernicus	Newton
He proposed the three laws of motion.			✖
He said the Sun was a star.		✖	
He invented the telescope.	✖		
He lay the foundation for scientific thought and experimentation.	✖		

17. D: As mentioned, the selected statement implies that Brahe is important in any discussion of the history of astronomy, even if some of his ideas were incorrect. Choice A is incorrect because she said he *is* still important, Choice C is incorrect because she is confirming that some of his ideas were incorrect, and Choice B is incorrect because "evolution" in this context isn't referring to human evolution or genetics, but the evolution or growth of our understanding of astronomy and how it is has changed over time.

Recording #4: Lecture and Discussion

18. C: The main topic of the lecture is why rubies are rare and how they form. Choice A, the scientific method and how to conduct experiments, is discussed, but is not the main focus of the talk. Choices B and D are barely touched upon, and are therefore incorrect.

19. A: Penn State University Geosciences professor Peter Heaney referred to rubies as a "minor geological miracle" because the conditions must be perfect for them to form and this is rare. This is, essentially, what the lecture discussion is all about. As the male student, Xavier, says, "Basically, he's

saying um...that the formation of rubies is essentially a perfect storm and a rare occurrence. It's like a miracle that they ever form." The professor elaborates: "Corundum is rare, the elemental substitutions are rare, chromium itself is rare, and even *more* rare is the fact that this cannot occur in the presence of silica or large amounts of iron, and silica is one of the most abundant elements in the crust and iron is common too but must be in very low concentrations to form rubies. This can kind of be visualized as hmmm...like a Venn diagram of increasingly more rare occurrences and just a tiny overlapped center where the formation of this gemstone is actually possible."

20. C: The professor states: "Rubies are a specific type of the rare mineral corundum, which is composed of densely packed aluminum and oxygen atoms. These atoms are normally colorless, but when other atoms, like in this case chromium, are substituted for a some of the uh...aluminum ones, the deep red color of rubies is produced. Other substitutions cause the bright colors of other gemstones such as sapphire from the substitution of um, uh...from titanium and iron." This means that gemstones get their colors via the various elemental substitutions to the normal arrangement of aluminum and oxygen atoms.

21. D: Listeners should recall that the professor says the following: "Scientists typically only address one question at a time so that they can use the scientific method...By focusing on just one hypothesis, scientists should only manipulate a single variable at a time, called the independent variable, and then examine its results on the dependent variable." Using this information, test takers can review the proposed experiments in the answer choices and select the one that only manipulates one variable at a time, which is Choice *D:* An experiment that uses the same exact recipe but bakes them for different lengths of time. The other experiments were changing multiple factors at one time, which contradicts the premise of the scientific method.

22. A & C: According to the discussion, rubies are gemstones and "are a specific type of the rare mineral corundum." Choice *B* is incorrect because they are not readily formed; in fact, they are rare. Choice *D* is incorrect because the professor says that "Geologists can even date the formation of these gemstones with the tectonic movements."

23.

Titanium	
Molten granite	✖
Salt	✖
Silica	
Chromium	✖
Sapphire	

Recording #5: Conversation

24. C: The student is having an issue with her bill. It is higher than she predicted. She starts the conversation by saying, "Hi. Is this the right place to ask about a problem with my bill?" Then she later says, "So, I received my bill for the semester and it says I owe $18,000. I thought I had a scholarship so there's no way I can pay this bill."

25. A, B, & C: The financial aid officer says, "I see the tuition billed to your account is $8,500. Your meal plan and housing in the dorms is $7,000 this semester, and there is a technology fee and other posted

fees including your parking permit totaling $2,500." There is no mention of a specific activities fee, Choice D.

26. According to the advice from the financial aid officer, the necessary order is the following:

1	E. Register to fill out the FAFSA
2	F. Input prior year's tax information
3	C. Evaluate financial aid package
4	B. Apply for a campus job
5	D. Pay balance on the account
6	A. Register for classes

27. B: The correct answer is Choice B. The financial aid officer has just explained what a work-study is. We can guess that the student makes the statement to express interest in the work-study opportunities and to show that she has some experience in the area of computer programming. Choice A is incorrect. There is no glitch in the system and she never offers to fix anything. Choice C is incorrect. The student is figuring out what she needs to do to pay her bill and register for classes. Though this answer choice may be a true statement if that situation occurs, that's not mentioned in the conversation. Choice B is the more likely reason for the statement. Choice D is incorrect. She made the statement after the financial aid officer explained work-study, not financial aid. The financial aid officer goes into more detail about financial after she makes this statement.

28. B: The student is most likely to apply for a job at the computer lab. Listeners can select this response based on the student's comment: "Back home I worked as a computer programmer at my mom's software company."

Listening Transcripts

Recording #1: Conversation

(Julia) Hey, Aaron! How's it going?

(Aaron) Oh, hey Julia! I've been a bit busy studying for my finals, but otherwise I'm doing okay! How about yourself?

(Julia) I've been crazy busy, haha. Studying, planning, volleyball, I can barely catch a break!

(Aaron) Wow, that's crazy, yeah. I couldn't even handle half that much myself.

(Julia) Well, I'm kind of used to it. If anything, I'm worried that I'm going to completely fail the economics final...

(Aaron) Whoa, really? No way, not happening. You're one of the best students in our class there, you'll do fine.

(Julia) I know, I'm just a bit worried since I can't ever seem to find the time to study for it.

(Aaron) Well, with a schedule as full as yours is, I'm not surprised. Hey, maybe I can help. We can study together whenever you've got time.

(Julia) Oh, I really appreciate the offer! I might take you up on that, but I have to warn you, I have no idea when I'll find the time...

(Aaron) Oh, I'm usually pretty free! Just shoot me a text or something at least an hour beforehand if you can and I'll wrap up whatever I'm doing and meet up with you.

(Julia) Alright, I'll be sure to remember that! Oh, before I forget, we're actually planning a surprise party for Professor Evans after the final! He always does so much for us, so we wanted to give something back.

(Aaron) Oh that's right, he's retiring after this semester! That's nice of you, who's helping with it?

(Julia) Myself, Lisa, Jimmy, and Thomas. And we managed to convince a couple of the other econ professors who had some free time to come too!

(Aaron) That's awesome! Anything I can help with, or something I should bring?

(Julia) Actually, yeah! Nobody's had a chance to place an order for a cake yet, do you think you could do that for us? Professor Evans likes strawberry cheesecake, and we'll all chip in to pay you back.

(Aaron) Sure thing, I'll order it the day before the final.

(Julia) Thanks, you're a lifesaver, Aaron! Oh, shoot, practice starts in 10 minutes, I have to run!

(Aaron) Oh, no problem! Get going, Julia, and I'll text you later!

(Julia) Sure thing, Aaron, thanks!

Recording #2: Lecture
(Narrator) Listen to the following part of a lecture on Executive Functioning Disorder from a psychology class.

(Professor) Today, we are going to pick up where we left off last class talking about learning disabilities. Now, we will turn our attention to another common learning disability known as Executive Functioning Disorder. Some people um...equate executive function with the CEO of the brain because the role of executive function is to plan, organize, and manage tasks, processes, and deadlines. Let's see...essentially, it is the sum total of mental processes that enable an individual to connect their past experiences with current and future situations. Individuals with executive functioning disorder may struggle with time management, organization, planning and forethought, um...follow through, memory, prioritizing, and getting started on tasks, among other challenges. Many students with executive functioning difficulties also struggle to apply previously learned ideas and information to new concepts or to solve problems. They also may find analyzing ideas and identifying when and how to seek help to be a challenge. Let's see...heeding attention to and remembering details is also encumbered. These difficulties can greatly impact a child or adult in school, work, and even with daily tasks that involve time management or multiple steps. Uh...students may lack the ability to plan work or change their plans, wait to be called on or to hear directions before proceeding, manage their time and space, get started on projects, switch between tasks efficiently, ask for guidance when they are confused, memorize and especially retrieve things from their memory, and turn in assignments in a timely manner.

123

I know many of you have expressed an interest in teaching someday so uh...it's important to think about how this will affect students in your classrooms. Let's see...students may need accommodations for assessments and test taking. For example, they may be permitted to provide oral answers rather than circling or filling in bubbles or writing. They may be provided with the test format ahead of time so they can understand what will be asked of them and just focus on the content during studying. They may be allowed additional time during test taking or they may be provided with outlines of a lesson prior to sitting through it. This helps, uh...because then they only need to focus on listening rather than uh...writing and listening.

Now, there are also things that teachers can do. Because of the challenges planning and following steps, teachers are encouraged to uh...give step-by-step instructions that students should repeat back to demonstrate listening and understanding. Um, the number of steps should remain reasonable and simple instructions, uh like those given in written form, should be provided. Depending on the age of the students and their reading abilities, a written outline of the lesson and any directions can also be provided. This is particularly important to assist with note-taking during a lesson and uh...help key students into the main points versus the details. Using directed phrases like, "this is important because..." can also help students identify key points and begin making connections as to why something is important. Like in our class, teachers should review prior material briefly before building upon it in the new lesson. To help keep students on task and meeting deadlines, teachers can provide daily to do checklists, encourage an assignment notebook that parents must review with their child. Lastly, to optimize success with assessments, teachers should explain what an ideal assignment or test looks like and provide a model.

While executive functioning issues alone can have a significant impact on an individual, I want you to think about how it often um...appears concurrently with other learning disorders like ADHD or dyslexia. Remember? We talked about these last class. This can make it, uh...especially challenging.

Recording #3: Lecture
(Narrator) Listen to part of a lecture from astronomy class and then answer the questions.

(Professor) We are continuing our discussion today of the history of astronomers from ancient times working up to the present day. So, remember, we are talking about the key contributors that have helped build our understanding of astronomy today. Let's pick up now with Nicolaus Copernicus. Copernicus, in many ways, can be thought of as the first in the modern astronomy scientists because he overturned the geocentric model of the solar system that had stood for over two thousand years, and instead, correctly (but shockingly at the time) suggested that the sun was the center of the solar system and the planets revolved around the sun. This was basically the birth of our present understanding of the solar system – the Heliocentric model. Before we go on, I want to remind you about the geocentric model we talked about last class. Remember, the ancient Greeks believed in a geocentric model of the universe, such that the planets and stars rotated around the central, stationary Earth. But Copernicus recognized that the uh...that the moon rotated around the Earth and that the Earth is just one of several planets revolving around the Sun. He also noted that the Sun is a star, the closest star, and other stars are much further away, that Earth rotates around its axis every day in addition to its yearly revolution, and that closer planets have shorter "years." Pretty important discoveries, huh?

Then we have Tycho Brahe. Now, Brahe was instrumental in determining the positions of fixed stars, unaided by telescopes, which were not yet invented. He made astronomical tools to help with mapping and understanding the "heavens" and the Solar System. He thought the Earth was not moving and that

124

the Sun and Moon revolved around the stationary planet, so we know now that this part was off-base, but he's still a key player in our evolution.

Johannes Kepler was interested in math and astronomy and felt that geometric figures influenced the universe. He built upon Copernicus' heliocentric model and you've probably heard of his three Laws of Planetary Motion. The first law states that planetary orbits are elliptical, not circular, and the Sun is at one of the foci and not the center. The second law says that the planetary speed is faster near the sun and slower when it is more distant. The third law is somewhat similar. This one states that um...that the larger the orbit of a planet, the slower its average velocity.

Next, we have Galileo Galilei. That's a fun name to say. Well, Galileo made many advancements to our thinking and to our ability to make further discoveries, like he invented the telescope. He used it to observe sunspots and discovered that the lunar surface, like Earth, had mountains and valleys. Let's see...he also noted that the Milky Way galaxy had separate stars, he discovered moons around Jupiter, and designed instruments such as a compass and this neat little calculating device. These discoveries helped prove the universe was dynamic and changing. Perhaps most importantly, he lay the foundations for scientific thought and process, the importance of logic and reason, and how to do experiments.

Lastly, Sir Isaac Newton. Remember, Newton was the one that proposed the three laws of motion that I'm sure you've heard in physics class: an object in motion stays in motion and an object at rest stays at rest unless acted on by an external force, force equals mass times acceleration, and every action has an equal and opposite reaction. He also proposed the Universal Law of Gravitation, which states that gravity is a force and that every object in the Universe is attracted to every other object. The magnitude of this force is directly proportional to the product of the masses of the objects and inversely proportional to the square of the distances between them.

Recording #4: Lecture and Discussion

(Narrator) Listen to the following portion of a lecture and discussion from a geology class.

(Professor) So now I want to turn our discussion to your homework assignment, Anne Sasso's article in *Discover* magazine called "The Geology of...Rubies." This article discussed how rubies are formed, why they have been so enamored throughout history, and what causes their brilliant red color, which, as I hope you read, is due to the ultraviolet light from the Sun causing the chromium in rubies to glow. Geologists are still searching for reasons as to how the existence of rubies came to be. Do you remember how Penn State University Geosciences professor Peter Heaney referred to rubies as a "minor geological miracle"? Can anyone tell me why Dr. Heaney says this?

(Student #1) Basically, he's saying um...that the formation of rubies is essentially a perfect storm and a rare occurrence. It's like a miracle that they ever form.

(Professor) Exactly, Xavier. Rubies are a specific type of the rare mineral corundum, which is composed of densely packed aluminum and oxygen atoms. These atoms are normally colorless, but when other atoms, like in this case chromium, are substituted for a some of the uh...aluminum ones, the deep red color of rubies is produced. Other substitutions cause the bright colors of other gemstones such as sapphire from the substitution of um, uh...from titanium and iron. Corundum is rare, the elemental substitutions are rare, chromium itself is rare, and even *more* rare is the fact that this cannot occur in the presence of silica or large amounts of iron, and silica is one of the most abundant elements in the crust and iron is common too but must be in very low concentrations to form rubies. This can kind of be

125

visualized as hmmm...like a Venn diagram of increasingly more rare occurrences and just a tiny overlapped center where the formation of this geode is actually possible.

Does anyone remember from the article how rubies form?

(Student #2) Was that the part about how they are used for jewelry and even people centuries ago marveled at their beauty?

(Professor) Well that's more about their importance or our interest in them. I'm looking for how they are created geologically.

(Student #2) Oh! Oops. Yeah, they form through plate tectonics, particularly at the boundary by the um, um...Himalayas, where deposits of the sedimentary rock limestone get pushed under the other plate and metamorphosed into the marble.

(Professor) Exactly Claudia! Molten granite in magma percolates in and infiltrates the forming marble. This limestone and granite interaction contains the chemical elements we now know are present in rubies. Importantly, this process removes the silica but leaves the aluminum. Geologist can even date the formation of these gemstones with the tectonic movements. Even more recently, teams of scientists have found that salt played an integral role in the formation of the rubies because it allowed the aluminum atoms to be fluid enough to get displaced occasionally by chromium.

Does anyone have any questions?... Yes, Xavier.

(Student #1) Have geologists done experiments to try to recreate all these conditions at once to make all different kinds of gemstones in the lab?

(Professor) Well, kind of. Remember...scientists typically only address one question at a time so that they can use the scientific method. This method establishes a rigorous process of investigation so that it can be uh...replicated by other scientists to verify results. By focusing on just one hypothesis, scientists should only manipulate a single variable at a time, called the independent variable, and then examine its results on the dependent variable. What would happen if scientists didn't carefully isolate variables?

(Student #2) Well, if scientists were to manipulate multiple variables, it would be impossible to know which change resulted in the observed effects.

(Professor) You got it! If scientists were to work to investigate multiple questions or change more than one variable when conducting an experiment, the research would be scattered, unfocused, and unable to prove anything.

Recording #5: Conversation

(Narrator) Listen to the following conversation between a student and the school's financial aid officer.

(Student) Hi. Is this the right place to ask about a problem with my bill?

(Officer) Yes. This is the financial aid office so I can assist you with any tuition and billing questions.

(Student) Great. So, I received my bill for the semester and it says I owe $18,000. I thought I had a scholarship, so there's no way I can pay this bill. Plus, now there's a hold on my account, so I can't seem to register for classes and I'm worried they are going to fill up.

126

(Officer) Ok let's see. Do you have a copy of your bill with you?

(Student) No. I left it in my dorm by accident.

(Officer) No problem. Can I see your student ID? I can pull it up in our system.

(Student) Yeah. Here it is. Don't mind the picture. I didn't know I was going to be photographed that day!

(Officer) Oh, don't worry...you look nice! Ok. Let me just take a look here at your bill and see what's going on. Hmm...Yes, I see the tuition billed to your account is $8,500. Your meal plan and housing in the dorms is $7,000 this semester and there is a technology fee and other posted fees including your parking permit totaling $2,500. The total amount posted to your account is $18,000.

(Student) Right. So, what about my scholarship?

(Officer) Well, it looks like you have a scholarship that is pending in your account for the amount of tuition, the $8500. It has not been applied because we are waiting on your financial aid application. Did you fill out the FAFSA? We need a current copy of that on file.

(Student) No. I didn't know I needed to do that.

(Officer) You'll definitely want to get that in as soon as possible. That way we can process your scholarship and also if you qualify for additional financial aid, we can set up a package for you. Some students get additional scholarships based on financial need, or there are loans and work-study opportunities.

(Student) Oh, that sounds helpful. What is a work-study?

(Officer) Work study refers to campus- based jobs where your compensation comes directly off of your bill. There are a variety of available positions for students around campus like in the library, at the sports center, or even one of the administrative offices.

(Student) Ok cool. Back home I worked as a computer programmer at my mom's software company.

(Officer) Well we have lots of office positions too. So, what you need to do first is to fill out the FASFA on the website. You'll need to put in last year's tax information, so make sure you have that as well. Then, they will evaluate your financial aid package to determine what your needs are. If you want to do a work-study, you can apply for a campus job. Lastly, make sure you pay the remaining balance on your account so you can register for classes.

(Student) Ok thanks. I better get going on this!

127

Speaking

Listen to all of these passages by going to testprepbooks.com/bonus/toefl, or by scanning the QR code below:

Sample Responses

Recording # 6

Question 1

Recording #7

Question 2

Recording #8

Question 3

Recording #9

Question 4

Speaking Question Transcripts

Listen to all of these passages by going to testprepbooks.com/bonus/toefl, or by scanning the QR code below:

Recording #6

1. Some students perform better on essays or research papers when they get to choose their own topics, while others do well when professors assign the topics. Do you think students should be required to work on topics that are chosen by the professor or do you think they should be allowed to choose their own topics? Explain the reasons for your opinion.

Recording #7

2. **(Female Student)** Oh no, the chess club is banned from meeting anymore!

(Male Student) What happened?

(Female Student) They said there have been reports of cheating online.

(Male Student) How many people were guilty?

(Female Student) One team captain and two members were cheating.

(Male Student) Well, that seems unfair. The chess club has three hundred members. They shouldn't all suffer because a few people were being shady. Instead of disbanding the entire club, they should have put a temporary ban on online matches. There's nothing wrong with playing in person!

(Female Student) You're right. They could create an officer role within the club to make sure everybody is following the rules. There were also reports of the team captains hazing new members.

(Male Student) That's terrible. They should ban the team captains and appoint new ones. A few corrupt people shouldn't ruin the entire group. They also don't seem to be offering any help to the students who experienced the hazing. That was probably a terrible experience for the new members, and now they're being punished for it instead!

(Female Student) They deserve a counselor they can talk to. I can't believe the school is treating them and the club as a whole this way!

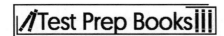

Recording #8

3. **(Professor)** Supervolcanoes are a recent topic of discussion among geologists. One example of a known supereruption occurred around 75,000 years ago in Sumatra, Indonesia. It happened at present-day Lake Toba. There are arguments that the eruption causes a volcanic winter, where the Earth's temperature drops by a few degrees. This hypothesis has not been proven true or false. It is believed that the eruption killed a significant amount of the human population and caused a population bottleneck. The most famous example of a supervolcano is the Yellowstone hotspot. There have been numerous supereruptions in this area, which is located across multiple U.S. states. The hotspot's last supereruption was about 640,000 years ago. It resulted in the Lava Creek Tuff, which is a type of rock formation. The hotspot also had supereruptions 1.2 million years ago and 2.1 million years ago. Scientists are not entirely sure when the next supereruption will be, but it is unlikely to be anytime soon. Scary, right?!

Recording #9

4. **(Professor)** Good morning class. Today we'll begin our discussion on minor members of the solar system. Minor members of the solar system are those objects that are too small to be classified as planets, yet in aggregate, they make up a large percentage of the "stuff" in our solar system. Asteroids, meteors, and comets are examples of minor members. In addition to being smaller than planets, asteroids and comets have more irregular orbits and can even enter the Earth's atmosphere and collide with Earth, the moon, the Sun, or other planets.

Asteroids and comets are thought to be remnants from the same giant cloud of gas and dust that condensed to create the Sun, planets, and moons about 4.5 billion years ago during the Big Bang. Some people even theorize that the main asteroids, which lie in a tight belt between Mars and Jupiter, may all be fragments from another planet that was forming there that suffered some sort of major collision and broke into thousands of little pieces. Comets tend to be more scattered and found in the far-reaching edges of the Solar System. However, both of these minor bodies are subject to changes in gravitational pulls or perturbations, which can alter their trajectories and cause various collisions and changes in course.

Generally speaking, comets are smaller than asteroids and are not as confined to a particular region. They also tend to be more elliptical in shape and have chemical components that vaporize when heated, perhaps because they contain more ice than asteroids, which are mostly composed of chunks of rock. Some people describe them as "fuzzy looking," when observed through a telescope because they grow tails as a function of their elliptical orbit that the sun illuminates. Comets are not always visible in the night sky, although they sometimes streak across in bright glows, such as Halley's comet. Because of the irregularity of their orbits, they are subject to impacts with Earth. Astronomers also believe that there is a concentration of comets near Neptune in what is called the Kuiper belt. Asteroids also can enter our atmosphere but many are quite small and burn up in the atmosphere on their way down. It is theorized that such a collision from a massive asteroid caused the extinction of the dinosaurs.

Speaking Sample Response Transcripts

Listen to all of these passages by going to testprepbooks.com/bonus/toefl, or by scanning the QR code below:

Recording #10

1. In my opinion students should be able to choose their topics as long as it relates to the subject being taught in the class. I have found it to be hard to focus on the topic when I'm not very interested in it and I end up putting off doing the assignment for too long. When I've been able to choose my topic, I feel like I put more time and effort into it. Also, my writing is better when I choose my topic, and if we're being graded on writing skills more than our knowledge of the topic, I think it's easier to do good writing when I'm really into the topic I've chosen. I know that when I can do a good job on a writing assignment it makes my confidence about writing better. So, to get the best out of students, I think teachers should let them choose topics to write about.

Recording #11

2. The student does not like how the university has handled the situation. He doesn't seem happy about this announcement. He feels like a lot of students are being punished and that it's not fair because only a few of the students were the ones who did something wrong. The university is banning all chess competitions on campus. Instead of banning all of the chess competitions on campus, since the cheating was done during online matches, he thinks that online competitions should be banned but only temporarily. Also, instead of punishing everyone for the hazing, he thinks that the captains who were involved should be removed and replaced. He thinks that the new members who were hazed already had it bad from that experience and that they shouldn't have to suffer more by not being allowed to compete on campus.

Recording #12

3. Supervolcanoes have eruptions that are level 8, which is the highest on the explosion scale. These are called supereruptions. They make calderas. These are craters. The Earth has maybe 20 of these supervolcanoes, but it isn't common to see them erupt. The last time there was an eruption it was over 26,000 years ago. 75,000 years ago, a supervolcano made a supereruption in Indonesia. It probably killed a lot of people and maybe it made the temperature of the Earth drop some, but we don't know if this is true or false. There's a supervolcano at the Yellowstone hotspot that is across many states. Lots of eruptions have happened there. The last one was 640,000 years ago. It created a rock formation. Some

131

eruptions were over one and two million years ago. Even scientists don't know when one will happen again.

Recording #13

4. This lecture described asteroids and comets, which are both minor members of the Solar System. This means that they are smaller than planets. Both asteroids and comets have more irregular orbits than the planets and they can enter the atmosphere and collide with the moon, Sun, Earth or other planets. In fact, it was likely an asteroid collision that caused the extinction of the dinosaurs! Scientists think asteroids and comets are ice and rock remains from when the planets formed during the Big Bang. Asteroids are mostly concentrated in one area between Mars and Jupiter, while comets tend to be more scattered throughout the Solar System and some are much further away. Comets are usually smaller than asteroids, more elliptical instead of round, and have tails, which make them look fuzzy when viewed through a telescope. They can streak across the sky. Asteroids are made of less ice and more rock than comets. Many small ones enter our atmosphere but they burn up before reaching the surface of the Earth.

Writing

Listen to all of these passages by going to testprepbooks.com/bonus/toefl, or by scanning the QR code below:

Sample Integrated Writing Response

The reading passage and the lecture give opposing views of zoos. The reading passage talks about good aspects such as conservation and advocacy, breeding, and rescue and rehabilitation. The lecture describes some negative aspects that actually reverse these supposed contributions of zoos.

In the lecture, the person says that animals are held hostage for humans to enjoy and that seeing these exotic animals makes people want them as pets. This encourages the exotic pet trade. Animals are sold to people as well as to zoos. With individuals, these animals end up dying. However, in the passage, the author says that zoos educate people about poaching and that they learn to protect and appreciate the animals. Also, visitors to zoos are supposed to be helping financially to support the care for these animals, but they're just learning that it's ok to pay a fee for the entertainment value of the animals.

Other problems that the lecturer sees with zoos are the health issues that come from limited genetic diversity and inbreeding. This contradicts what the author says in the passage about zoos giving supplements and providing a good diet to help with strong breeding, preventing illness, and working to

increase a healthy population of offspring. The lecturer says that the offspring aren't released into the wild, so this does not affect the wild population. However, the author of the passage believes that zoos can help prevent endangerment and extinction.

The lecturer disagrees with the author about rescue and rehabilitation. The lecturer says that many animals don't survive after being placed back into the wild after rehabilitation, which is the opposite of the author's view that animals that are rescued are kept alive but would have died if left in their natural habitat. The author also points out that animals are rescued because of physical ailments, but the lecturer argues that animals that are kept captive can't build natural immunities. While some animals are helped by rescue and rehab of zoos, according to the author, others don't receive as much benefit from zoos, according to the lecturer.

Sample Academic Discussion Response

I think the main reason that journalism has changed is the popularity of social media. People from younger generations are no longer turning on the television to watch the news. They are using social media platforms to see what people are saying about current events. This means that anybody can post anything which leads to the spread of misinformation very quickly.

In order to restore faith in journalism, there need to be unbiased news outlets that utilize social media effectively. Additionally, social media outlets should be held accountable for allowing misinformation to spread so easily. As a society, we should all be dedicated to the truth, and allowing people to promote lies should be condemned by all institutions.

Integrated Writing Lecture Transcript

Recording #14

(Professor) While zoos make claims about being dedicated to education and conservation, they are some of the biggest contributors to animal exploitation and neglect. The animals found in zoos are often depressed and forced to entertain visitors. This can lead to premature death that could have been prevented if the animals were not kept in captivity.

Zoos claim to be educational advocates for animals. However, they are guilty of the very things that they advocate against. Zoos keep animals in captivity and charge an entrance fee for access to them, teaching people that it is acceptable to hold animals hostage for human enjoyment. This contributes to the exotic pet trade, which supplies animals to both zoos and individuals. Suffering, neglect, and exploitation are common in this trade, which is built purely around profit. Millions of animals die because zoos make people want animals that are not appropriate to keep as pets. This goes against zoos' mission statements.

Zoos breed animals as a form of conservation, but this type of breeding reduces the genetic diversity of endangered animals. The offspring are often kept captive and are not released into the wild. This means that the actual wild population is not affected by breeding programs. Practices such as this increase health problems due to inbreeding. While zoos claim that they are feeding the animals a perfect diet and keeping them healthy, they also use drugs to keep the animals subdued. Zoo environments don't provide the animals with enough comfort. Their enclosures are often too small, loud, and exposed. Zoos breed animals into miserable conditions.

Zoos take pride in the fact that they rehabilitate and rescue animals that would have died otherwise. However, one could argue that zoos are playing God and should not interrupt the natural course of nature. Additionally, there are studies showing many animals do not survive their transition into the wild. Being in zoos does not expose the animals to diseases and illnesses that they need to build immunity against. Zoos cannot effectively vaccinate animals against every illness. When zoos have aging animals that they cannot release or use for entertainment anymore, they sell those animals for profit. Zoos make claims about rehabilitation and rescue, even when their strategies are known to end in failure.

Reading

Questions 1–10 are based on the following passage:

Mangroves are a type of woody growth that is very important to the ecosystems in which it lives. They include groups of shrubs and trees that grow along coastlines in tropical and subtropical areas (coastal wetlands). *Mangrove* can refer to a group of trees and shrubs or to the mangrove tree itself. Taking into consideration the various mangroves and other plants that exist alongside them, there are over eighty species in all. Mangroves have a distinct ability to thrive in extreme conditions. They are adapted to soils with low-oxygen levels and water that is extremely salty, both of which would kill most plants. They can live in freshwater but are much more commonly found in saltwater due to the varying levels of competition along freshwater and saltwater coastlines. Because mangroves can withstand conditions along saltwater that many plants cannot, they are much more likely to be found in saltwater. Since freshwater coastlines have more plants to compete with, mangroves are less likely to be found there.

Not only are they more likely to be found in saltwater, but they are also more likely to exist in areas with extreme conditions in general. This includes areas that see frequent flooding, hurricanes, waves, and so on. There is variety in how mangroves grow because they are able to thrive in a variety of environments including bays, lagoons, basins, and rivers. Their only real restriction is temperature, as they do not handle freezing temperatures well and are quickly killed. The ability to withstand such environments has come from millions of years of adaptation, as they have existed since the late Cretaceous epoch (145 to 66 million years ago). **A**

Mangroves are important to the ecosystems that they live in, as they provide many benefits to the land and animals around them. Due to their resilience and their existence along coastlines, mangroves can prevent erosion. They can also soften the impact of extreme weather events. For instance, they can absorb the impact of a hurricane as it passes through a coastline that contains mangroves. Mangrove roots alone provide many benefits. Their above-ground roots benefit the soil beneath them. They are dense, which slows the flow of water and in turn allows sediment to accumulate and bind, preventing erosion. These roots also improve the quality of the water that they reside in, as they filter various pollutants. **B** Mangroves are important to various animals as well, providing habitat, food, and an area to breed. Not only do they provide benefits for the environments that they are near, but they also help the world in general. They not only clear pollutants from the water, but they also help to clean the air. Mangroves can absorb very large amounts of greenhouse gases and carbon dioxide that have been emitted and store it in their soils. With the levels of carbon emissions and greenhouse gases today, mangroves are vital in containing some of these emissions. However, in the past forty to fifty years, nearly half of the world's mangrove forests have been lost. Some areas, namely southeast and south Asia, have lost more of their

135

mangroves than other areas due to factors like deforestation, urban development, and agriculture. **C**

Mangroves reproduce via vivipary, which is unique compared to the way many other plants reproduce. Vivipary means the offspring stays connected to the parent as it begins to grow, rather than being first disseminated and then growing upon finding the right environment. **D** Mangrove flowers are first pollinated for seedlings to be produced. These seedlings, or propagules, are then carried by the waves of whatever body of water is near. The propagules can spend days floating until they are soaked with water, which causes them to sink. Upon sinking, they stick in the soil. The amount of time that the propagules spend floating depends on the type of mangrove it is, and there are limits on how much time each type has before it is no longer able to grow. Because propagules can be carried by the water, they are able to establish and grow away from other mangroves and start a new forest. After this, it can take years for the mangrove to flower and become a forest of its own. The length of time it takes depends on the growing conditions that surround the plant.

1. The use of the word *development* in this passage is closest in meaning to:
   a. Evolution
   b. Infrastructure
   c. Stagnation
   d. Event

2. The phrase *they are dense* in paragraph 3 refers to:
   a. Mangroves
   b. Ecosystems
   c. Mangrove roots
   d. Propagules

3. Which of the following choices best communicates the important information of the sentence that is highlighted? Incorrect answer choices exclude pertinent information or misrepresent information.
   a. Mangrove propagules can spend different amounts of time floating, depending on what type of mangrove they are.
   b. There is a limit to how long mangrove propagules can float until they can no longer grow, but each mangrove propagule floats for the same amount of time.
   c. Mangrove propagules can float for various amounts of time and there is no limit on how long they can float, as they are still able to grow.
   d. Different kinds of mangrove propagules spend different amounts of time floating and have a limited amount of time to float before they are unable to grow.

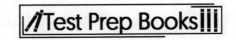

4. Find the four areas where the letters **A**, **B**, **C**, and **D** are located. These spaces indicate where the following sentence might be added to the passage.

> Unfortunately, replanting mangroves is not an option, as once they're lost, the coastline they once protected changes in a way that makes it much more difficult for them to grow.

In which area does the sentence best fit?
   a. A
   b. B
   c. C
   d. D

5. Which of the following can be inferred about agriculture based on paragraph 2?
   a. Some types of agriculture hurt nearby mangrove populations.
   b. Agriculture can be used to help mangrove populations.
   c. Agriculture is not as harmful to mangrove populations as urban development is.
   d. The expansion of agriculture is important to replanting mangrove populations.

6. According to paragraph 4, all the following are true about mangrove reproduction EXCEPT:
   a. Mangroves reproduce through vivipary.
   b. The propagules of different kinds of mangroves float for differing amounts of time depending on what type they are.
   c. The conditions in which the propagules plant themselves are a big factor in the speed with which they flower.
   d. Mangroves do not grow at all until they find the correct environment.

7. In paragraph 3, why does the author describe the root system of the mangrove?
   a. To illustrate the importance of mangroves to the environment they live in
   b. To explain why mangroves are more important than other plants
   c. To explain why mangroves are so resilient
   d. To note the way that mangroves benefit from their surroundings

8. According to paragraph 1, what is true about mangroves?
   a. Mangroves did not exist until around 10 million years ago.
   b. Mangroves have adapted over many years to harsh conditions that would kill most plants.
   c. Freezing temperatures are difficult for mangroves, but they can withstand them.
   d. Mangroves are more commonly found in freshwater than in saltwater.

9. In paragraph 4, why does the author include information about vivipary?
   a. To refute the idea that mangrove populations do not grow quickly
   b. To explain how mangrove populations can grow following the reduction in their population
   c. To note how different mangrove reproduction is from the reproduction of other plants
   d. To illustrate what vivipary is by explaining how mangroves reproduce

137

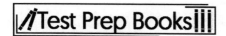

10. An opening sentence is provided to create a summary of the given passage above. Choose THREE answer choices that state the important ideas of the passage.

Mangroves are very resilient plants adapted to live in harsh conditions along tropical and subtropical coastlines.

1.

2.

3.

a. Mangroves provide various benefits to the water, air, and animals that surround them.
b. There has been a great decrease in the number of mangroves in the world within the past four to five decades due to development, agriculture, deforestation, and more.
c. Mangroves have existed for many years since the late Cretaceous epoch.
d. Mangroves reproduce through vivipary, which can take years from pollination all the way to flowering and creating a new forest.
e. Mangroves can store massive amounts of carbon and their dense roots clean the water by absorbing various pollutants.
f. After the propagule is lodged in new soil, it can take years before flowering and growing a new mangrove forest.

Questions 11–20 are based on the following passage:

Various types of systems exist within the human body, such as the nervous system, the cardiovascular system, and the digestive system. The nervous system consists of two different parts: the central nervous system and the peripheral nervous system. The spinal cord and the brain comprise the two aspects of the central nervous system. The peripheral nervous system is made up of two systems—the autonomic nervous system (ANS) and the somatic nervous system (SNS). The role of the ANS is to balance the physiological operations that occur involuntarily, such as blood pressure and digestion. The SNS is involved with both the senses and movement and consists of the nerves that are all around the body. The body's sense organs are a part of the SNS.

There are five different sense organs—the skin, nose, tongue, ears, and eyes. They are specialized to help us perceive the world around us. Another aspect of our senses is the vestibular and proprioceptive systems. The vestibular system is the human body's system for balance. Proprioception is the ability to perceive our body's location, actions, movements, and so on. Each sense organ has receptors that allow information to be communicated to the brain. When a sensory stimulus comes into contact with the body, it's picked up by that organ's receptors. The receptors then communicate the

138

information through nerve signals sent to the brain, which allows for the perception of the various senses. The part of the brain that is most involved with the senses and their perception and interpretation is the parietal lobe. It allows us to make sense of what we feel and the environment that surrounds us. Each sense organ is responsible for communicating about a particular sense. **A**

The skin is the body's largest organ and is responsible for our perception of touch. The skin has various receptors that pick up the sensations of pain, pressure, touch, temperature, force, and more. There are receptors located within different layers of the skin, such as Merkel cells found in the top layer of the skin, the epidermis. The nose is responsible for the body's sense of smell. **B** Its receptors are in the top of the nasal cavity. When a chemical binds to them, the information is passed to the olfactory bulbs, which then pass the information on to the brain via the olfactory nerve. **C** The tongue is responsible for our sense of taste. Tastebuds are contained within the papillae of the tongue. Chemicals contact the tastebuds and their gustatory cells, which then send the signal through the receptors to the brain. **D** Although tastebuds are responsible for sending messages to the brain about taste, the perception of flavor can be affected by the olfactory sense, such as when a person is sick and their sense of smell is diminished.

The eyes are responsible for sight. First, light enters the eye. Light is bent through the cornea of the eye and then passes through the aqueous humor. Based upon the amount of light present, the pupils adjust by changing size. After the pupil, light travels through the lens of the eye to the retina. The signal is then sent to the brain. The rods and cones of the eye work together to portray a complete picture in terms of light and color. The ears are responsible for our sense of sound. There are three parts of the ear: the outer, middle, and inner ear. The outer ear consists of the external ear, the ear canal, and the tympanic membrane (the eardrum). Sound waves first reach the outer ear through the ear canal. They travel through the stapes, malleus, and incus of the middle ear to the inner ear. Upon reaching the inner ear, the cochlea picks up the stimuli, which then sends the information through the auditory nerve.

Certain nerves are specialized for different aspects of sensation. The olfactory nerve is involved with the sense of smell. The cochlear nerve is responsible for communicating auditory information. Two of the nerves involved in the sense of taste include the glossopharyngeal nerve and the vagus nerve. The vagus nerve is a part of the parasympathetic nervous system and is involved with various involuntary functions of the body.

11. The use of the word *involuntary* in this passage is closest in meaning to:
    a. Mandatory
    b. Reflexive
    c. Prescribed
    d. Deliberate

139

12. The phrase *when a chemical binds to them* in paragraph 3 refers to:
    a. The nose's receptors
    b. The olfactory nerve
    c. Merkel cells
    d. The tympanic membrane

13. Which of the following choices best communicates the important information of the sentence that is highlighted? Incorrect answer choices exclude pertinent information or misrepresent information.
    a. Chemicals reach the gustatory cells and tastebuds after traveling through the papillae.
    b. The signal for taste reaches the receptors, after which it is sent to the brain.
    c. The gustatory cells send a signal to the brain after coming into contact with chemicals.
    d. The signal is sent to the brain after chemicals encounter receptors through the tastebuds and gustatory cells.

14. Find the four areas where the letters **A**, **B**, **C**, and **D** are located. These spaces indicate where the following sentence might be added to the passage.

    The sense of smell and the sense of taste work together.

In which area does the sentence best fit?
    a. A
    b. B
    c. C
    d. D

15. Which of the following can be inferred about sight based on paragraph 4?
    a. Sight is the simplest of all the senses.
    b. Different parts of the eye contribute to different aspects of sight.
    c. The most important feature of sight is the ability to pick up various colors.
    d. Sight takes the most time for us to perceive due to the many steps light must go through.

16. In paragraph 5, why does the author include examples of nerves that are specific to the senses?
    a. To explain an additional aspect of the human body's sense perception
    b. To illustrate how these nerves developed their specializations
    c. To contrast certain senses from other senses through different nerves
    d. To illustrate the greater system of the sensory experience

17. According to paragraph 3, all the following are true of the sense of smell EXCEPT:
    a. Merkel cells play a large role in picking up chemicals for our perception of smell.
    b. The top of the nasal cavity is where the nose's sense receptors are located.
    c. The olfactory bulbs are involved in our sense of smell.
    d. The olfactory nerve is what passes on the information from the olfactory bulbs to the brain.

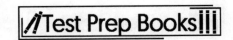

18. According to paragraph 1, which of the following is true about the nervous system?
    a. The nervous system consists of two parts: the brain and the spinal cord.
    b. The autonomic nervous system is involved in helping the body keep balance.
    c. The somatic nervous system helps to manage the body's involuntary processes such as blood pressure.
    d. The central nervous system and the peripheral nervous system are the two aspects of the nervous system.

19. According to paragraph 2, all the following are true of the body's sensory system EXCEPT:
    a. Sense organs are designed to help us discern what is happening in the environment around us.
    b. Each sense has the same receptors that allow information to travel to the brain.
    c. The sensory process first begins with a stimulus encountering the body.
    d. The parietal lobe is involved in perceiving and understanding the senses.

20. Choose the two correct answer choices for each category below:

The Ear	•
	•
The Eye	•
	•
The Skin	•
	•

    a. This is the largest organ of the body.
    b. This sensory organ contains the tympanic membrane.
    c. This sensory organ contains Merkel cells.
    d. The aqueous humor is a part of this sensory organ.
    e. The first step of this sensory organ's sense is picking up light.
    f. There are three different parts of this sensory organ.

Listening

Directions: The Listening section measures your ability to understand conversations and lectures in English. In this test, you will listen to several pieces of content and answer questions after each one. The questions typically ask about the main idea and supporting details. Some questions ask about a speaker's purpose or attitude. Answer the questions based on what is stated or implied by the speakers.

Listen to all of these passages by going to testprepbooks.com/bonus/toefl, or by scanning the QR code below:

Note that on the actual test, you can take notes while you listen and use your notes to help you answer the questions. Your notes will not be scored.

For your convenience, the transcripts of all of the audio passages are provided after the answer explanations. However, on the actual test, no such transcripts will be provided.

Recording #1: Conversation

1. Why does the student meet with the teaching assistant?
    a. To discuss the placement of the thesis statement in an essay
    b. To discuss a couple questions he has about the assignment
    c. To discuss the function of a thesis statement in an essay
    d. To discuss his choice for a major

2. Based on the information given to the student by the teaching assistant, put an "X" in each box next to the descriptions that correctly describe a thesis statement.

Located in a body paragraph	
Functions as a summary	
Directly answers the question the essay is asking	
Typically the last sentence of the introduction	
Located in the conclusion	
Located in the introduction	
Functions like a road map	
Directly asks the question the essay answers	

3. Which statement most accurately characterizes the teaching assistant's attitude toward the student?
    a. The teaching assistant is being friendly while maintaining a supervisory role.
    b. The teaching assistant is trying to remain impartial while still being helpful.
    c. The teaching assistant is behaving more like a friend than a supervisor.
    d. The teaching assistant is expressing frustration with the student.

4. While speaking with the teaching assistant, the student narrows down their topic to which of the following?
   a. Cold War
   b. Cuban Missile Crisis
   c. Korean War
   d. Iran-Contra Affair

5. According to the teaching assistant, what would the professor love to see as part of the presentation?
   a. A 10-minute presentation
   b. An audiovisual component
   c. The discussion of a broad topic
   d. A road map

Recording #2: Lecture

6. What is the main point of the lecture?
   a. The main point is to describe how volcanoes vary in appearance because there are three different types of volcanoes.
   b. The main point is to describe how volcanoes form differently based on the type of lava flow.
   c. The main point is to describe the various factors that contribute to the formation and appearance of volcanoes.
   d. The main point is that lava flow underwater varies based on the type of volcano.

7. How is the lectured mainly structured?
   a. Causes and effects
   b. Sequential
   c. Lists and descriptions of information
   d. A problem followed by a solution

8. What reason does the professor give for cinders cones collapsing?
   a. Their shape
   b. Basaltic rock
   c. Their size
   d. Ash composition

9. Based on the information given in the lecture, why could one infer that lava flows with lower viscosity cause more damage?
   a. They spread far and fast.
   b. They're hotter than lava flows with high viscosity.
   c. They're rockier than high-viscosity lava flows.
   d. They move more slowly.

143

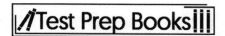

10. Why does the professor say, "Were we truly to think of volcanoes, we might think more of their origins."?
    a. The is professor is accusing the class of not putting much thought into the origin of volcanoes.
    b. The professor is ending the lecture and preparing the students for the upcoming lecture the next time they meet.
    c. The professor is creating a segue into a more detailed explanation of volcano formation.
    d. The professor is questioning the amount of research that has been done on volcanoes.

11. In the lecture you heard about the different characteristics of the two types of lava. In the table below, write either *a a* or *pahoehoe* next to the characteristics they match with.

Characteristic	Lava Type
Contains earthen debris and rock	
Comes from shield volcanoes	
Smooth	
Comes from composite volcanoes	
Smooth	

Recording #3: Lecture

12. What is the main point of the lecture?
    a. To persuade students to support genomic research
    b. To inform the class on the changes in medicine due to DNA mapping
    c. To describe medical treatments that use genomics
    d. To prove the value of scientific research

13. Why does the professor mention the BRCA gene?
    a. To discuss treatment of cancer
    b. To demonstrate its role in disease eradication
    c. To explain the benefit of tailored medicine
    d. To demonstrate the benefit of genomics in preventive medicine

14. What strategy does the professor use throughout the lecture to demonstrate the value of the Human Genome Project?
    a. She discusses genetic mutations
    b. She gives concrete applications for the research
    c. She cites medical researchers
    d. She presents and refutes the opposition

15. Cas9 will facilitate which of the following?
    a. Pharmacogenomics
    b. Disease diagnosis
    c. Gene editing
    d. Disease detection

16. Based on the language used in the lecture, how does the professor feel about genomic research?
    a. Hopeful
    b. Resigned
    c. Opposed
    d. Concerned

17. Based on the lecture, why has genomic research been so successful?
    a. We've been able to develop medicines to treat disease.
    b. Disease identification was a struggle prior to the research.
    c. We were able to map, sequence, and link genes.
    d. Many diseases are related to changes in our genes.

Recording #4: Conversation

18. What does the professor stop the student to talk about?
    a. The group project due next week
    b. An opportunity to work with the professor
    c. Why his grades are dropping
    d. The next test

19. Who is currently in the hospital?
    a. Daniel's mother
    b. The professor's wife
    c. Another student in class
    d. Daniel's sister

20. What attitude is the professor trying to express when he says, "You've seemed distracted during class as well. Is everything alright?"?
    a. Contention
    b. Disbelief
    c. Anger
    d. Concern

21. Which of the following is a likely outcome if the student accepts the professor's offer?
    a. Daniel will get a chance to study and catch up in class.
    b. Daniel will have to find another part-time job.
    c. The professor will have to fail Daniel out of the class later.
    d. Daniel's mother will need another week to recover in the hospital.

22. What can be inferred from the professor saying, "Hmm… Well, I don't know about that just yet."?
    a. The professor can help Daniel find another class to take.
    b. Daniel may not need to drop the class.
    c. Dropping the class is the only option.
    d. The upcoming test provides an alternative solution to Daniel's dilemma.

145

Recording #5: Lecture

23. What is the main idea of the lecture?
    a. Without the Silk Road, many places wouldn't be populated today.
    b. The Silk Road is responsible for the sharing of science and math.
    c. The Silk Road was responsible for exchanging far more than trade goods.
    d. The Silk Road is still in use today for a variety of reasons.

24. Based on the passage, what was an unintended consequence of Silk Road trade?
    a. Enabling gun proliferation
    b. Strengthening the Mongols
    c. The colonization of wild spaces
    d. Spreading disease and illness

25. Based on the passage, how does the writer feel about the influence of the Silk Road?
    a. Indifferent
    b. Positive
    c. Negative
    d. Disappointed

26. What is a popular misconception about the Silk Road?
    a. It was only on land.
    b. It was a myth.
    c. It was started by the Chinese.
    d. It was used only for trade goods.

27. Why does the professor mention World religions?
    a. To argue that the Silk Road brought goods from the East to the West.
    b. To give an example of how the Silk Road traded more than tangible goods.
    c. To emphasize that the Silk Road had limited impact.
    d. To explain that the Silk Road helped spread world religions.

28. Based on information in the lecture, why would sites on the Silk Road be World Heritage Sites?
    a. They are in danger of being destroyed by a trans-Asian highway.
    b. They have cultural and historical significance to the world.
    c. The road is still in use today.
    d. There are many towns and cities in those locations.

146

Speaking

Listen to all of these passages by going to <u>testprepbooks.com/bonus/toefl,</u> or by scanning the QR code below:

Recording #6

1. Listen to the following audio recording and then answer the question:
   - Preparation Time: 15 seconds
   - Response Time: 45 seconds

Recording #7

2. Read the following announcement and then listen to the conversation. Lastly, answer the question that follows them.

University to Lower Tuition Costs

Today, we are proud to announce that tuition costs will be lowered by 15 percent for the upcoming semester. These are difficult times and we have noticed that students are struggling. The cost of housing around campus has risen exponentially. We know that students are finding it difficult to pay for both tuition and housing.

In addition to the issue of rising housing costs, the number of students applying to our school has decreased. We hope that lowering tuition will encourage more students to attend and keep our school competitive. We are proud of this change and hope that you join us in celebrating.

Listen to the following conversation:

What is the female student's opinion about this announcement made by the university and why does she feel this way?

Recording #8

3. Read the following academic passage and then listen to the conversation. Finally, follow the instructions below.

Evolutionary Biological Mimicry

147

Evolutionary biological mimicry is when a plant or animal resembles another type of organism to increase its survival chances. It can occur within an entire species or between individuals within a species. This mimicry can be defensive or attractive in nature. Mimicry is more common in animals than it is plants. There are many different classifications of mimicry that denote the specific function. One of the major classifications, Batesian mimicry, is when a harmless species mimics a dangerous species. This helps survival by scaring off predators. Mimicry primarily fools the visual sense but it can deceive auditorily as well.

Listen to the following lecture:

Instructions: Explain evolutionary biological mimicry and discuss the examples provided by the professor.

- Preparation Time: 30 seconds
- Response Time: 60 seconds

Recording #9

4. Listen to the following excerpt from a lecture and follow the instructions afterward:

Instructions: Using the details given by the professor in the lecture, explain two types of symbiotic relationships that occur in the ocean.
- Preparation Time: 20 seconds
- Response Time: 60 seconds

Writing

Listen to all of these passages by going to testprepbooks.com/bonus/toefl, or by scanning the QR code below:

Integrated Writing

First, read the passage below:

Technology has irreversibly changed the world for the better. New technologies have allowed humans to do things that were never thought possible before. All sectors of

society have improved because of technological advances. Humans are more connected, knowledgeable, and capable because of technology.

One major way that technology has helped society is by connecting people across the world. Emails allow people to communicate with each other, and their use has changed the workforce. The same goes for video conferences. Video meetings can be conducted for personal reasons, or they can provide career opportunities, such as the ability to work from home. Social media allows friends and families to showcase the events of their lives. People can share their interests online and meet new like-minded people. This was not nearly as easy before technology advanced to this point. These advances in communication impact aspects of life. They can even help people with issues such as loneliness and social anxiety.

Another way that technology has helped society is through medical advancements. New machinery and treatments are available that were not possible years ago. Sick and/or elderly people do not have to suffer from many illnesses that were once debilitating or life-ending. Diseases are easier to diagnose, treat, and prevent. For example, blood tests are faster and more accurate than ever. Additionally, medical records are now mostly digital, which helps people keep track of family medical history and be more knowledgeable about their health.

The third way that technology has improved society is through education. Before computers and internet were widely available, people had to consult experts and go to libraries to learn about new subjects. Now the internet allows people to search for any information they want to know. Knowledge is now more accessible for whoever wishes to have it.

Now listen to the following lecture:

Recording #14

3. Prompt: Summarize the points presented in the lecture. Explain how they contrast with specific points in the reading passage.

You have 20 minutes to write your essay.

The following pages are provided for writing your essay.

_____

_____

_____

_____

_____

_____

_____

_____

_____

_____

_____

_____

_____

_____

_____

_____

_____

_____

_____

_____

_____

Academic Discussion

First, read the following online academic discussion between a professor and some students:

Instructor: Artificial Intelligence, or AI, is developing at a rapid pace. People are concerned about AI becoming uncontrollable or dangerous. Some have suggested anticipatory laws that prevent AI from negatively affecting humans. What do you think should be done about AI as it evolves?

Student 1: AI should be regulated. The danger to the human race is becoming apparent very quickly. Technological singularity would destroy the world. This is when technology becomes impossible to control. The technology would become super-intelligent, perhaps even sentient. Some scientists are claiming that this could lead to human extinction! Governments around the world need to work together to put a stop to this rapid evolution of AI.

Student 2: I don't think that there is anything that can be done about AI evolving in negative ways. Corporations will forever try to become more efficient and make more money. Government militaries may use AI in deadly ways, such as drones that can remotely drop bombs. Even if one country enacts laws to prevent this, there will always be AI developed somewhere else that is doing the bidding of the self-interested. The topic has already become too complex for the world to solve.

Next, add your opinion to the conversation using 100 words or more.

You have 10 minutes to write your response.

The following pages are provided for writing your essay.

Answer Explanations #2

Reading

Recording #1

1. B: The use of *development* in this passage is in relation to urban development, which involves construction in new areas for urban uses. Because of this, *infrastructure* is the most fitting option of all the choices. Choices *A* and *D* are similar to *development*, but not in the context that it is used within the passage. *Stagnation* is the opposite of *development*, so Choice *C* is also incorrect.

2. C: The phrase *they are dense* in paragraph 3 refers to the roots of the mangroves. They are a part of the mangrove, though it is not the mangrove, in general, being referenced. How the mangrove contributes to its ecosystem is described in paragraph 3, but it is not specifically referenced at that point in the paragraph. Propagules are not mentioned until paragraph 4.

3. D: Choice *D* states the two pieces of important information within the sentence: different mangrove propagules float for different lengths of time, and after a certain amount of time they can no longer grow. Choice *A* only states part of the information and Choices *B* and *C* contain incorrect information.

4. C: Choice *C* follows an explanation of the loss of mangroves over the past four to five decades, which is the most appropriate place to explain that they cannot be simply replanted. It is then followed by the next paragraph, which explains how mangroves can grow. Choice *A* is incorrect because it does not contain information directly relevant to any mangrove loss or growth. Choice *B* is incorrect because it does not work in the context of that part, which explains how mangroves help the ecosystem they live in. For Choice *D*, the sentence would be placed in the middle of explaining how mangroves grow and reproduce, which is not an appropriate place for the sentence.

5. A: The only choice that can be inferred is that some agriculture can hurt mangrove populations, as it has been one reason for the decline in the world's mangroves. Choices *B* and *D* imply that agriculture can be used to help mangrove populations, which cannot be inferred based on the provided information. Choice *C* makes a comparative statement that cannot be inferred based on the passage, as there is not enough information provided for this.

6. D: Choice *D* is the only option with incorrect information—mangroves reproduce through vivipary, which means they first start growing while still attached to the parent plant (they do not wait until they find the right environment). The other choices contain correct information regarding the reproduction of mangroves: they reproduce through vivipary, different types float for different amounts of time, and the factors they plant themselves in impact the time it takes for them to continue to grow.

7. A: The author describes the root system of mangroves to explain their importance within the environment. Choice *B* is incorrect, as there is no judgment or comparison that is made to support them being more important than other plants. Choice *C* is incorrect because it does not explain why they are so resilient to such harsh conditions. Choice *D* is incorrect because any benefits that they receive are not described within the passage.

8. B: Choice *B* is the only correct statement about mangroves. They have existed for many years and are adapted to conditions other plants cannot survive. The other choices are all incorrect: mangroves have existed for longer than 10 million years, they cannot survive freezing temperatures, and they are more commonly found in saltwater than in freshwater.

9. C: Choice *C* is correct, as it is mentioned that mangroves reproduce uniquely from many other plants, contrasting their reproduction with the way other plants reproduce. Choice *A* is incorrect because while the time the growth takes is mentioned, it can vary greatly, and there is no mention of how quickly or slowly they grow in relation to any standard amount of time. Choice *B* is incorrect, as it is not explained how their natural reproduction could help them grow. Also, the loss of parent plants hurts their ability to reproduce. Choice *D* is incorrect because vivipary is not explained for the sake of vivipary, but for the sake of explaining how mangroves reproduce. In addition, because vivipary is mentioned as being unique from other plant reproduction methods, Choice *C* is a more appropriate answer.

10. A, B, D: The correct answers are Choices *A*, *B*, and *D*: Mangroves provide various benefits to the water, air, and animals that surround it; there has been a great decrease in the number of mangroves in the world within the past four to five decades due to development, agriculture, deforestation, and more; mangroves reproduce through vivipary, which can take years from pollination all the way to flowering and creating a new forest. Any of the other choices would leave out vital information from the summary.

Recording #2

11. B: The use of *involuntary* in this passage is in relation to bodily processes that occur unconsciously. Because of this, *reflexive* is the most similar choice. *Mandatory* and *prescribed* are similar to *involuntary*, but they imply an intention or an imposition. *Deliberate* is the opposite of involuntary.

12. A: The phrase *when a chemical binds to them* refers to the nose's receptors. The olfactory nerve is not referenced there, as the chemical does not directly bind to the nerve. Merkel cells are also not referenced there, as they are mentioned earlier in relation to the skin. The tympanic membrane is also not referenced there, but rather later along with information about the ear.

13. D: The correct answer is Choice *D*, as it contains the information of the original sentence in a more concise way—the gustatory cells and tastebuds encounter a chemical that allows for the signal to be sent to the brain. The other choices leave out important information, such as the signal being sent to the brain, or the fact that the tastebuds and the gustatory cells are involved in the experience of taste.

14. D: Choice *D* is correct because the given sentence includes both the sense of taste and the sense of smell. This allows for the sentence to follow the explanations of the sense of taste and sense of smell and to preface a statement about how they work together. Choice *A* is not the correct placement because the specifics of the sense organs have not yet been explained at this point. Choice *B* is not the correct placement because placing this sentence here would interrupt the explanation of smell. Choice *C* is not the correct placement because while it could work, the sentence is better placed following the explanations about smell and taste and before information about how they work together.

15. B: The correct inference is that different parts of the eye contribute to different aspects of sight because the roles of different parts of the eye are explained. It cannot be inferred that sight is the simplest of all senses, as each sense has its own similar-yet-different process. It also cannot be inferred that one feature of sight is the most important, as it is an opinionated statement. It cannot be inferred

that sight takes the most time to process, either. Although there were more steps explained regarding the process of sight, there was not an explanation of the time it takes to process any of the senses.

16. A: The author included explanations of the nerves that are specific to the senses to explain an additional aspect of the human body's sensory perception. Choice *B* is incorrect because the passage does not explain how these nerves became specialized for these senses. Choice *C* is incorrect because the nerves are not listed or explained in a way that contrasts with the senses as they were previously explained. Choice *D* is incorrect because they are not explained in a way that ties in the greater system regarding the senses, but rather as additional information about the sense organs.

17. A: The correct choice is the one incorrect statement regarding smell: Merkel cells are a part of the skin and therefore are a part of the sense of touch rather than smell. The other choices are all correct statements about the nose and sense of smell. The nose's receptors are in the top of the nasal cavity; the olfactory bulbs are involved in perceiving smell; and the olfactory nerve is what relays the information to the brain from the nose.

18. D: The last choice is the correct statement about the nervous system, which is that the central nervous system and the peripheral nervous system make up the nervous system. The other choices are incorrect—the nervous system is made up of more than the brain and spinal cord; the autonomic nervous system is not involved with helping the body keep balance; and the somatic nervous system is not involved with involuntary bodily processes such as blood pressure.

19. B: The one statement that is not true regarding the body's sensory system is that each sense has the same receptor that allows information to travel to the brain (rather, each sense organ has its own unique receptors). The other statements are all true: sense organs are designed to help us discern what is happening in the environment around us; the sensory process begins with a stimulus encountering the body; the parietal lobe is involved with the perceiving and understanding of the senses.

20. The ear: B, F; the eyes: D, E; the skin: A, C: The ear consists of three different parts and contains the tympanic membrane. The eyes contain the aqueous humor, and the first step of the eye's sense (sight) is picking up light. The skin contains Merkel cells and is the largest organ of the body.

Listening

Listen to all of these passages by going to testprepbooks.com/bonus/toefl, or by scanning the QR code below:

Recording #1: Conversation

1. B: Choice *B* is correct. The student clearly states at the beginning of the conversation that he has a couple questions about the assignment. Choice *A* is incorrect. The student is admittedly confused about the placement of the thesis statement, but this is only one detail that he wanted to discuss with the teaching assistant. The more accurate reason for the meeting with the teaching assistant is Choice *B*. Choice *C* is incorrect. The teaching assistant offers this information without being asked. The student's question was about placement, not function, of the thesis statement. Choice *D* is incorrect. The teaching assistant asks the question about the student's major toward the end of the conversation.

2. In the table below, the boxes that are marked with an "X" match up with the descriptions of a thesis statement there were given by the teaching assistant in the conversation.

Located in a body paragraph	
Functions as a summary	
Directly answers the question the essay is asking	✖
Typically the last sentence of the introduction	✖
Located in the conclusion	
Located in the introduction	✖
Functions like a road map	✖
Directly asks the question the essay answers	

3. A: Choice *A* is the correct answer. The teaching assistant is certainly being friendly, but she's still acting in a supervisory capacity. Therefore, Choice *C* is incorrect. The teaching assistant is not being strictly impartial. For example, telling the student about the professor's preferences for presentations provides an advantage over other students. So, Choice *B* is incorrect. Choice *D* is incorrect because the teaching assistant isn't frustrated with the student.

4. D: After the teaching assistant says the Cold War might be too broad, the student narrows down his topic to focus on the Iran-Contra Affair. Thus, Choice *D* is the correct answer. The Cold War is the student's initial topic, but the teaching assistant advises the student to focus on an individual event. So, Choice *A* is incorrect. The Cuban Missile Crisis occurred during the Cold War, but it doesn't come up

160

during the conversation. Therefore, Choice *B* is incorrect. Likewise, the Korean War isn't discussed during the conversation, so Choice *C* is incorrect.

5. B: Choice *B* is the correct answer. The teaching assistant suggests adding an audiovisual component to the presentation, and when asked by the student if this is a requirement, she states that it's not a requirement but that the professor would love it. Choice *A* is incorrect. The teaching assistant says that a 10-minute presentation is long enough to defend a thesis without losing the attention of the audience. Nowhere is it stated that the professor would love to see a 10-minute presentation. Choice *C* is incorrect. The teaching assistant tells the student that his current topic is too broad for the assignment. Choice *D* is incorrect. The teaching assistant never says to include a road map in the presentation. The term *road map* was used to describe the function of the thesis statement.

Recording #2: Lecture

6. C: Choice *C* is the correct answer. The lecture begins with the professor telling the class that most people think of the cone of the volcano when they think of volcanoes, but he goes on to explain how there is more to a volcano than just the cone. He explains how the different types of volcanoes are created. He also describes how the type of lava determines how the volcano will look. He even discusses the different types of underwater lava flow. Choice *A* is incorrect. Although he does describe the different volcano types, there is more to the lecture than this. This is only one portion of the lecture that contributes to the main point of the lecture. Choice *B* is incorrect. As with Choice *A*, this information is discussed, but only to support the main point, not as the main point itself. Choice *D* is incorrect. Underwater lava flow is explained near the end of the lecture and is only a part of the lecture that supports the main point that there are many factors that contribute to the formation and appearance of volcanoes.

7. C: The professor lists information related to volcanoes and lava flows. First he lists and describes volcano types, then he lists and describes types of lava, and finally he lists and describes types of underwater lava flow. Choice *A* is incorrect because the passage opens with how we think about volcanoes, and it does not end with any effect or impact of these thoughts. Choice *B* is incorrect. It does not appear to go in any specific categorizable order. Choice *D* is incorrect. There is no problem; it is a fact that there are volcanoes.

8. B: When the professor discusses cinder cone volcanoes, he explicitly states that basaltic rock weakens cinder cone volcanoes. Choice *A* is incorrect because the cone shape is not the cause of its structural weakness. Choice *C* is incorrect because size does not seem to impact the integrity of the volcano. Choice *D* is incorrect. Ash and rock are considerably different and can spew from the same volcano. It's the rock, not the ash, that makes a cinder cone unstable.

9. A: Choice *A* is correct. Lava flows with low viscosity are more fluid. There is not much in the way of rock or debris to slow the flow, so it can move fast and spread far. Choice *B* is incorrect. The professor did not mention temperature as it relates to the lava flow. Choice *C* is incorrect as a rocky lava flow would have a higher viscosity. Choice *D* is incorrect. Low viscosity means there is little to no friction in the flow and so it can move more quickly.

10. C: Choice *C* is correct. He says this as an introduction to a lecture that gives details about the various origins of volcanoes and describes how this determines the type of volcano that results. Choice *A* is incorrect. The purpose of the statement is to introduce the main topic of the lecture, not to accuse the

class of anything. Choice *B* is incorrect. This statement is made at the beginning of the lecture to prepare the students for the topic that he will be discussing. The statement is not made at the end of the lecture, and the intention is not to prepare the class for the lecture of an upcoming class. Choice *D* is incorrect. The amount of research done on volcanoes is never in question. It's quite the opposite. The professor uses information from research that has been done to provide more knowledge about volcanoes to his class.

11.

Characteristic	Lava Type
Contains earthen debris and rock	A a
Comes from shield volcanoes	Pahoehoe
Smooth	Pahoehoe
Comes from composite volcanoes	A a
Smooth	Pahoehoe

Recording #3: Lecture

12. B: The professor discusses gene research and the application so the students can learn how DNA mapping changed medicine. Choice *A* is incorrect. There is no language to persuade students to support or oppose further gene research. Choice *C* is incorrect. Although medical treatments are described, it's done to support the overall goal of showing how DNA mapping has changed medicine. The procedures are not described in enough detail to make this the main point. Choice *D* is incorrect. That goal is very general, and the passage is quite specific and related to gene research and medicine.

13. D: The ability to identify the BRCA gene enables doctors to prevent cancer by removing the site of the cancer. As such, it functions as preventive medicine. Choice *A* is incorrect. Knowing which gene mutation causes breast cancer does not help with treatment because the cancer can still occur if preventive action isn't taken. Choice *B* is incorrect. Being able to identify the gene and prevent the disease from forming does not eradicate it. Choice *C* is incorrect. Tailored medicine enables doctors to tailor treatments based on a person's genetic makeup. Identifying the BRCA gene does not enable tailored medicine because the treatment is used on any and all individuals with the gene mutation.

14. B: The professor gives the very real and concrete changes to medicine introduced and created based on genomic information. Choice *A* is incorrect. Genetic mutations and their identification are valuable; however, it's the treatment and response to those mutations that demonstrate the true power of genomics. Choice *C* is incorrect. Medical researchers are not cited. Choice *D* is incorrect. The professor does not discuss the opinions of those who oppose such research.

15. C: The professor states clearly that the potential of Cas9 is to enable gene editing to eradicate diseases before they start. Choice *A* is incorrect. Cas9 is a naturally occurring enzyme and does not need

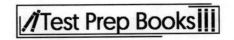

pharmaceuticals. Choice *B* is incorrect. Cas9 facilitates treatment, not diagnosis. Choice *D* is incorrect because, again, it facilitates treatment, not detection.

16. A: The last sentence spoken by the professor indicates that she is hopeful for future advancements. Choice *B* is incorrect. Resigned would suggest defeated, and the professor is the opposite of that. Choice *C* and Choice *D* are incorrect. The professor is neither opposed nor concerned. Both of these would contradict the hopeful tone and language used in the lecture.

17. D: The professor clearly states that genomic research has been so successful because most diseases are related to mutations, or changes in our genes. Choice *A*, Choice *B*, and Choice *C* are all incorrect. Although true, they all represent a single outcome of genomic research, and genomic research does much more than any one of those single outcomes.

Recording #4: Conversation

18. C: The professor wants to talk with the student about why his grades have recently been dropping. There is no upcoming group project mentioned in the conversation, so Choice *A* is incorrect. The opportunity discussed is for the student to stay with the professor while his mother recovers, not to work with the professor, so Choice *B* is incorrect. The conversation does mention retaking the previous test near the end, but it isn't the main focus of the conversation, so Choice *D* is incorrect.

19. A: Daniel reveals in the conversation that his mother is in the hospital. The professor's wife and Daniel's sister are mentioned, but neither are in the hospital, so Choices *B* and *D* are incorrect. There is no mention of any other students in the class, so Choice *C* is incorrect.

20. D: The professor is primarily concerned about how the student is doing. He isn't trying to be confrontational, upset, or angry, so Choices *A*, *B*, and *C* are all incorrect.

21. A: If Daniel decides to accept the professor's offer to stay with him, the most likely outcome of these is that he will be able to study more and catch up in the class. Choices *B*, *C*, and *D* are all options that are more likely to happen if Daniel declines the offer instead, so they are all incorrect.

22. B: The professor's statement implies that Daniel may not need to drop the class. Choice *A* could be possible, but as the conversation continues, it becomes clear that he doesn't want Daniel to fail or drop the class, so it is incorrect. Choice *C* is also incorrect because the wording suggests the professor doesn't want Daniel to drop the class. There's no mention of an upcoming test, so Choice *D* is incorrect.

Recording #5: Lecture

23. C: Many people know of the Silk Road because of trade goods such as spices, and the professor seeks to educate the students on the fact that it was responsible for spreading far more than trade goods. Choice *A* is incorrect. Although many places may have remained uninhabited without the Silk Road, that's not the main idea of the lecture. Choice *B* and Choice *D* are incorrect. Although true, they are supporting details, not the main idea.

24. D: The passage notes that, unfortunately, the Silk Road is considered to be one of the major ways the plague was spread. Choice *A* is incorrect. Although the Chinese did provide gunpowder to the West, it's not responsible for gun proliferation. Choice *B* is incorrect. The Mongols did receive horses through the route, which bolstered their military prowess. However, *unintended* implies it was accidental, but

163

the trade was intentional. Choice *C* is incorrect. Although remote places were developed into small communities, wild spaces being colonized is not mentioned as a concern in the passage.

25. B: The passage notes that most of the impact from the Silk Road was positive, and then, in the final paragraph, the writer notes a continued positive outcome moving forward. Choice *A* is incorrect. Language throughout the passage indicates the writer's interest in the Silk Road's ability to spread and share beneficial goods and ideas. Choice *C* is incorrect. The author notes some negative impacts but does not strike a negative tone. Choice *D* is incorrect. The author seems hopeful in the last paragraph about continued efforts to utilize the Silk Road land route. Furthermore, the author notes the preservation via World Heritage Sites.

26. A: Many believed the Silk Road to be only an on-land trade route. The first paragraph notes the existence of routes via the sea. Choice *B* is incorrect. Clearly, the impact of the Silk Road establishes its existence. Its impact was real and significant. Choice *C* is incorrect. Trade along the Silk Route went in both directions, and it's not clear where it was initiated. Choice *D* is incorrect. The passage includes many other elements brought by the Silk Road.

27. B: World religions demonstrate how the Silk Road was responsible for trading more than tangible trade goods and commodities. Choice *A* is incorrect. Goods along the Silk Road traveled in both directions. Choice *C* is incorrect. It is the opposite of what the Silk Road did, and world religions demonstrate that. Choice *D* is incorrect. There is a larger point being made regarding the impact of the Silk Road.

28. B: Places along the Silk Road are steeped in rich world history and are important culturally, not just to the regions they are in but those along the route as well. Choice *A* is incorrect. Although a trans-Asian highway is in discussion, these sites would be protected. Choice *C* is incorrect. The road is still in use today, but that wouldn't be reason enough to preserve them. Choice *D* is incorrect. Towns or cities must have significant cultural and historical importance to qualify for World Heritage Sites. Existing along a significant trade route isn't enough.

Listening Transcripts

Recording #1: Conversation

(Narrator) Listen to a conversation between a student and teaching assistant, and then answer the questions that follow.

(Student) Thank you for meeting with me. I have a couple questions about the upcoming assignment

(Teaching Assistant) Sure thing. Are you talking about the essay or presentation?

(Student) Both, I think; that's where I'm confused. Is the presentation supposed to be a summary of the essay? Or is the presentation allowed to primarily focus on one part of the essay?

(Teaching Assistant) That's a good question. The presentation is graded based on how well you defend your thesis. So it's similar to a summary of the essay, assuming you've followed the guidelines I provided. Have you written your thesis statement yet?

(Student) No, I've started writing the essay, but I'm confused about where the thesis statement should appear in the essay.

(Teaching Assistant) Your thesis statement functions like a road map because it explains to readers how you will be analyzing and interpreting the evidence that follows. Additionally, your thesis statement should directly answer the question that essay is asking. So, your thesis statement must be in the introduction, and it's typically the last sentence before the body paragraphs begin.

(Student) Gotcha. So it's a part of the introduction, not the whole thing, right?

(Teaching Assistant) Yeah, you should try to limit it to one sentence.

(Student) That makes sense.

(Teaching Assistant) Remind me, what's your topic?

(Student) I'm writing about the Cold War.

(Teaching Assistant) That's a little too broad for this assignment. Have you considered narrowing it down to a single event?

(Student) I've been very interested in the Iran-Contra Affair. Maybe I could write about that within the broader context of the Cold War?

(Teaching Assistant) Yeah, that sounds great. It also helps that that's a relatively recent event, so you could add some terrific audiovisual components into your presentation.

(Student) Is that a requirement?

(Teaching Assistant) No, but, between you and me, Professor Ramirez would love it. He's always talking about the persuasive power of video.

(Student) Wow, well thanks for the tip. I've watched some of Oliver North's congressional testimony, and I'm sure I could find some short clips of it for the presentation.

(Teaching Assistant) That'd be phenomenal.

(Student) How long should the presentation be?

(Teaching Assistant) There's no time limit, but I think 10 minutes works best. You want to have enough time to defend your thesis without losing your audience's attention. How have your other classes been going? You're a history major, right?

(Student) No, I'm only minoring in history. My major is political science. Those classes have been a little abstract and dry.

(Teaching Assistant) I felt the same way in college, which is why I opted for history over political science for graduate school. Let me know if you're ever thinking about applying to the graduate program. I'd be more than happy to write you a recommendation.

(Student) Awesome, I might just take you up on that. Thanks for all your help.

(Teaching Assistant) No problem.

Recording #2: Lecture

(Professor) Perhaps it's because it takes so long for the process to complete that many of us, when we think of volcanoes, think only of the cone. Although that triangular cone at the top of a volcanic mountain is formed during an eruption as rock, dust, and ash build up on the edges of the vent, it's not the only shape volcanoes take.

What we see of a volcanic mountain likely took anywhere from ten thousand to fifty thousand years and, possibly, tens of thousands of eruptions to form. If we truly thought of volcanoes, we might think more of their origins. We might think of vents at the bottom of the oceans—fissures and cracks—that erupt over and over, building layer upon layer. As the lava erupts, the water cools it rapidly, hardening it until an island breaks the surface of the water.

However, every volcano is different. There are three types of volcanoes, and even those can vary in what spews during an eruption. The three primary types of volcanoes are shield, composite, and cinder cone.

Shield volcanoes: These volcanoes have a sloping hill shape leading downward from the vent. The hill is formed gradually as layer after layer of a low-viscosity lava, which can flow for longer distances than other types of volcanoes.

Composite volcanoes: These volcanoes are the shape most envision. Because the lava forms in alternating layers of what's called *tephra* (rock fragments, earth, and ash), it piles higher than the shield volcano, often rising to a point at the vent. As a result, its slopes are steeper, but its diameter is smaller.

Cinder cone volcanoes: These volcanoes resemble craters. In appearance, they are almost a mix of the other two. Although the eruptions spew rock like the composite volcano, a rock made from the basaltic lava spews from a shield volcano; basaltic rock is fairly weak. As a result, it's unable to pile as high as a composite volcano but still higher than a shield volcano.

Just as there are three types of volcanoes, there are also different types of lava. The names of the lava flows come from the Polynesian culture. Lava flows on land are called either *a'a* (pronounced "ah-ah") or *pahoehoe* ("paw-hoy-hoy"). A'a lava flows are often from composite volcanoes, loaded with earthen debris and rock. In contrast, pahoehoe lava flows are smooth and fast running and come from shield volcanoes.

Lava flows in water are a bit different. Although most underwater flows resemble pahoehoe flows, they vary based on the speed and force of the eruption as well as the grade of the sea floor near the eruption. There are three recognized types of undersea lava flows: pillow lava flows, lobate flows, and sheet flows.

Pillow lava flows appear in large bumps, like a lumpy pillow or overstuffed cushion, and can be both fairly long (several kilometers) and quite high (tens of meters). As the lava erupts from an undersea fissure, the outer layer cools almost immediately, creating a shell under which lava continues to flow.

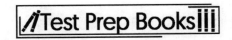

The flow underneath puts stress on the "shell," causing it to bubble out. New pillows are formed when that pressure is enough to break a previously formed pillow, starting the process all over again.

Lobate flows are most similar to on-land pahoehoe flows. However, they often appear as if air has been injected below the flow itself, giving it a puffier appearance.

Sheet flows occur when there is a fast eruption with low viscosity. As a result, the flow spreads out, pooling in lower-lying areas and spreading far and wide, flowing much like a river.

Recording #3: Lecture

(Professor) Over a period of nearly fifteen years, genetic scientists worked diligently to map out the human genome. An international effort, the goal of which was not perhaps clear to many laypeople at the start, the Human Genome Project sought to identify, map, and sequence all genes found in human DNA to better understand the function and form of each genetic marker. More specifically, the goal was to garner a stronger understanding of everything from disease and predisposition to specific diseases to physical and personality traits. As a result of this work, we've seen significant impact across medical and health fields, which have been able to apply the knowledge to improving both human health and physiological performance.

Over the course of the project, scientists were able to determine that there are approximately 20,500 human genes. In identifying these, scientists were also able to determine their order and then further establish their locations and create linkage maps that help connect the genes to different characteristics that are observable over several generations of a family.

As a result of the work, there have been major advances in medicine that have facilitated the treatment of disease. Because many diseases are related to changes in our genes, scanning and searching for those mutations can help detect diseases early. Early detection is vital in the treatment of many diseases, such as cancer. In addition, genetic testing can identify a predisposition toward a certain disease or condition and, in turn, individuals can act preemptively to address the issue. For example, many women who test positive for a mutation in a BRCA gene, the breast cancer genes, have opted to get mastectomies prior to developing cancer. In this way, genomics works toward helping to prevent diseases in the first place.

Similarly, genomics can help with the diagnosis of disease, particularly when it's something incredibly rare. The research has enabled scientists to identify approximately 2000 different disease genes. What this means for doctors is that when patients come in with an array of symptoms, yet a diagnosis still seems to elude them, genomic research has enabled patients to be diagnosed more quickly and more accurately—in seconds—facilitating faster treatment.

Those treatments, with the help of genomic research, are growing more effective as well. Prior to this research, we've all likely witnessed medication having different effects on different people, and genomic research explains that. Pharmacogenomics, specifically, researches how genes impact the liver's ability to metabolize different drugs. These variations are normal, but until this research, they were unpredictable, meaning sometimes doctors were unsure if a medication dose would be beneficial, toxic, or have no positive impact at all. Now, doctors are able to respond to these differences and modify dosages. Similarly, pharmaceutical researchers are able to develop more effective medications. In fact, more than 250 medications come with pharmacogenomic information, so doctors can appropriately prescribe medication based on a patient's genetics.

167

Perhaps one of the most significant medical changes is the potential shift from treating to curing when it comes to disease management. Most medicine—even modern medicine—is designed to treat or mitigate conditions. However, a greater understanding of genomics means doctors can identify the gene mutation or variation responsible for the disease and remove it. Using enzymes—in one case, the Cas9 enzyme—doctors can attack the specific part of the gene that carries the mutation and ultimately remove the disease. This kind of gene editing may be the future of medicine, especially as it becomes more affordable.

All in all, genomic research has single-handedly changed the current landscape for medicine, with even more hope on the horizon.

Recording #4: Conversation

(Professor) Alright, that's it for today, class. See you tomorrow! ...Oh, Daniel? Could I talk to you for a minute?

(Daniel) Ah... sure thing, professor. What is it?

(Professor) I wanted to talk to you about your performance on the last test.

(Daniel) Oh...

(Professor) You started off this semester very strong, but the last two weeks your grades have been steadily slipping. And your performance on the last test was barely passing.

(Daniel) I'm sorry, professor.

(Professor) I'm not here to admonish you, Daniel. I just wanted to check on you. You've seemed distracted during class as well. Is everything alright?

(Daniel) Um... Well, to tell the truth, professor, no. My mother, she was just suddenly hospitalized a couple of weeks ago.

(Professor) I'm sorry to hear that. Is she going to be alright?

(Daniel) I don't know. She's stable, I know that much, but the doctors won't tell me much. I'm worried about her... It's just me, her, and my sister.

(Professor) I see... So you've been having to suddenly support your sister too?

(Daniel) Yeah. I've barely had time to study or practice. She's only eight, so I have to make dinner and help her with her homework too. I'm sorry I can't focus on class, professor. I may have to drop out later.

(Professor) Hmm... Well, I don't know about that just yet. It would be a shame to see a great student like you held back by unfortunate events beyond our control. I'll have to consult with my wife first, but... perhaps you and your sister can stay with us for the time being.

(Daniel) What? Are you sure, professor? I'm not sure what my mother would think, and I wouldn't want us to impose...

(Professor) Oh, you wouldn't be imposing in the slightest. Our kids are grown up and on their own, and we haven't moved out of the old home yet. The extra bedrooms might be a bit messy, but we'd have more than enough space for you two while your mother recovers.

(Daniel) I see, um... That's awfully kind of you, but I'll have to see what my mother thinks.

(Professor) Of course. I'm sure she's worried about you and your sister as well, so you should make sure this idea is okay with her too.

(Daniel) I really appreciate the offer, professor. Maybe I can get a chance to retake the test?

(Professor) Haha, let's not get ahead of ourselves. I can certainly help you catch up to get your grades back up, but as far as what's already happened, we'll see about that.

(Daniel) Haha, fair enough. Thought it might be worth asking anyway. I've got to go, or I'll be late for my work shift.

(Professor) Alright, Daniel, take care! Send me an email later and we can schedule a time during my office hours to talk some more.

Recording #5: Lecture

(Professor) For many, the Silk Road means the overland trade of silk, from China to Rome, or wool and precious metals, such as gold and silver, making the trek to China from the West. However, the history and trade on the Silk Road were far more expansive than that. There were many routes, including some via sea, and many items for trade.

The first thing to really know is that prior to discovering land routes, the Silk Road was predominantly made up of maritime spice routes. Spices such as cinnamon were making their way from the East to the Arabian Peninsula. Along with the spices came knowledge and understanding as these port cities became trading destinations. As information and wares spread, demand grew, requiring more frequent travel and additional routes.

The overland Silk Route was a 4000-mile trade pathway that traversed some of the most challenging landscape in that region. From mountains to deserts, the harsh terrain and lack of government control over the routes made travel incredibly dangerous. As a result, routes were shortened, traders traveled in caravans, and both inns and couriers popped up along the trail to offer rest and delivery services. All of these enabled traders to return more quickly to their homes to start the route again with more in-demand goods. Among those in-demand goods were silk and spices as well as tea, porcelain, textiles, precious stones, glassware, livestock, horses, and other manufactured goods.

However, the Silk Road routes tended to share far more than goods. In fact, these routes are largely credited with spreading knowledge that encouraged growth in both science and math. These two fields would then significantly impact the communities and cultures they were introduced to. Similarly, religion and concepts of belief were able to travel this way as well. China was influenced by Christianity, and Buddhism was largely influenced by Hinduism.

Although these introductions were largely deemed positive, the Silk Road was also responsible for influences that may be seen less positively. For example, the Chinese received horses, which significantly

shaped the military might and power of the Mongol Empire. In turn, China introduced gunpowder to the West, forever transforming how wars were fought in Europe and beyond.

In addition to changing the way nations and cultures engage in war, the Silk Road is thought to, at least in part, be responsible for the spread of the Black Death plague, which ravaged Europe in the mid-fourteenth century. As traders, couriers, opportunists, entrepreneurs, and others flocked to the popular routes, returning to small towns and communities, more than spices spread.

Furthermore, as travelers and goods filled the inns along the route, towns and villages began to develop. This forever changed the region and continued to encourage the growth of trade. In fact, the Silk Road overland route is still on the radar for further development.

The parts of the route that exist today include World Heritage Sites, but, more importantly, they connect regions that could benefit economically and from stronger connections. As a result, the United Nations has suggested both a trans-Asian highway and a railroad system to improve the socioeconomic status of these regions.

Much like travelers throughout history bringing in business, a completed and maintained highway and railroad promise to do the same. The Silk Road has and will continue to evolve over time to facilitate multicultural and international cooperation.

Speaking

Listen to all of these passages by going to <u>testprepbooks.com/bonus/toefl,</u> or by scanning the QR code below:

Sample Responses

Recording # 6

Question 1

Recording #7

Question 2

Recording #8

Question 3

170

Recording #9

Question 4

Speaking Question Transcripts

Recording #6

1. Some people prefer to go on vacation with their families and some people prefer to go on vacation with their friends. Which one would you prefer? Give reasons for your preference.

Recording #7

2. **(Female Student)** This is great news! The school is lowering tuition by 15 percent.

(Male Student) Wow. I am in total support of this.

(Female Student) Me too. When I came in as a freshman, my rent was $300 a month. Now that I'm a senior, it's triple that amount! As a full-time student, I don't have time to work every day, so I'm not bringing in a lot of money. I can't afford housing on top of tuition, and I know many other students can't either.

(Male Student) I bet that will make a lot more people want to come to this college!

(Female Student) They said that they've noticed fewer students are applying. They want the lowered tuition to make the college more competitive. This makes total sense to me. There are a lot of super intelligent students who will choose our school over others because they'll be saving money.

(Male Student) I can't wait!

Recording #8

3. **(Professor)** Biological mimicry is one of the most fascinating forms of evolution. One example of an animal that uses mimicry is the kingsnake. Kingsnakes live in southeastern North America and are harmless. They are hunted by numerous predators, including hawks. To improve their chances of survival, they have evolved to have the same colors and markings as the coral snake, which is highly venomous and deadly. This visual evolution sends a signal to potential predators that the kingsnake is dangerous, even though it is not.

The mimic octopus is an even more impressive example of biological mimicry. It can mimic three different dangerous animals in the ocean. It changes its colors and poses on demand. It can resemble a lionfish, sea snake, or banded sole. All of these mimicked sea creatures are either venomous or poisonous. Predators now avoid the harmless mimic octopus due to this deception. Scientists believe it can mimic even more creatures than what is currently known. Additionally, the mimic octopus can camouflage itself to blend in with its environment and avoid detection altogether. Cool!

 Speaking|Answer Explanations #2

Recording #9

4. **(Professor)** Today, we will discuss symbiotic relationships, particularly through examples that exist within the ocean. There are different types of symbiosis, but generally it can be defined as a long-term and close relationship between two different species. In symbiotic relationships, one or both species will benefit from the relationship. The two types of symbiotic relationships that we will focus on today are commensalism and mutualism.

In a commensal relationship, one species is unaffected by the relationship, while the other species benefits. An example of a commensal relationship in the ocean is that of remora and sea turtles. Remora are a fish that attach themselves to larger animals such as sea turtles. Through this relationship, remora benefit through transportation, food scraps, and protection, while the species they are attached to are unharmed by this attachment. Another example of a commensal relationship is the relationship between Imperial shrimp and sea cucumbers. The Imperial shrimp benefits, while the sea cucumber is unaffected. Imperial shrimp ride on the sea cucumber, relying on it for food and transportation. In mutualist symbiotic relationships, both species that are involved benefit from the relationship. One example of a mutual symbiotic relationship is that of the pistol shrimp and goby. Pistol shrimp will both dig and maintain a burrow, during which the shrimp will feed the goby through invertebrates that are disturbed in the process. The shrimp will then eat what is left after the goby feasts. In return, the goby provides protection to the pistol shrimp, being that the goby has much better eyesight. The goby will place its fin on the antennae of the shrimp when they are outside of the burrow. If the goby senses danger, it will flip its fin which signals to the shrimp to return to the burrow. Another mutual relationship is that of clownfish and sea anemones. The clownfish are safe from the sting of the anemone, which allows them to live within sea anemones, providing them with shelter and protection. The sea anemone benefits through the clownfish providing food and protection from predatory fish and parasites.

Speaking Sample Response Transcripts

Recording #10

1. I think I like the idea of having a vacation with friends. In my family, people are all different ages and so they have different abilities or things they want to do. My little sister is three years old and my grandmother lives with me and would have to join the vacation. I probably wouldn't be able to go rock climbing or do more active and hard activities if they are with me. My friends are close to my age and we have similar hobbies and can physically do the same things, so I think a vacation with them would be more fun. I like to get out and be active on a vacation. My friends are the same way. However, my family more enjoys relaxing and napping. It would be better with friends.

Recording #11

2. The student is happy to hear to that the university is lowering tuition by 15 percent. The university says that it's hard times for students because the cost of housing has gone up. The student says that this is true. She knows because her rent was lower when she started college. It was $300 then. Now it is tripled. Wow, that's $900! Since she goes to school full time, she doesn't have time to work and make enough money to pay for school and also a place to live. The university also hopes that lower tuition will

172

make more people apply to the college. She thinks that this is a great idea because people will want to save money so they will choose this school over other ones.

Recording #12

3. Evolutionary biological mimicry is what harmless plants or animals do to have a good chance of surviving. They survive better by scaring away predators. It fools predators visually and auditorily. One animal that does this is the kingsnake. The hawk is its predator. The king snake evolved so that it looks like a coral snake. Coral snakes are venomous, so looking like a coral snake makes the kingsnake seem dangerous to the hawk, but it is really harmless. Another animal that does biological mimicry is the mimic octopus. It's able to make itself look like at least three other animals in the ocean that are poisonous. These are the lionfish, sea snake, and banded sole. This makes predators avoid the mimic octopus. It can probably look like more creatures.

Recording #13

4. Symbiosis is when two species have a relationship that is beneficial to at least one of them. In the ocean, two types of symbiotic relationships can happen. Commensalism is the type where one species is helped and the other one isn't affected. An example is when a Remora fish attaches to a sea turtle and uses it as transportation and to get food. It doesn't help or hurt the turtle, but the fish is protected by the turtle. Another example is when the imperial shrimp rides on the sea cucumber. A mutual symbiotic relationship is the other type. Both species benefit. An example is the Pistol Shrimp and the Goby fish. The shrimp digs a burrow and disturbs invertebrates that the fish will eat. Then the shrimp eats the leftovers. The shrimp can't see good so the fish helps it by using its fin to let the shrimp know if there is danger. Clownfish also have this type of relationship with the sea anemone. It can't be stung by the anemone so it lives in the anemone so predators can't get to it. It brings the anemone food, so the anemone benefits too.

Writing

Listen to all of these passages by going to testprepbooks.com/bonus/toefl, or by scanning the QR code below:

Sample Integrated Writing Response

The effects of technology on society are the topics of the passage and the lecture. The lecture describes ways that technology has had a negative impact, while the passage describes how it has made a positive impact.

The first thing discussed in the lecture is the negative impact that technology has had on society due to the internet and social media. Things like cyberbullying and photoshopping are causing mental health problems for people. Rather than connecting people and helping with loneliness and social anxiety, which are discussed as positive benefits of technology in the reading passage, the lecture states that people who use the internet actually have more anxiety and depression than those who don't use it.

Next, the lecture explains how more aspects of health are impacted by technology. The internet and video games can be very addictive, so people spend more time sitting doing that than getting up and exercising. Looking at screens can make the eyes strain. In children who use screens a lot, they have less attention span and do worse in school. On the other hand, the passage describes how technology has helped in the area of health by making blood tests accurate and fast and how people can keep track of their medical history and records with electronic health records.

The last thing about technology is education. The person giving the lecture says that since anyone can post anything on the internet, people get bad information and spread it and that this is harmful to society. In contrast, the author of the passage says that being knowledgeable is easier due to technology because people no longer have to go to the library or talk to an expert if they want information.

Sample Academic Writing Response

I believe that the rise of AI is inevitable. Technology is already taking over jobs and automating tasks that have long been the responsibility of humans. For example, cashiers are being replaced by self-checkout stations. It would be in the best interest of everybody for lawmakers to come up with restrictions for AI. Otherwise, AI will take over more jobs such as teachers, therapists, and accountants. Without people working, our economy will suffer, and the quality of life will decline for everybody. What will people do once they lose their jobs, their sense of purpose, and their ability to contribute to their community? This cannot continue.

Integrated Writing Lecture Transcript

Recording #14

(Professor) Although technology has undeniably helped society, the effect of its advancement is largely negative. Different facets of life have been damaged by technology, including the physical and mental well-being of technology users. These downfalls show that technology is often not worth the positive changes it can have.

Technological advancement has led to new forms of communication, such as email and social media. While some might argue that these are positive means of connecting with other people, they have been undeniably damaging to a large portion of society. Social media leads to cyberbullying, where people are judged and ridiculed online. Photoshopping and catered content has enforced unrealistic beauty

174

standards. This can be damaging for young people exploring the internet. People on social media tend to feel more anxiety and depression than those who are not.

While technology has helped the medical field advance, it has also hurt the physical well-being of individuals. The internet, video games, and other forms of media can be highly addictive. This means that people want to spend more time being sedentary online than maintaining their physical health with exercise. Merely using technology can be damaging. Eye strain from too much screen time is a common physical ailment for technology users. There is also a connection between children using screens too much and poorer attention spans and performance in school. Social media's beauty standards can lead to eating disorders and issues with body image. These are all physical and mental health problems that technology has directly caused.

The third way that technology has been harmful is through education. While the internet allows people to gain access to knowledge of all types, it has also led to misinformation and disinformation. People can post nearly anything that they want to on the internet. This means that they can put out false statements and lies with no consequences. Misinformation is shared and spreads to many people who believe what they are reading. This is problematic for news regarding politics, health, history, and more. This type of disingenuous discourse is harmful to society.

Reading

Questions 1–10 are based on the following passage:

The Maya were one of the indigenous civilizations who inhabited Mesoamerica prior to the colonization by the Spanish in the sixteenth century. Mesoamerica was comprised of the areas that are currently known as Mexico and Central America. In comparison to other indigenous groups of a similar time and place, the Maya had a more concentrated population rather than a scattered population. They lived in the areas that are modern-day Mexico, Belize, Guatemala, and parts of El Salvador and Honduras. Within the larger area that they populated, there were three general sub-areas: the Southern highlands and the Central and Northern lowlands. The Maya established many cities here. One example is Nakbe in modern-day Guatemala, which was dated to sometime around 750 BC. **A**

Chichen Itza is an important archaeological site located on the Yucatan Peninsula in Mexico, which placed it within the Northern lowlands. **B** *Chichen* means "at the mouth of the well." It was a sacred city established during the fifth century AD (the classical period of archaeology) by the Itza, who were Mayan. The exact time of its establishment is uncertain. **C** Studying this site and others like it has helped researchers better understand the life of the Itza/Maya. It is generally believed that the city was founded due to the cenotes it contained. A cenote is a sinkhole in which a cave's ceiling has collapsed, revealing the water within it. The Xtoloc cenote and the Sacred cenote are two examples within Chichen Itza. It is believed that the Maya used cenotes to make offerings. During ceremonies, they would throw objects and sometimes human sacrifices into a cenote. **D**

The Chichen Itza also contains the pyramid El Castillo, also known as the Pyramid of Kukulkan. It was constructed in honor of Kukulkan, the feathered serpent god of storms, rain, wind, and life. The Maya believed that Kukulkan brought the winds and rain. There are various ways that El Castillo shows aspects of Mayan life, including its representation of their calendar. The spring and autumn equinoxes were an important part of Mayan agriculture. Corn, for example, was to be planted at the time of the spring equinox and harvested at the time of the autumn equinox. During these equinoxes, there is an effect that is created by the light and shadows that are cast across the pyramid. As the sun sets, the light and shadows work together to give the appearance of a snake traveling down the stairs of the pyramid. These diamond-shaped shadows lead down to the serpent heads at the base of the stairs. Not only does this effect occur at the equinoxes, but other aspects of its design are also connected to the calendar. El Castillo is a four-sided pyramid with ninety-one steps on each side. These 364 steps, in addition to the one platform at the top, make 365 for the number of days within a year. The four sides also connect to the two solstices (winter and summer) and the two equinoxes (spring and autumn). There are eighteen months within the Mayan religious calendar. This is represented by El Castillo's eighteen terraces. The pyramid also has

fifty-two panels that represent the Maya's solar and religious calendar's fifty-two-year cycle. It has also been discovered that there is a cenote hidden underneath El Castillo that was intentionally sealed off by the Maya.

Chichen Itza also shows something about Maya life through its sacbeob. Sacbeob are the paved paths or roads that connected the various buildings of Chichen Itza. These roads predate the roads of ancient Italy that led to Rome. Another notable detail is that researchers believe that, while with time they have worn down to the stone's gray, the buildings were once painted in bright colors. Researchers continue to explore the site to learn about the life of the Maya. While Chichen Itza was a major point for many years, researchers believe it began to decline partly due to drought, during which a nearby city called Mayapán began to flourish. Eventually, the Spanish arrived and conquered Chichen Itza as part of their colonization of the Americas.

1. The use of the word *offering* in this passage is closest in meaning to:
   a. Tribute
   b. Donation
   c. Contribution
   d. Bidding

2. The phrase *studying this site* in paragraph 2 refers to:
   a. Nakbe
   b. El Castillo
   c. Chichen Itza
   d. The Northern Lowlands

3. Which of the following choices best communicates the important information of the sentence that is highlighted? Incorrect answer choices exclude pertinent information or misrepresent information.
   a. In Chichen Itza, the buildings are believed to have been painted bright colors before fading over time.
   b. Researchers believe that the buildings were once brightly painted before fading to the stone's natural gray.
   c. It's believed that some of the buildings of Chichen Itza and other Mayan cities were once brightly painted.
   d. Researchers are continuing to work to understand what Mayan life was like, including what the infrastructure that they built likely looked like at the time.

4. Find the four areas where the letters **A**, **B**, **C**, and **D** are located. These spaces indicate where the following sentence might be added to the passage.

   While others found the site of Chichen Itza before them, in 1841 John Lloyd Stephens and Frederick Catherwood's travels through the site were the first to be documented.

In which area does the sentence best fit?
   a. A
   b. B
   c. C
   d. D

177

5. According to paragraph 3, all the following are true of El Castillo EXCEPT:
    a.   Various features of El Castillo are representative of the Mayan calendar.
    b.   On the equinoxes, an optical illusion is created by how light and shadows bounce on El Castillo.
    c.   El Castillo was created in honor of the feathered serpent god called Kukulkan.
    d.   El Castillo has four sides, which represent the four agricultural seasons.

6. Which of the following can be inferred about the archaeological research of the Maya based on paragraph 4?
    a.   The next step in researching the Maya is to focus research on Mayapán.
    b.   There is still much to learn about the Maya through continued research.
    c.   There are many conflicting reports regarding the use of sacbeob in Mayan cities.
    d.   Researchers believe there is little left to learn from Chichen Itza.

7. According to paragraph 1, which of the following is true of the Maya?
    a.   The Maya established various cities that thrived within the three sub-areas in which they lived.
    b.   The Mayas lived dispersed throughout Central and Latin America.
    c.   One of the general sub-areas in which the Maya lived was the Southern lowlands.
    d.   The Maya established Chichen Itza around the year 750 BC.

8. In paragraph 2, why does the author include information about cenotes?
    a.   To explain what a cenote is
    b.   To illustrate an aspect of Mayan life through one natural feature
    c.   To support the explanation of Mayan ceremonies
    d.   To explain the purpose of cenotes in Mayan life and city establishment

9. The use of *contained* is closest in meaning to:
    a.   Accommodated
    b.   Included
    c.   Comprised
    d.   Held

10. An opening sentence is provided to create a summary of the given passage above. Choose THREE answer choices that state the important ideas of the passage.

> The Maya, an indigenous civilization of Mesoamerica, inhabited parts of modern-day Mexico and Central America leading up to the Spanish colonization of the sixteenth century.

1.

2.

3.

a. Chichen Itza, an important archaeological site, is now studied to learn about the life of the Maya through its various buildings and the land it was founded upon.
b. The Mayan city of Chichen Itza, now an archaeological site, was established in the Yucatan Peninsula in Mexico near cenotes, which were used as a part of ceremonies.
c. The light and shadow effects that arrive with the equinox on El Castillo were likely connected to agricultural markers for the time of planting and time of harvest.
d. El Castillo is a pyramid honoring Kukulkan that contains representations of the Mayan calendar through its various features, including an illusion that occurs with the equinoxes.
e. With the decline of Chichen Itza, another nearby city called Mayapán was able to thrive until the Spanish colonization of the sixteenth century.
f. Chichen Itza eventually declined prior to colonization, and now researchers are piecing together what life there was like, including how the buildings were painted and the existence of paved roads.

Questions 11–20 are based on the following passage:

Air pollution is created when chemicals and other pollutants fill the air. It is damaging to the Earth and the health of the beings that inhabit it. There are both natural and man-made pollutants. Some natural pollutants include ash, salt spray, radon, and sulfur dioxide. Man-made pollutants, or anthropogenic sources of pollution, come from various human activities. They are by-products of different activities such as the burning of fossil fuels or the production of chemicals. One example is vehicular transportation, which can emit carbon dioxide, nitrogen dioxide, and more. Air pollution can take different forms including gases and liquid droplets.

A lot of air pollution occurs within cities. Smog is one type of air pollution that is more common in urban areas. The term *smog* was created by a physician Dr. Henry Antoine Des Voeux from London, England in the early 1900s. In 1905, he released a paper using the word to describe the mix of smoke and fog that was seen often in industrial areas. There are two types of smog. The first is sulfurous smog, which is created by the burning

of fossil fuels that contain sulfur, such as coal. **A** Smog of today is different from the smog described by Dr. Des Voeux. It is photochemical and created by the sunlight reacting with volatile organic compounds (VOCs) and nitrogen oxides. **B** These come from the emissions of fossil fuels being burned by cars, factories, and more. This process creates ground-level ozone, which is different from the ozone layer of the Earth.

The ozone layer is a layer within the Earth's atmosphere. The Earth's atmosphere contains multiple layers going from the Earth and outward: the troposphere, the stratosphere, the mesosphere, the thermosphere, and the exosphere. The ozone layer is within the stratosphere. The higher it is in the stratosphere, the warmer it is due to the absorption of UV rays and radiation from the sun. There are two types of UV rays: UVA rays and UVB rays. Due to the release of chlorofluorocarbons (CFCs) from plastic into the stratosphere over many years, the ozone layer has thinned out. The thinning of the ozone layer allows more UV radiation into the troposphere, which is harmful to people's health. **C** Too much exposure to air pollution is also harmful to human health, particularly lung health. People may experience different effects depending on the length of exposure. Short-term exposure can cause symptoms such as headache and difficulty breathing, as well as conditions such as pneumonia. Long-term exposure to various types of air pollution can cause more serious issues, including cancer, damage to the cardiovascular or nervous systems, and harm to other organs such as the lungs and liver. It also impacts the health of animals and plants. The harmful effects are similar in animals and humans, as pollution causes animals to have respiratory issues as well. It can also cause animals to develop neurological issues. Air pollution harms plants by damaging the stomata, the cells within leaves that allow them to absorb carbon dioxide and release oxygen. Some plants are more vulnerable to damage than others. Air pollution also contributes to the creation of acid rain. Rain that is not contaminated usually has a pH of around 5.6, making it slightly acidic. The pH of acid rain is usually 4.5 or lower. Acid rain occurs when pollution from nitrogen oxide and sulfur dioxide combines with rainwater.

Air pollution does not only occur outdoors but can occur indoors as well. This comes from substances being burned, from radon building up within homes, or from potentially harmful materials that are used within homes. **D** Many of the emissions that contribute to air pollution are created by companies. These corporations could create fewer emissions by using different sources of energy and different materials. The specific steps that could be taken depend on the type of corporation in question. Even though individuals create fewer emissions than corporations do, there are ways for individuals to further limit their contributions to pollution as well. Some of these measures include limiting fires and only burning firewood; taking public transportation; working from home rather than driving; and using fewer appliances, vehicles, and tools that are powered by gas.

11. The use of the word *exposure* in this passage is closest in meaning to:
    a. Introduction
    b. Subjection
    c. Divulgence
    d. Publication

12. The phrase *these come from* in paragraph 2 refers to:
    a. Carbon dioxide
    b. Sulfur and nitrogen oxides
    c. VOCs and nitrogen oxides
    d. Volatile organic compounds

13. Which of the following choices best communicates the important information of the sentence that is highlighted? Incorrect answer choices exclude pertinent information or misrepresent information.
    a. Air pollution can cause respiratory issues in animals and humans.
    b. Air pollution can lead to similar issues in both animals and humans.
    c. Pollution can lead to respiratory issues in various animals.
    d. Pollution causes issues to humans, plants, and animals; in particular it causes respiratory issues in humans and animals.

14. According to paragraph 4, which of the following is true of indoor air pollution?
    a. Pollution of indoor air primarily comes from outdoor air entering buildings.
    b. Indoor air pollution can be caused by burning things inside of homes.
    c. Air pollution indoors only comes from harmful materials that are used in construction.
    d. Indoor air pollution can come from chemicals such as ozone building up within homes.

15. Which of the following can be inferred about the ozone layer based on paragraph 3?
    a. Exposure to ozone is far worse than exposure to the various chemicals in air pollution.
    b. The ozone layer plays an important role in maintaining the health of the people and animals that inhabit the Earth.
    c. The ozone layer plays a larger role in maintaining the habitability of the Earth than other layers of the Earth's atmosphere.
    d. The thinning of the ozone layer likely does not cause any large issues, as this occurs naturally.

16. According to paragraph 3, all the following are true of smog EXCEPT:
    a. The term was created by Dr. Des Voeux in a 1905 paper.
    b. Photochemical smog consists of a reaction of VOCs and nitrogen oxide with sunlight.
    c. Much of today's smog is created by the burning of fossil fuels and creates ground-level ozone.
    d. The smog of today is called sulfurous smog and is created by burning coal.

17. Find the four areas where the letters A, B, C, and D are located. These spaces indicate where the following sentence might be added to the passage.

> While much of the world is exposed to pollution, the severity of pollution varies in different parts of the world.

In which area does the sentence best fit?
    a. A
    b. B
    c. C
    d. D

181

18. In paragraph 3, why does the author include information about the health effects of air pollution?
    a. To illustrate the issues that much of the world is facing
    b. To note the effect that the ozone layer thinning has on people
    c. To explain one of the effects that air pollution has on the world
    d. To support the explanation of the thinning of the ozone layer

19. According to paragraph 3, all the following are true of the impact of air pollution on rain EXCEPT:
    a. Because rain is already slightly acidic, all rain is acid rain and air pollution doesn't impact it.
    b. Acid rain is created by the combination of rainwater with nitrogen oxide and sulfur dioxide.
    c. Rain that is not contaminated by pollution has a pH of about 5.6.
    d. Acid rain generally has a pH of 4.5 or lower.

20. An opening sentence is provided to create a summary of the given passage above. Choose THREE answer choices that state the important ideas of the passage.

> Air pollution comes from both natural and man-made sources, such as sulfur dioxide and the emissions created by burning fossil fuels respectively.

-
-
-

a. Sulfurous smog is created by burning fossil fuels such as coal, which contains sulfur.

b. The smog of today is photochemical and made by sunlight's reaction with VOCs and nitrogen oxides; it is different from the sulfurous smog that Dr. Des Voeux was discussing when he coined the term.

c. Pollution contributes to acid rain, the thinning of the ozone layer, and air pollution, which can have a negative effect on the health of people, animals, and plants.

d. The Earth has multiple layers within the atmosphere. The ozone layer, which absorbs UVA and UVB rays, is within the stratosphere.

e. Some of the potential long-term effects of air pollution on people include damage to the nervous or cardiovascular systems or harm to organs such as the liver or lungs.

f. Pollution occurs both inside and outside and is largely contributed to by corporations, though there are ways in which individuals can lower their emissions, such as by taking public transportation.

Listening

Directions: The Listening section measures your ability to understand conversations and lectures in English. In this test, you will listen to several pieces of content and answer questions after each one. The questions typically ask about the main idea and supporting details. Some questions ask about a speaker's purpose or attitude. Answer the questions based on what is stated or implied by the speakers.

Listen to all of these passages by going to testprepbooks.com/bonus/toefl, or by scanning the QR code below:

Note that on the actual test, you can take notes while you listen and use your notes to help you answer the questions. Your notes will not be scored.

For your convenience, the transcripts of all of the audio passages are provided after the answer explanations. However, on the actual test, no such transcripts will be provided.

Recording #1: Lecture

1. What is the professor discussing in this lecture?
   a. Why people play games
   b. Chess grandmaster Magnus Carlsen
   c. How play can influence us
   d. The concept of instrumental play

2. How does the professor define instrumental play?
   a. Play serving as a means to a goal
   b. Play with musical instruments
   c. Play with no specific purpose
   d. Play as a career

3. What does the professor mean when he says, "A natural assumption, but goals and play are like peanut butter and jelly."?
   a. Play can be very messy.
   b. Having a goal when you play helps keep you satisfied.
   c. Goals and play are heavily related to each other.
   d. Playing in pursuit of a goal is nutritious.

183

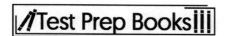

4. What makes up the conclusion of the professor's lecture?
   a. Asking a lot of hypothetical questions
   b. Asking the students why they play
   c. Defining the concept of instrumental play
   d. Justifying instrumental play as an idea

5. What is the likely effect of the professor asking so many hypothetical questions about play to the students?
   a. The students might be overwhelmed or confused.
   b. The students start frantically taking notes.
   c. The students reply without waiting for a prompt to respond.
   d. The students get up and leave the classroom in disgust.

6. What does the professor imply when he says, "Now, you might be naturally thinking that play isn't supposed to have a goal."?
   a. The students aren't thinking critically about the subject.
   b. Play should never have a goal.
   c. Goal-oriented play is superior to free play.
   d. People assume play isn't a complex subject.

Recording #2: Lecture

7. What is the professor discussing in this lecture?
   a. What the President does every day
   b. How a bill becomes a law
   c. How members of Congress get elected
   d. What a member of the Senate does every day

8. How many votes are required to pass a bill in the House?
   a. 145
   b. 200
   c. 218
   d. 256

9. Why does the professor mention cloture?
   a. To explain a solution to filibusters
   b. To start a debate with students
   c. To clarify a detail from earlier in the lecture
   d. To share an interesting fact

10. What does the professor imply when he says, "This is where the term "filibuster" comes up, and it's a bit of a controversial one."?
    a. Filibusters are a bad thing.
    b. Filibusters have nothing to do with debate.
    c. Debate should encourage the use of filibusters.
    d. There are different opinions about filibusters.

11. What step of the process for a bill passing the House goes in the blank?

Proposed -> Relevant Committee(s) ->___?___-> Debate -> Vote

   a. Speaker of the House
   b. Presidential review
   c. Debate committee
   d. Rules committee

12. What does the professor mean when he says, "At this point it's sort of like a group project for the committee."?
   a. The committee will have to grade each other's work.
   b. The committee is incapable of working together.
   c. The committee will have to work together on the bill.
   d. The committee needs to divide the work evenly.

Recording #3: Conversation

13. Why has the professor asked the student to stay after class?
   a. She wants to see if there is any way she can help him since she has noticed that his performance is not as good as it usually is.
   b. She wants to schedule a time before basketball practice to provide tutoring to the student.
   c. She wants to give him some suggestions to help with his bedtime routine.
   d. In order to commit to her New Year's resolution of not playing video games during her spare time, she's finding other ways to spend her downtime.

14. What is the professor's attitude when she says, "Education should come first, but I see your point."?
   a. She is angry and sarcastic.
   b. She is hesitant yet understanding.
   c. She embarrassed and apologetic.
   d. She is stubborn and committed to her opinion.

15. Which of the following did the professor wrongly assume?
   a. That the student is staying with friends and family.
   b. That the student recently moved into a new apartment.
   c. That the student is effectively homeless.
   d. That the student's parents bought a new house.

16. What does the teacher usually do during her downtime?
   a. Grades homework assignments
   b. Plays games on her phone
   c. Prepares lesson plans for the rest of the week
   d. Talks to students about their personal lives

17. What does "bouncing between friends' and relatives' homes" most likely mean?
   a. The student is excited about having more sleepovers.
   b. The student is temporarily staying with their relatives' friends.
   c. The student is moving between homes after short stays.
   d. The student is exploring options before deciding where to stay permanently.

Recording #4: Conversation

18. Why does the student meet with the academic advisor?
    a. The student needs to get the paperwork to change majors.
    b. The student is considering changing majors.
    c. The student needs to schedule her general education classes.
    d. The student wants to stay a fifth year to complete her degree.

19. If the student majors in creative writing and minors in British literature, which courses will she need to take for each? Place an "X" in the appropriate boxes.

	British Literature	Creative Writing
Three 100-level courses		
Four 100-level courses		
Two 300-level courses		
Three 300-level courses		
One 400-level course		
Two 400-level courses		
Capstone course		

20. Why does the student want to finish their classes before 3:00 p.m. next semester?
    a. The student needs more time to study for their new major and minor.
    b. The student plans to work more hours to pay for the summer semester.
    c. The student has several extracurricular commitments in the evenings.
    d. The student is trying to complete their degree in four years.

21. What is the student's attitude when she says, "Oh man, I didn't realize I'd be so far behind."?
    a. The student is angry.
    b. The student is embarrassed.
    c. The student is disappointed.
    d. The student is excited.

22. Why does the academic advisor tell the student that she could minor in British literature?
    a. He is recommending a way for the student to not lose the credits she has already acquired.
    b. He is disagreeing with her desire to change majors.
    c. He is agreeing that creative writing is a better major.
    d. He is suggesting ways to bring in more money for the university.

Recording #5: Lecture

23. What is the main idea of the lecture?
    a. Roman life was captured by the eruption of Vesuvius.
    b. Preservation is more important than excavation in Pompeii.
    c. Excavations of Pompeii are revealing but must be done properly.
    d. Digging in Pompeii has been damaging to the ruins.

24. What claim made during the beginning of the lecture is supported by the discovery of a horse at the Villa of the Mysteries? Select two answer choices.
    a. Ash from the eruption preserved the area.
    b. Pompeii would have more to reveal.
    c. Many were killed quickly from heat.
    d. The city was left in decay.

25. How is the lecture organized?
    a. The professor defines a term and follows with examples.
    b. The professor gives a chronological explanation of excavations and discoveries.
    c. The professor discusses the cause and then the effects of the volcanic eruption.
    d. The professor compares various excavation techniques.

26. Based on the lecture, how does the professor feel about Pompeii?
    a. Disinterested
    b. Intrigued
    c. Protective
    d. Hopeful

27. What method did researchers use to reveal body shapes?
    a. Finding mummified remains
    b. Filling voids with plaster
    c. Discovering remains preserved in ash
    d. Finding intact skeletons

28. Why is the Villa of Mysteries so well known?
    a. It's well preserved.
    b. It has a dog's skeleton.
    c. It has beautiful frescos.
    d. It has mummified remains.

Speaking

Listen to all of these passages by going to testprepbooks.com/bonus/toefl, or by scanning the QR code below:

1. Listen to the following audio recording and then answer the question:
    • Preparation Time: 15 seconds

187

• Response Time: 45 seconds

2. Read the following announcement and then listen to the conversation. Lastly, follow the instructions below.

Maplewood Food Hall Closure Due to Repairs and New Murals

As of Friday, Maplewood Food Hall will be closed for an indefinite amount of time. This is for two reasons. On Thursday night, multiple students engaged in a violent food fight that damaged tables, chairs, serving equipment, and windows. We must make the necessary repairs to ensure that Maplewood is a safe environment again. The second reason is that we will be taking this time to renovate the space with new murals, which will take months to complete.

In the meantime, please feel free to continue using Oakwood Food Hall on South Campus. It is about a twenty-minute walk from Maplewood Food Hall. We apologize for this inconvenience and hope that you will enjoy the coming changes.

Listen to the following conversation between two students:

Question: What are the female student's opinions regarding the announcement made by the university? Be sure to address her comments regarding both of the reasons given for the food hall closure.

• Reading Time: 30 seconds
• Response Time: 45 seconds

3. Read the following academic passage and then listen to the lecture. Finally, follow the instructions below.

Animal Hibernation

Hibernation is what some animals do to conserve energy to survive the winter. It can last anywhere from days to months. Some animals must hibernate because food may be scarce in the winter. Also, the environment may be harsh with cold temperatures and wind. By hibernating, the animal slows down their metabolism and lowers their body temperature. These physiological changes conserve the animal's energy. This means that they do not have to hunt and/or forage for food. Before hibernation, some prepare by eating large amounts of food to store energy in fat deposits. Some animals go into hibernation while pregnant and give birth during or soon afterwards.

Listen to the following lecture:

Instructions: Explain animal hibernation and discuss the examples provided by the professor.

• Preparation Time: 30 seconds
• Response Time: 60 seconds

Question 4. Listen to the following excerpt from a lecture and follow the instructions below:

188

Instructions: Using details and examples provided in the lecture, explain opportunity cost and the ways it can be calculated.

- Preparation Time: 20 seconds
- Response Time: 60 seconds

Writing

Listen to all of these passages by going to testprepbooks.com/bonus/toefl, or by scanning the QR code below:

Integrated Writing

First, read the passage below:

The Civil War is one of the most impactful events in American history. It began due to fundamental differences between states, yet in the end it brought together the entire nation. It changed the United States for the better in multiple ways.

One of the major accomplishments of the Civil War was the freeing of millions of slaves. In 1863, President Abraham Lincoln signed the Emancipation Proclamation, which freed all the slaves in Confederates states. He did so in the face of great opposition. The Union Army's purpose at that point was to liberate any enslaved people. This emergence of freedom and justice was one of the major victories that came out of the Civil War. It put the U.S. on a path to granting African American citizenship and uniting all people of the nation.

The Civil War helped the United States establish a more powerful federal government. The Civil War was an expensive endeavor, and the government was forced to abandon the gold standard. Paper money was put into circulation. The creation of national banking furthered the power of the federal government. Additionally, the government implemented national conscription and personal income tax. These changes made the government more centralized and powerful. This would be especially important on the world stage. The United States would become one of the most powerful countries on the planet due to its newfound governmental strength.

The Civil War changed the economy into something new. As mentioned, a new currency, banking system, and taxation system were formed. Before the war, the U.S. was an

189

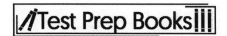

agricultural economy. The Civil War changed this, especially since the slave system and plantations were no longer an option. A free market emerged, and new industries boomed. Industrialization took the country by storm and people no longer relied on agriculture to support themselves. This new free market economy continued and still functions today.

Now listen to the following lecture:

3. Prompt: Summarize the points presented in the lecture. Explain how they relate to specific points in the reading passage.

You have 20 minutes to write your essay.

The following pages are provided for writing your essay.

190

Academic Discussion

First, read the following online academic discussion between a professor and some students:

Instructor: Fossil fuels power much of the world as we know it. However, some fossil fuels undeniably hurt the environment. Alternatives are more costly to develop and may not be as effective for powering large areas, such as the United States. Should there be a focus on moving away from fossil fuels?

Student 1: I don't believe that we should be pursuing alternative energy methods right now. The United States is already suffering from enormous debt. The infrastructure that we use every day is failing. Bridges, roads, and railways are deteriorating. The country cannot keep up with maintenance. The future is important, of course, but this country needs to focus on problems that are far more pressing than developing new energy sources that we ultimately don't need at this very moment.

Student 2: I believe that we should focus on utilizing all energy options. While it might not be feasible to use renewable energy for 100 percent of the country, it wouldn't hurt to implement it in certain areas. Solar energy could be used in areas that get a lot of full sun coverage year-round. Wind energy can be used in areas that often experience high winds. There is no reason to not decrease our reliance on fossil fuels. They are not renewable and will not last forever.

Next, add your opinion to the conversation using 100 words or more.

You have 10 minutes to write your response.

The following pages are provided for writing your essay.

Answer Explanations #3

Reading

Recording #1

1. A: The use of *offering* in this passage is closest in meaning to Choice *A, tribute*, as these offerings are part of a ceremony. The other choices, though similar in meaning, do not accurately represent the intentions of these offerings as being part of a ceremony.

2. C: The phrase *studying this site* in paragraph 2 refers to Chichen Itza, as it describes the purpose of studying a site like Chichen Itza. Nakbe and El Castillo are not being referenced at this point. Chichen Itza is within the Northern lowlands, but the city/site of Chichen Itza is being specifically referenced here.

3. B: The sentence that best incorporates all the important information accurately and more precisely is Choice *B.* Choices *A* and *C* are not as precise and don't include the mention of researchers believing that the buildings were once painted. Choice *D* doesn't portray the information within the highlighted sentence.

4. C: Choice *C* places the sentence in relation to the mention of how the site of Chichen Itza is studied and includes further information about the first study of it that was documented. Choice *A* is incorrect, as it places the sentence prior to the mention of Chichen Itza. Choice *B* is incorrect, as it places the sentence prior to the mention of the site being studied. Choice *D* is incorrect, as it places the sentence following information about cenotes and ceremonies. Because of this, Choice *C* is the most appropriate placement of this sentence.

5. D: The correct choice is the one statement that is incorrect regarding El Castillo: its four sides are representative of the two equinoxes and two solstices and are connected to agriculture. Choice *D* states that it is representative of the four agricultural seasons. The other choices are all accurate statements about El Castillo: various features are representative of the Mayan calendar, an optical illusion is created on the equinoxes, and it was created in honor of Kukulkan.

6. B: The statement that can be inferred is that there is still much to learn about the Maya through continued research. The other choices cannot be inferred because there is no direction implied for future research to go, there is no mention of conflicting research, and there is more research that can be done.

7. A: The only true statement within the given choices is Choice *A,* that the Maya established various cities that flourished within three general sub-areas. The other choices are inaccurate because the Maya had a more concentrated rather than scattered population, the Southern sub-area was the Southern highlands, and Nakbe was established around 750 BC.

8. D: Information about cenotes is first mentioned in relation to why Chichen Itza was likely established in the area that it was and what the Maya used cenotes for. Because of this, Choice *D* is the correct answer, as the purpose of cenotes in Mayan life and cities is the reason for their inclusion. Choice *A* is incorrect, as while it is explained what cenotes are, that is not why they were included within the

passage. Choices *B* and *C* are incorrect because they only include part of the purpose of including cenotes.

9. B: The use of *contained* within the passage is closest in meaning to *included*, as it is used to explain sites that are included in Chichen Itza. *Accommodated*, *comprised*, and *held* do not accurately portray the idea that these buildings and other structures are included within the area of Chichen Itza.

10. B, D, F: The correct choices for the summary are Choice *B,* Choice *D,* and Choice *F:* the Mayan city of Chichen Itza, now an archaeological site, was established in the Yucatan Peninsula in Mexico near cenotes, which were used as a part of ceremonies; El Castillo is a pyramid honoring Kukulkan that contains representations of the Mayan calendar through its various features, including an illusion that occurs with the equinoxes; Chichen Itza eventually declined prior to colonization, and now researchers are piecing together what life and cities were like, including the buildings being painted and the existence of paved roads. Including other choices within the summary would leave out important information from the passage.

11. B: The use of *exposure* within this passage is closest in meaning to *subjection*, as people are subjected to or exposed to air pollution. *Introduction*, *divulgence*, and *publication* are all similar to *exposure* but have different implications. Being introduced implies being introduced intentionally to something new, divulgence would mean to reveal something, and publishing something would involve making information known.

12. C: The phrase *these come from* in paragraph 2 refers to VOCs and nitrogen oxides because the sentence explains where *these* come from, and *these* are VOCs and nitrogen oxides, which come from burning fossil fuels and are a part of photochemical smog. Choice *A*, carbon dioxide, is not referenced at this point in the passage. Choices *B* and *D* include one portion of what is being referenced but are not correct, as they do not mention both VOCs and nitrogen oxides.

13. A: Choice *A* is correct, as it contains all the important information in the given sentence: air pollution can cause respiratory issues in animals and humans. The other choices leave out important aspects or include other information. Choice *B* does not reference respiratory issues; Choice *C* doesn't mention that pollution can cause respiratory issues in humans as well; and Choice *D* also includes plants, which are not included in the original sentence.

14. B: Choice *B* is correct, as indoor air pollution can be caused by burning things inside. The other choices are incorrect statements about indoor air pollution: indoor pollution can come from various things, not just outdoor pollution or harmful materials, and ozone is not mentioned as being a chemical that builds up as a part of indoor pollution.

15. B: The thinning of the ozone layer contributes to potential health issues; therefore, it can be inferred that the ozone layer plays a part in maintaining the health of people and animals. Choice *A* is incorrect because there is no information regarding what pollutant is worse than others, and ground-level ozone (smog) is a part of air pollution. Choice *C* is incorrect, as there is no information given about the roles of other layers of the atmosphere, therefore a judgment cannot be made about the importance of the different roles they play. Choice *D* also cannot be inferred because there are issues attributed to the thinning of the ozone layer, and it is occurring due to fossil fuel emissions, which are not natural.

16. D: Choice *D* is correct, as it is the only incorrect statement about smog. Photochemical smog is generally what is found today, not sulfurous smog. The other choices are incorrect, as they are all true

statements about smog: the term was created in a 1905 paper by Dr. Des Voeux; photochemical smog is a combination of VOCs and nitrogen oxides and their reaction with sunlight; and much of today's smog is created by burning fossil fuels, which creates ground-level ozone.

17. C: The given sentence best fits in Choice *C*, as it places a sentence about much of the world being exposed to air pollution along with an explanation of the health effects of exposure. Choice *A* is incorrect, as it places the sentence next to information about sulfurous smog. Choice *B* is incorrect, as it places the sentence next to information about photochemical smog. Choice *D* is incorrect, as it places the sentence next to information about pollution and how it can be reduced.

18. C: The author includes information about the health effects of air pollution to explain one effect that air pollution has on the world. Choice *A* is incorrect ,as while air pollution can affect many, the passage does not focus on general issues of the world but on information about air pollution. Choice *B* is incorrect because it is not just the effect of ozone, but of air pollution in general. Choice *D* is incorrect because the information about air pollution's health effects is about more than the ozone layer, and the thinning of the ozone layer adds to the explanation of what makes up air pollution.

19. A: Choice *A* is correct because it is the one incorrect statement about air pollution's impact on rain. Not all rain is acid rain, acid rain is rain that is contaminated with chemicals and has a pH of 4.5 or lower. The other choices are all correct statements about acid rain: acid rain is created by rain combining with nitrogen oxide and sulfur dioxide, rain that is not contaminated by pollution has a pH of about 5.6, and acid rain generally has a pH of 4.5 or lower.

20. B, C, F: The correct choices are Choice *B,* Choice *C,* and Choice *F:* The smog of today is photochemical and made by sunlight's reaction with VOCs and nitrogen oxides, which is different from the sulfurous smog discussed by Dr. Des Voeux when he coined the term; pollution contributes to acid rain and to the thinning of the ozone layer, which adds to air pollution that can have a negative effect on the health of people, animals, and plants; pollution occurs both inside and outside and is largely contributed to by corporations, though there are ways in which individuals can lower their emissions, such as by taking public transportation. Including the other choices within the summary would exclude important information from the summary.

Listening

Listen to all of these passages by going to testprepbooks.com/bonus/toefl, or by scanning the QR code below:

Recording #1: Lecture

1. D: The professor's lecture is about explaining the concept of instrumental play. It's about a more specific idea than just why people play games, so Choice *A* is incorrect. The lecture does mention Magnus Carlsen, but he is not the main focus, so Choice *B* is incorrect. The lecture does discuss some ways play can influence people early on, but it is not the main focus either, so Choice *C* is incorrect.

2. A: The professor says that instrumental play is any kind of play in service of a specific goal. It isn't play with musical instruments, so Choice *B* is incorrect. Play with no purpose is essentially the opposite of instrumental play, so Choice *C* is incorrect. Play as a career could be considered a type of instrumental play, but is too specific to be the definition, so Choice *D* is incorrect.

3. C: The professor intends to suggest that goals and play are two heavily related concepts by referring to peanut butter and jelly since this is a a common combination for a sandwich. He isn't trying to suggest that play is messy, so Choice *A* is incorrect. He isn't implying that goals during play keep someone satisfied or are somehow nutritious, so Choices *B* and *D* are both incorrect.

4. B: The professor concludes his lecture by asking his students a direct question about why they play, giving them something to consider for the future. The professor's hypothetical questions make up the latter part of his lecture but aren't really the conclusion, so Choice *A* is incorrect. Choice *C* is incorrect because defining instrumental play is one of the first things he does in the lecture. Choice *D* is similarly incorrect since the professor justifies instrumental play after defining it.

5. A: The professor doesn't really give the students time to think or expand on the hypothetical questions he is asking, so the most likely outcome of this is that the students become a bit confused or overwhelmed by having to switch what they're thinking about so often, making Choice *A* correct. Choice *B* is possible, but the professor is not following up on most of his questions to allow students to take notes on them, so it's incorrect compared to Choice *A*. Choice *C* is unlikely since the professor is not giving the students any opportunity to respond, so it is incorrect. The professor is not saying anything especially negative or demeaning that would suggest that the students would want to leave the class, so Choice *D* is incorrect.

201

6. D: By addressing a counterargument here, the professor is trying to imply that play is a more complex subject than people tend to think. He isn't trying to say anything specific about the students, so Choice A is incorrect. The professor isn't trying to state that play should never have a goal in mind, so Choice B is incorrect. He also isn't trying to imply that goal-focused play is somehow superior to free play, so Choice C is also incorrect.

Recording #2: Lecture

7. B: The purpose of the professor's lecture is to explain the process of how a bill becomes a law. It doesn't discuss the President's daily actions, so Choice A is incorrect. It doesn't discuss the process of electing members of Congress, so Choice C is incorrect. While Senate members are involved, the lecture's focus is not really about the Senate members, so Choice D is incorrect.

8. C: The lecture mentions that 218 votes are necessary to pass a bill in the House. 145 and 200 are too low, so Choices A and B are incorrect. 256 is too high, so Choice D is incorrect.

9. A: The professor starts to talk about cloture as an answer to filibusters being a problem in debate, so Choice A is correct. He doesn't start a debate with students about cloture, so Choice B is incorrect. The professor doesn't refer back to an earlier detail when talking about cloture, so Choice C is incorrect. The tone of the lecture doesn't imply that cloture is simply a side fact, but instead that it is relevant to the current topic, so Choice D is incorrect.

10. D: The professor is implying that there are different opinions about filibusters that make it a nuanced issue. Choices A, B, and C are incorrect because the professor focuses on the factual explanation of filibusters and how they are used, and doesn't insert his own opinion about whether the filibuster is a good or bad thing.

11. D: The lecture explains that after being refined in relevant House committees, the bill goes to the House Rules committee before it goes on to debate on the House floor. It has to go to Rules before going to the Speaker of the House, so Choice A is incorrect. The President doesn't review the bill until much later in the process, so Choice B is incorrect. There isn't a specific committee for debating a bill, so Choice C is incorrect.

12. C: By referring to a group project, the professor is implying that members of the committee will have to work together when discussing and editing a bill. He doesn't mean that committee members will have to evaluate each other, so Choice A is incorrect. He also isn't implying that the committee is unable to work together at all, so Choice B is incorrect. Choice D is similar, referring to how the committee will have to split the work evenly. However, it is more accurate to say that the committee will have to work together rather than splitting the work, so Choice C is more correct here than Choice D.

Recording #3: Conversation

13. A: Choice A is correct. She says, "Your performance on our last few assignments has not been up to your usual standard. Is there anything I can help you with?" Choice B is incorrect. They do discuss the times that each would be available to meet, and basketball practice is mentioned, but the professor does not ask the student to stay after class to ask about meeting with him specifically before basketball practice. Choice C is incorrect because the professor doesn't know until the conversation has started that the student's sleep schedule is off. Therefore, this cannot be the reason that she asked him to stay after class. Choice D is incorrect. The professor's New Year's resolution is brought up near the end of

conversation as part of her explanation for why it would be no trouble to meet with the student during her free time on Tuesday mornings.

14. B: When the professor says, "Education should come first," her tone indicates that she is hesitant to put more importance on anything besides education, but when she says, "I see your point," she shows understanding for the student's wishes to keep his home life separate from basketball. Choice A is incorrect. No anger or sarcasm can be detected in her tone of voice or what she says. Choice C is incorrect. The professor does not sound embarrassed and she doesn't apologize or sound sorry. Choice D is incorrect because the professor offers to meet with the student at a different time instead of insisting to meet with him before basketball practice. Additionally, her tone does not sound like she's being stubborn and the fact that she says, "but I see your point," proves that she is not committing to opinion and being stubborn.

15. D: After the student mentions that his family is in the process of moving, the professor wrongly assumes the student's parents bought a house. Thus, Choice D is the correct answer. It's true the student is staying with friends and family, so this can't be an incorrect assumption. Therefore, Choice A is incorrect. The professor asks if the student was moving to an apartment, which isn't an assumption. Therefore, Choice B is incorrect. The student is effectively homeless, but the professor doesn't make this assumption. Therefore, Choice C is incorrect.

16. B: When the student says he doesn't want to trouble the professor by meeting with her, the professor explains that it's not a problem because she typically wastes time playing games on her phone during her downtime. Thus, Choice B is the correct answer. The professor doesn't mention grading homework assignments or preparing lesson plans. Therefore, Choice A and Choice C are both incorrect. The professor talks about the student's personal life during this conversation, but the professor doesn't say that's what she typically does during her downtime. Therefore, Choice D is incorrect.

17. C: The student says he's been "bouncing between friends' and relatives' homes" after his family was evicted. This most likely means the student is staying with a number of different people on a temporary basis. Thus, Choice C is the correct answer. The student mentions that he's excited to have sleepovers with his cousins, but that doesn't explain the meaning of this phrase. Therefore, Choice A is incorrect. The student is temporarily staying with friends and relatives, but he doesn't mention relatives' friends. Therefore, Choice B is incorrect. Choice D is incorrect because the student doesn't characterize this issue as a search for a permanent home.

Recording #4: Conversation

18. B: The student meets with the academic advisor because she is considering changing majors, so Choice B is correct. Choice A is incorrect. The reason for the meeting with the academic advisor is not to get the paperwork to change majors. The advisor mentions that it will be needed, but this is not the reason for the conversation. Choice C is incorrect. The student does ask if her general education credits will count toward her new major, but this isn't the reason for her conversation with the academic advisor. Choice D in incorrect. The student mentions that she does not want to stay a fifth year. Although she wants to change majors and she will need to take extra classes, she does not meet with the academic advisor to discuss staying a fifth year to complete the degree.

19.

	British Literature	Creative Writing
Three 100-level courses		✖
Four 100-level courses		
Two 300-level courses	✖	
Three 300-level courses		✖
One 400-level course		
Two 400-level courses		
Capstone course		✖

Since the student has already taken several British literature courses, the academic advisor suggests minoring in British literature because the student would only need to take two 300-level courses. There are no other course requirements for the minor, so none of the other answer choices apply for a minor in British literature. The student is only just beginning a creative writing major, so there are significant course requirements. The academic advisor mentions the student needs to complete three 100-level courses, three 300-level courses, and a capstone course. The academic advisor never mentions 400-level courses.

20. B: The student asks the academic advisor whether they can finish their classes before 3:00 p.m. in order to pick up night shifts at work. Thus, Choice *B* is the correct answer. The student never mentions their study schedule or extracurricular commitments, so Choice *A* and Choice *C* are incorrect. The student does want to complete their degree in four years, which is why the student wants to take classes over the summer. However, the desire to finish classes earlier in the day is more directly related to their work schedule and finances, so Choice *B* is the better answer. Therefore, Choice *D* is incorrect.

21. C: The tone of the student's voice and the statement shows that she is disappointed about how far behind she'll be if she changes majors, so Choice *C* is correct. Choices *A*, *B*, and *D* are not the feelings conveyed in her statement. She does not sound angry, she does not seem to be embarrassed, and she's certainly not excited about being behind. Disappointment most accurately describes her attitude in the statement.

22. A: The student has asked if her British literature credits can count towards the general education requirements. Since they cannot, the advisor recommends minoring in British literature. It can be inferred that the student wants these credits to count toward something, and this is the best solution for the student to not lose the credits she's already worked for. Therefore, Choice *A* is correct. The academic advisor hasn't said anything to indicate that he disagrees with her choice to change majors, and recommending British literature certainly does not support Choice *B* as a correct answer. Choice *C* is incorrect because the advisor never shares an opinion on the subject, and his recommendation does not prove that he believes creative writing is a better major. Choice *D* is incorrect. Although additional classes taken by students will no doubt bring the university more money, the student's question about using her British literature credits for general education credits leads us to believe that the academic advisor sees that she does not want to lose her credits and that this is the reason he recommends British literature as a minor.

Recording #5: Lecture

23. C: A good portion of the lecture is focused on errors in excavation and efforts to both preserve what is there and be more mindful regarding future excavations. Choice *A* is incorrect. Roman life was

204

captured in the ash, but the focus of the lecture goes well beyond that fact. Choice *B* is incorrect. According to the professor, both are important, but the focus is mostly on excavation efforts. Choice *D* is incorrect. This fact is true, but the focus is too narrow. The professor discusses excavation successes, goals, and so forth.

24. A, B: Choice *A* is correct. This fact is true, and the professor discusses the preservation. However, the horse demonstrates more than preservation. At the beginning of the lecture, the professor claims that Pompeii has more to reveal, and discoveries in the last five years, such as the horse, prove that to be true, so Choice *B* is correct as well. Choice *C* is incorrect. The fact is established in the beginning of the lecture, but there is no indicator that the horse died from the heat. Choice *D* is incorrect. The ability for researchers to make new discoveries suggests that the entire city is not in decay.

25. B: Choice *B* is correct. After the professor introduces the topic and explains how ash preserved the area, she continues to give a chronological explanation of the various excavation efforts and discoveries that have been made, starting with the first efforts soon after the eruption and ending with discoveries made in 2021. Choice *A* is incorrect. The professor does not define nor give examples of terms. Choice *C* is incorrect because the professor does not discuss the cause of the volcanic eruption. Choice *D* is incorrect because the lecture isn't structured around comparisons of excavation techniques.

26. C: Throughout the lecture, the professor stresses both the mistakes made and efforts to protect the site and its value. This suggests that the professor feels protective toward Pompeii. Choice *A* is incorrect. The level of detail and concern in the professor's tone does not suggest disinterest. Choice *B* is incorrect. The professor does seem intrigued, but there's a greater focus on preservation and protection. Choice *D* is incorrect. The end of the lecture suggests hope regarding better effort to preserve and protect. In other words, the overwhelming feeling is still protective.

27. B: The professor explains that the researchers used plaster to fill voids and re-create body shapes. Choice *A* is incorrect. Mummified remains were found elsewhere. Choice *C* is incorrect. Most of the city was preserved in ash, so this method would have been unnecessary. Choice *D* is incorrect. Skeletal remains were found, but they were not used to help re-create body shapes.

28. C: Paragraph 7 notes that the Villa of Mysteries is well known for its beautiful frescos. Choice *A* is incorrect. It's true that the Villa is well preserved, but so are many other areas. Choice *B* and Choice *D* are incorrect. Although a dog's skeleton and mummified remains were found there, they were not found in the Villa.

Listening Transcripts

Recording #1: Lecture

(Professor) Let's talk about play. As humans, we need some form of play. It may not be what you think of when you think of an essential need, but play is extremely important. The act of play helps us build our imaginations and cognitive skills. It helps us build social and conversational skills and confidence. Children benefit massively from good, constructive play, but adults benefit from play too. It gives us a direction for our imagination and creativity and lets us explore the world around us.

There are many ways we can describe play, but today we're going to focus on a specific type of play. Today's focus is called instrumental play. Now, I'm really going to break this down, because understanding the concept and definition of instrumental play is important. When we say something is

instrumental, we mean it was an important means of pursuing a result. If we say that the CEO was instrumental to the company's success, we mean the CEO was a means by which the company gained success. You with me so far? Now, instrumental play has a similar definition. We mean that the act of play serves as a means to obtaining a specific result. Or, in simpler terms, that it is play in service of a goal. When someone engages in instrumental play, it is because they seek something from the act of play.

Now, you might be naturally thinking that play isn't supposed to have a goal. Otherwise it's not play, right? Play should be "uninhibited" or "free" and not have a reward attached to it. A natural assumption, but goals and play are like peanut butter and jelly. At the most basic level, an adult might engage in play to unwind, to de-stress, to feel more relaxed. That's a form of instrumental play—engaging in play to achieve the goal of feeling relaxed. Maybe someone joins in a game at a party to connect with others. That can be instrumental play too—engaging in play to achieve social satisfaction. Play doesn't have to have a tangible, physical reward to be considered instrumental play. So long as there is a reason—a purpose—behind the play, it is instrumental.

Now, let's say you have a competitive game. Chess, for example. Some people play chess for fun. It lets them flex parts of the brain that they may not get to use every day, such as parts that focus on strategy and forward thinking. Some people play chess as a casual hobby. It stimulates them, provides a comfortable space of rules and goals that are familiar to them. Now, here's a thought for you. Why do you think chess grandmaster Magnus Carlsen, the highest rated chess player in the world, plays chess? Is it because he finds familiarity in it? Maybe because he enjoys the strategy and has memorized it all by heart? We can't know for certain unless we were to have him here with us right now and ask him, but we can at least say this much: he has something that he seeks from it, a goal he pursues through the act of playing chess.

Competitive players of any game have to have a goal they seek through the act of playing it. Do they seek the glory of being named the best in the world amongst their peers? If so, then why would someone continue after that point? Do they just really, really like playing the game so they've just followed whatever path allows them to keep playing? Consider then why there are organizations, teams, entire tournaments and markets of people dedicated to the act of play. What are the goals that each individual person seeks in play? And is one person's goal any more or less valid than another's? What are the goals that drive professional baseball players to sign multi-million-dollar contracts to play in the most challenging leagues of their peers? Are their goals any more or less valid than the kids putting together a game of baseball after school who just want to have fun and pass the time?

I know I've given you all a lot to think about, but don't feel like you have to have answers to all these questions now. We'll talk more in depth over the semester about play. I just want to get you all in the right mindset of thinking about the biggest question we're going to discuss together. That question is, why do you play?

Recording #2: Lecture

(Professor) A law may start as a bill in either the House or the Senate. We'll start with the House of Representatives. It can be proposed by any member of the House. From there, the Speaker of the House will refer this bill to the relevant committee to be discussed. Depending on the bill's contents, it could be referred to multiple committees. Once it's in committee, it'll get discussed, refined, and edited. At this point it's sort of like a group project for the committee. They work through the merits of the bill and set more specifics, like if they want the bill to regulate something after a threshold, and then the committee

206

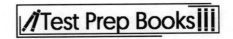

will do research and decide on what that threshold should be. This is a process that can take a while, but when the committee finally agrees on the version of the bill they want to submit, they will all vote on it, and if the committee passes it, then the bill is moved up to the House Rules committee.

Now, the Rules committee is a bit special. They don't make any edits to bills that come to them. Instead, they decide on a plan for how the House of Representatives will debate the bill. So they'll set the rules for debate, and from there the bill moves to the House floor. Then, it sits in a pile with all the other bills that have reached this point. The Speaker of the House is responsible for deciding what bills the House discusses and setting the schedule. When our bill is selected, it enters the floor of the House for full debate. Members of the House will have to follow the rules set by the Rules committee, so eventually debate will come to an end and the House will vote on it. The House vote needs a simple majority, so it just needs 218 votes out of 435 House members to be able to pass. If the bill passes at this point, it either moves to the Senate or to Conference Committee.

All of this explains the process for proposing a bill in the House, but there is a slightly different process for proposing a bill in the Senate. A bill that passes in the House still has to pass in the Senate, and likewise from the Senate to the House. So let's take a look at how a bill passes the Senate. There's a little more formality here; to introduce a bill in the Senate, you basically have to get the approval of the presiding officer of the Senate first. Once you do, it gets sent to the Senate's version of committees, and it goes through the same process as committees in the House. Now, in the Senate, they don't have a Rules committee, so once the individual committee or committees have agreed on edits to the bill, it gets sent straight to the Senate floor. The Senate Majority Leader sets the schedule for what bills are discussed and when, and when the time comes, our bill comes up for debate in the Senate.

The Senate has far fewer rules for debate, and technically, debate on a single bill can last forever. This is where the term "filibuster" comes up, and it's a bit of a controversial one. See, because debate is unlimited in the Senate, if one Senator decides they really, really don't like a bill, they can use their debate time to talk about whatever they want. As long as they don't leave the floor, they can go on for hours and hours about anything—it doesn't even have to be related to the bill in question. This is a tactic used to force changes or concessions on a bill, or even outright kill it at this point. Many critics have called for an end to this tactic, but there is a method to deal with it. At any time, the Senate can call for a cloture vote, which forces all debate to end in thirty hours and puts the bill up for vote. Cloture requires sixty of the one hundred senators to concur, which is a little more than a simple majority. Regardless of whether debate ends naturally or by cloture, the Senate will vote on the bill. If another simple majority votes in favor of the bill—in this case fifty-one out of a hundred—then the bill passes the Senate.

A single bill has to pass both the House and the Senate in these ways. Now, if both the House and the Senate pass the exact same bill with no changes, the bill goes straight to the President. This almost never happens, though, so instead it goes to a Conference Committee. Here, members from both the House and the Senate work to create a compromise bill that is sort of a middle ground of both versions. That compromise bill goes back to both the House and the Senate for votes, and when the same version passes in both places, it goes to the President. The President either does not sign the bill, sending it back to the House and the Senate with reasons why, or signs it and our bill finally becomes a law.

Recording #3: Conversation

(Narrator) Listen to a conversation between a professor and student, and then answer the questions that follow.

(Professor) Thank you for waiting after class. I've been meaning to speak to you for a while.

(Student) No problem, I have some time before basketball practice. What's up?

(Professor) Your performance on our last few assignments has not been up to your usual standard. Is there anything I can help you with?

(Student) No. My sleep schedule is just really off.

(Professor) That happens to me sometimes, too. It's really helped me to get into a bedtime routine, and to limit my screen time as I wind down for the night.

(Student) Thanks, but that's not the problem.

(Professor) Okay. What is the problem?

(Student) Our family has been in the process of moving.

(Professor) Oh, I see. That's great your parents were able to buy a house. Interest rates are historically low right now.

(Student) Well, they didn't buy a house.

(Professor) Oh, I see. Sorry I assumed; that was wrong of me. Did you move into an apartment?

(Student) Kind of.

(Professor) What does that mean?

(Student) My mom lost her job last month, and we were evicted from our apartment. We've been bouncing between friends' and relatives' homes ever since.

(Professor) I'm sorry to hear that. Are you doing okay otherwise?

(Student) Yeah. It's a nice change of pace to have sleepovers with my cousins, but I don't like not knowing where I'll be staying every night. It stresses me out.

(Professor) That's very understandable. Is there anything I can do to help?

(Student) Could I have extra time on my tests? I always have difficulty finishing in time.

(Professor) I can't do that without a doctor's note, but I have office hours every Monday and Wednesday at six o'clock. Why don't you stop by?

(Student) I have basketball practice in the evenings, and coach benches us if we're late. I need to stay on the court to have a chance at playing professionally.

(Professor) What if I talked to your coach?

(Student) No! That'd make everything worse. I don't want him to know I'm struggling in class or anything about my home life. Basketball is my escape from everything, and I need to keep it that way.

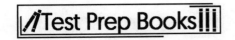

(Professor) Education should come first, but I see your point. Do you have any free time in the morning?

(Student) Yeah, I don't have class or work before 10:00 a.m.

(Professor) That's perfect. I have Tuesday mornings free. Why don't you stop by my office at around 9:00 a.m.?

(Student) No, you don't have to do that. I don't want to trouble you.

(Professor) It's no trouble at all. You're one of my best students, and I don't want to see you fall behind. Plus, my New Year's resolution was to stop playing games on my phone, and that's typically all I do during my downtime.

(Student) Well, in that case, I could use the help. Thank you so much. I really appreciate it.

(Professor) No problem. I'll see you next Tuesday at 9:00 a.m.

(Student) Great, thanks again.

Recording #4: Conversation

(Narrator) Listen to a conversation between a student and an academic advisor, and then answer the questions that follow.

(Student) Hey, thank you for meeting with me. I have a couple questions about my major and schedule for next semester.

(Academic Advisor) Sure thing.

(Student) I'm currently majoring in British literature, but I'm thinking about switching to creative writing. Is that possible?

(Academic Advisor) Yes, that's definitely possible. They're in the same department, so all you'd have to do is file the paperwork to make it official. You won't need to reapply to anything.

(Student) Great, but will my credits count toward my new major?

(Academic Advisor) Let me pull up your transcript and take a look.

(Student) Thanks.

(Academic Advisor) Hmm, it looks like most will apply. British literature and creative writing both have the same general education requirements, so all of those will count the same as before. The only issue is some of the high-level British literature credits aren't applicable to creative writing.

(Student) So I should enroll in 300-level creative writing courses next semester?

(Academic Advisor) No, you need to start with 100-level courses. Once you complete three of those courses, you can start taking 300-level. Once you've taken three 300-level courses, then you'll qualify for a 600-level capstone course.

(Student) Oh man, I didn't realize I'd be so far behind. Can I take the 100-level and 300-level courses simultaneously? For example, next semester can I take all three 100-level courses and then one 300-level courses?

(Academic Advisor) No, like I said, the 100-level course requirement must be met before enrolling in a 300-level course.

(Student) Oh, man, I really can't afford to stay for a fifth year to complete my degree.

(Academic Advisor) We do offer an abbreviated semester over the summer. If you take the three 100-level courses in the Spring, then you could start taking 300-level courses this summer. That way, you could finish the 300-level courses next Fall and enroll in the capstone course the Spring semester of your senior year.

(Student) That could work. Can my British literature courses count as general education requirements?

(Academic Advisor) You've already completed English 101, so that won't work. British literature can't be substituted for the language, science, or math general education requirements that you're still missing. However, you could minor in British literature since you're only two 300-level courses short.

(Student) I'll definitely keep that in mind. Would it be possible to finish my classes by 3:00 p.m. next semester if I take the three 100-level creative writing classes and one class to meet my general education requirements? I'll need to pick up some night shifts if I'm going to take classes this summer.

(Academic Advisor) Yeah, but only if you take a language course. All the open math courses are in the evening.

(Student) Great, I'll sign up as soon as I get home. Thanks so much.

(Academic Advisor) You're welcome. Please let me know if you have any more questions.

(Student) Will do.

Recording #5: Lecture

(Professor) I'm sure that everyone here in class has heard of the ancient city of Pompeii. It's the Roman city that was buried under nearly 19 feet of ash and debris after a two-day eruption event at Mount Vesuvius. Many of the citizens were killed quickly, first by heat, and then others by ash suffocation. The ash preserved the area, providing a peek at daily life in a Roman city. Initial excavations occurred early on, and the city likely plundered. Further excavations by research and archaeological teams were banned after 1960 when preceding expeditions left the city largely in decay. However, Pompeii would still have much more to reveal.

After the eruption, it's believed that survivors as well as thieves visited the city to remove valuables, both personal and public. In fact, there was clear evidence, from graffiti to actual dig holes, that homes were excavated and searched for prior to official or sanctioned explorations. The city was largely undisturbed and remained buried for a long time after this initial period. Then, in the 1500 and 1600s, there were two encounters with the ruins, although nothing major came of it.

In the 1700s, the first major excavations were initiated after nearby Herculaneum was discovered. These led to several subsequent expeditions and major discoveries and a greater understanding of the

techniques and strategies that would best maintain the integrity of the site and reflect the moment when Pompeii was covered.

For example, one archaeologist determined that air pockets under the ash were likely the result of decomposed organic remains and that if they injected the void with plaster, they could re-create the body shapes. These advances were, unfortunately, matched by mistakes.

In the 1920s and later in the 1950s, excavations were made that nearly uncovered whole sections in their entirety. However, these excavations and subsequent attempted restorations were haphazard at best, and poor records were kept. As a result, further excavations were halted for several decades.

Eventually, additional exploration was permitted but only in previously unexplored areas or other designated regions. Still, these new expeditions, with more modern techniques and strategies, in part based on what we have already learned, are focused more on documenting and preserving than uncovering. That doesn't mean they haven't come without their own amazing discoveries.

For example, in 2018, a well-preserved harnessed horse was unearthed in the Villa of the Mysteries, a villa known for amazing frescoes. Subsequent discoveries in 2020 and 2021 have included slaves' quarters, a wealthy man and his slave, a ceremonial chariot, an inn that revealed much about the fare being served, a dog's skeleton, and a fully intact tomb with mummified remains thought to belong to a freed slave.

With so much left to be discovered, there's been a marked shift in strategies focused on preservation and conservation rather than continued digs. While buried, the city remained fairly well preserved because it was protected from the elements. Once digging started, it was exposed to all sorts of vulnerabilities from the natural world, including earthquakes, weather, erosion, water, and so forth. Similarly, it exposed the city and its treasures to humans. From poor excavation methods to vandalism and human traffic, the city has further deteriorated.

There was a time when it was believed the preservation attempts were not enough, but in the last few years, several buildings have reopened after restoration, giving some hope that both re-creation and restoration may be enough to show visitors the real Pompeii.

Speaking

Sample Responses

Recording # 6

Question 1

Recording #7

Question 2

Recording #8

Question 3

Recording #9

Question 4

Speaking Question Transcripts

Recording #6

1. These days, many people are allowed to work from home. Some people think there are too many distractions and that productivity is not best when working at home. Do you agree or disagree? Explain the reasons for your opinion.

Recording #7

2. **(Female Student)** This announcement says that they're closing Maplewood!

(Male Student) Isn't that our fault anyways? I heard there was a food fight.

(Female Student) The actions of a few students shouldn't result in punishment of the entire student body. They're choosing to renovate when classes are in session, instead of waiting until summer break. This is a big inconvenience.

(Male Student) Well, where are we supposed to eat?

(Female Student) They said that we can use Oakwood Food Hall instead.

(Male Student) What?! Isn't that super far away?

(Female Student) Yeah, it is. The lines for Oakwood will be super long now too, since every student will be eating there instead of splitting between the two food halls. I only have an hour between classes. I can't walk an extra twenty minutes and wait in longer lines.

(Male Student) They should rethink this decision. They could prevent this. How am I supposed to eat lunch now?

(Female Student) The repairs would only take a week; they should focus on that instead of the renovations that will last months. In the meantime, students should receive meal vouchers for the inconvenience. It's only right, since we're paying for access to both food halls!

Recording #8

3. **(Professor)** There are many animals that hibernate, and you might not expect some of them! Our friends the bumblebees enter hibernation in the winter. The entire colony dies except for the queen, so she is the only bumblebee in the colony that hibernates. The queen bees will hibernate for nine months, which is most of their lifespan. They dig a hole into the soil and stay there the entire time. She builds a wax pot, keeps a bit of honey and pollen in it, and then lays her eggs on it. She lies down on the eggs to keep them warm, a bit like a chicken. She emerges when it starts getting warmer outside and begins her new colony. Cool, right?

212

Another unexpected hibernator is the snail. Not all snails hibernate, but when they do, it's very strange. This is because their hibernation period can last up to three years, and they usually stay in groups. They can hibernate in the summer too, which is known as estivation. They also have built-in shelter, so they'll hide under rocks or plants and close their shell to the outside world with a mucus layer called an epiphragm. It dries out and hardens to act as a blockade. Their preparation is a bit more gross than a cute bumblebee's or bear's is. To prepare for hibernation, snails remove any liquids from their guts so those liquids don't freeze during the winter. They also make a type of antifreeze in their blood called glycerol.

Recording #9

4. **(Professor)** Today we will be learning about how to calculate opportunity cost. In economics, it is often necessary to decide between different investments. This investment analysis can be based on any resource, such as money, effort, or time. To make a decision, you must find out the opportunity cost of each option. In simple terms, the opportunity cost is what you are potentially losing by choosing one option over another.

So, let's begin. There are implicit and explicit opportunity costs. An implicit opportunity cost is intangible. An explicit cost has a dollar amount that can be accounted for. We will focus on explicit opportunity cost, since that is something that we can calculate. We need to know the returns of the two options being considered. Once we have those numbers, we need to subtract the return of the chosen option from the option not chosen.

Let's look at an example. An investor is planning to buy an existing business. They are deciding between a coffee shop and a donut shop. The coffee shop brings in a total revenue of $450,000 per year. The donut shop brings in a total revenue of $500,000 per year. To calculate the opportunity cost of choosing the coffee shop, you would subtract the total revenue of the coffee shop from the total revenue of the donut shop. That gives us an opportunity cost of $50,000. In other words, the investor would be losing out on $50,000 by choosing the coffee shop over the donut shop. This works with percentages as well. Let's say that the donut shop had a return of 10 percent and the coffee shop had a return of 4 percent. If we chose the coffee shop, the opportunity cost would be 6 percent.

This logic can be applied to any situation where you are choosing between two options, no matter the complexity. On the simpler end, if you are deciding between two jobs with different commute times, you could find the opportunity cost of the difference in commute time between the two options. In complex investment situations, an investor makes opportunity cost calculations on every possible return to determine the best option.

Speaking Sample Response Transcripts

Recording #10

1. I disagree with that statement. I think it all depends on what the environment where a person works is like. Some workplaces are quiet or at some jobs people don't have time to goof off, so it's good for getting things done. My experience is that when I'm at work, my coworkers are distractions. They talk a lot and joke around and they interrupt me when I'm busy. I never seem to get enough done. If I could work from home, I could turn off my phone while I work and have a quiet environment to do my work in. Or if it's too quiet, I could turn on music I like and that always helps me focus better. If I can focus

without all the interruptions, I think my productivity would be so much higher. So I think that distractions and low productivity can happen at a workplace just as much as at home, and sometimes more. I know I could work better at home.

Recording #11

2. The university is closing one of the food halls because there was a food fight and they need to fix the damage from that. They don't know how long it will be closed because they are also renovating it with murals while it's closed. The student doesn't like this because she thinks that the repairs could be done fast and that the renovations can wait until summer break. This isn't right for the students who were not involved in the food fight to have to go to another food hall for lunch. This is not convenient for students. For her, the food hall they will have to use instead is too far away and she doesn't have enough time to get over there and to wait in a line that will be longer. She thinks vouchers should be given to the students because they pay to use two food halls.

Recording #12

3. Hibernation is how animals conserve energy in the winter. There isn't much food in the winter and it's also cold. The metabolism is slower while an animal hibernates and their temperature is low. These things conserve energy. They eat a lot and store that energy in fat before they hibernate. Bumblebees hibernate, but it's only the Queen. She hibernates for nine months and that is most of her life. She stays in a hole and builds wax and there she puts honey and pollen. She lays eggs there. Then when it's warm she come out and starts a colony. Another animal that hibernates is a snail. A snail can hibernate for three years. They will get under a rock in a group and close up their shells with an epiphragm. This is a layer of mucus that gets hard when it dries. It blocks things. The liquid of a snail is removed first so the liquid can't freeze in the winter. In their blood is antifreeze called glycerol. Sometime they hibernate in the summer and it's called estivation.

Recording #13

4. Opportunity cost is a way to decide between two options, like investments or jobs. Before you make a decision, you see what the opportunity cost is. This is what you lose by choosing one thing and not the other. Two types of opportunity cost are implicit and explicit. Implicit is intangible. Explicit can be counted, like money. It can be calculated. After it's calculated, the two numbers are subtracted. So if you know the revenue of two businesses, they can be subtracted. An example is a coffee shop that makes $450,000 and a donut shop that makes $500,000. The difference is $50,000 and that's the opportunity cost if you choose to have a coffee shop that makes $450,000 instead of the donut shop that makes more money. Percents can also be used. Complex and simple things can use opportunity cost to help decide what to choose.

Writing

Sample Integrated Writing Response

In reading the passage and listening to lecture, we get two very different feelings about The Civil War. The passage introduces it as a good thing that brought the country together and changed the United States in a good way. Then the lecture introduces a different story of unnecessary devastation that made the country worse.

The lecturer tells us that former slaves had a hard time after the war because they had no necessities. There were outbreaks of illness that killed many because they didn't have the same resources and health care that white soldiers had. They could not vote and were not considered citizens. Although the outcome of the war was expected to bring positive changes, like we see in the reading passage, this is not truly what happened, according to the lecture. The passage says that after the war people were united. That it brought freedom and justice as victories of the war. The lecture shows this to not be true.

In the lecture we learn that the government was divided and did not know how to handle the former slaves or how much the federal government should control. This contradicts the passage that portrays the federal government as getting stronger and more centralized after the war. Both the passage and lecture agree that the war was expensive, but they disagree on the effects of this. The passage sees it as a positive thing that the government had to start using paper money. The lecture sees it as causing economics problems.

As the economy changed, it was hard for the South, as we see in the lecture. They had to rebuild what was destroyed during the war while they were also learning to live with a new kind of economy since they couldn't have slaves and plantations anymore. However, the passage notes positive effects of the new economy, like free markets and industrialization. In the lecture is says that these were only good for the North, not for the South.

The Civil War did have a great impact on the United States. The lecture shows how it was not easy for former slaves or for the South after the war and how things were still very much divided. The passage tells a different story of freedom and a new and better government and economy.

Sample Academic Discussion Response

It is imperative that we ban fossil fuels as soon as possible. They are destroying our Earth. For example, fracking for oil requires an almost total destruction of the landscape. The chemicals used may get into waterways and ruin the drinking source for many people, animals, and plants. How can we allow this to continue where there are alternatives? Solar, wind, and even nuclear power are all cleaner options. Oil companies have lobbied and led the public to believe that it is not worth the investment to pursue these options. I don't think we can put a price on the health of the Earth or its impact on future generations.

Integrated Writing Lecture Transcript

Recording #14

(Professor) The Civil War was an unnecessary time of death and destruction in the United States. It changed America primarily for the worse. Although the Civil War is credited with the great success of ending slavery, the brutality of the war left many of the states and their inhabitants in terrible situations.

Although the freeing of the slaves was the major victory of the Civil War, it was also tragic in many ways. The positive narrative about emancipation often overlooks the struggles of former slaves. They lacked the necessary items to live, such as food, shelter, and medical care. Many slaves died from disease outbreaks that spread across the South after the war. They were not afforded the same assistance that white soldiers received. They were not able to bury their loved ones due to a lack of sanctioned cemeteries. Freed slaves were not considered citizens or given the right to vote for many more years.

This fact, combined with the harsh post-war conditions that they faced, meant that freedom was not always the positive change it was promised to be.

The government changed greatly during and after the Civil War. However, it was not necessarily for the better. During the Reconstruction era, political tensions were high and corruption was rife. Politicians were divided on the topic of equal rights for black Southerners. The Ku Klux Klan confronted the new government, causing violence and tension. The most extreme incident was when President Abraham Lincoln was assassinated by a Confederate sympathizer. Nobody could agree on how to deal with the former Confederate states, how much federal control was needed, and how to treat freed slaves.

The Civil War cost billions of dollars and caused economic destruction. By getting rid of slavery, the South had lost its economic institution. While the North had the ability to industrialize and adapt to the economic changes, the South had no such opportunity. In addition to the economic changes, the South was facing huge infrastructure losses. Southern farms, buildings, roads, rail lines, and more were destroyed during the Civil War. The South was faced with repairing this damage and adapting to a new economy at the same time.

Dear TOEFL Test Taker,

We would like to start by thanking you for purchasing this study guide for your TOEFL exam. We hope that we exceeded your expectations.

Our goal in creating this study guide was to cover all of the topics that you will see on the test. We also strove to make our practice questions as similar as possible to what you will encounter on test day. With that being said, if you found something that you feel was not up to your standards, please send us an email and let us know.

We would also like to let you know about other books in our catalog that may interest you.

GRE Study Guide

This can be found on Amazon: amazon.com/dp/162845900X

GMAT Study Guide

amazon.com/dp/1637753829

MCAT Study Guide

amazon.com/dp/1637752997

We have study guides in a wide variety of fields. If the one you are looking for isn't listed above, then try searching for it on Amazon or send us an email.

Thanks Again and Happy Testing!
Product Development Team
info@studyguideteam.com

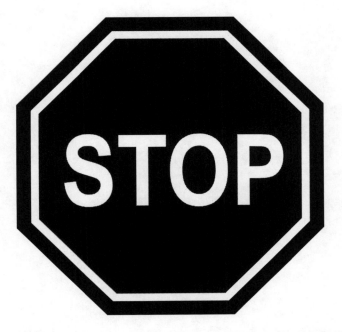

FREE Test Taking Tips Video/DVD Offer

To better serve you, we created videos covering test taking tips that we want to give you for FREE. **These videos cover world-class tips that will help you succeed on your test.**

We just ask that you send us feedback about this product. Please let us know what you thought about it—whether good, bad, or indifferent.

To get your **FREE videos**, you can use the QR code below or email freevideos@studyguideteam.com with "Free Videos" in the subject line and the following information in the body of the email:

      a. The title of your product

      b. Your product rating on a scale of 1-5, with 5 being the highest

      c. Your feedback about the product

If you have any questions or concerns, please don't hesitate to contact us at info@studyguideteam.com.

Thank you!

Made in the USA
Columbia, SC
23 September 2023

23278196R00124